INTRODUCTION TO Christian Worship

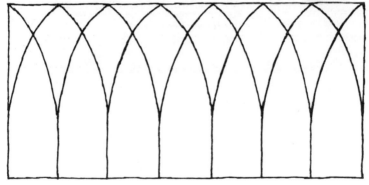

JAMES F. WHITE

ABINGDON
Nashville

INTRODUCTION TO CHRISTIAN WORSHIP

Copyright © 1980 by Abingdon

Library of Congress Cataloging in Publication Data

White, James F
  Introduction to Christian worship.
  Bibliography: p.
  Includes index.
  1. Liturgics. 2. Public worship. I. Title.
BV176.W48   264   79-21073

ISBN 0-687-19509-8

MANUFACTURED BY THE PARTHENON PRESS AT
NASHVILLE, TENNESSEE, UNITED STATES OF AMERICA

TO
Decherd H. Turner, Jr.

who has given his time
to help others write in theirs

Contents

Preface

After twenty years of teaching, one is bound to have made up one's mind on a few matters. Two more decades from now, I am sure my judgments on some matters will be more mature. But midstream seems to be a good time to pull together what I have taught and to anticipate what I have yet to learn. The experience of writing this book is a marvelous discipline of compressing everything I have done in a score of years into a single volume. Few were involved in teaching Christian worship when I embarked on this ministry. Now, nothing gives me greater joy than to have so many new companions in this work with whom to share where I have come and to look ahead to where they will go. I hope this book will aid them in their teaching until they find better ways to interpret Christian worship. With Peter Lombard, I can say, "If anyone can explain this better, I am not envious."

I have tried to set out in these pages in as brief a form as possible all that I regard as essential information to equip one for the ministry of worship leadership. I have attempted to include all one really needs to know in planning, preparing for, and conducting Christian worship except the details pertaining to one's own denominational service books or customs. The information in this book should be equally relevant both to ministers or priests and to lay members of worship committees. They will, of course, need to complement these materials with their own service books or customs.

To facilitate reference to specific service books, I have keyed this book to those most widely used, those familiar to the majority of English-speaking Christians in the United States. Frequent reference is made to the revised Roman Catholic books, especially the ritual, the sacramentary, and the pontifical. The new *Lutheran Book of Worship* appeared just as these pages were begun, and the new American *Book of Common Prayer* was given final approval just a few months prior to the publication of this book. So I have been able to refer to both. Since I am deeply involved in editing the United Methodist *Supplemental Worship Resources,* it has been possible to make reference to those volumes already published and to those yet to appear as well as to the 1965 *Book of Worship.* The reader is also directed to the Presbyterian *Worshipbook* of 1970 and the United Church of Christ *Services of the Church* (1969) and *Hymnal* (1974).

The time is appropriate for summarizing what has been accomplished in the post–Vatican II surge of liturgical revisions, now almost complete. On the tomb of Pope Martin V are carved the words: "His were times of happiness." This seems an apt description of the ecumenical situation in worship in our times. We can look at the past decade and a half of liturgical revision as a time of happiness when the churches of the world moved closer together by sharing their riches in worship with one another. There is no more concrete evidence of the ecumenical accomplishments of our times than the rapprochement that has occurred in Christian worship in the 1960s and 1970s. Thus it is now possible to write an introduction to Christian worship which, I hope, will be of as much service to Roman Catholics as to Protestants.

Study of Christian worship can provide a valuable means of understanding Christianity itself for any interested inquirer. There is no better way to discover the heart of Christianity than by becoming more aware of what Christians do when they gather to worship. Both Christian and non-Christian can learn much about Western culture's dominant religious tradition by becoming more knowledgeable about Christian worship.

This book is intended as an introduction to Christian worship. But it is also an interpretation of the subject. I have not hesitated to venture new insights and interpretations that I have come to, myself. Some of these, others can and will refute. What is valid in these interpretations will remain; what is not will be replaced by someone more perceptive. The basic organization of the subject and various details, I have tried and refined over the years through use with my students. It is exciting to anticipate that others will develop more satisfactory interpretations in the years ahead. Much research remains to be done in liturgical studies. Many areas are still mysterious, such as: the origins of the synagogue service, the sources of Epiphany, the details of the cathedral office, the Roman canon between Hippolytus and Ambrose, and the genesis of the normal Sunday service used in American Reformed, Methodist, and Free Church traditions. If this book can induce others to look forward with relish to subsequent research, it will have been a successful introduction and interpretation.

Though much of the book is of an academic nature, the whole thrust is always in a pastoral direction for strengthening the worship leadership of Christian communities. Much is written in a descriptive manner to describe what has been and why, but most chapters conclude with a normative section on what ought to be and why in the churches today. The descriptive sections give the background for the normative portions. Anyone charged with worship leadership has responsibility for much decision-making. But these decisions can only be well informed when made on the basis of all relevant factors. Hence, in every chapter, historical and theological information precedes the pastoral sections. When pastoral norms for action are stated, it is always in terms of what Christians have practiced and how they have reflected on these practices. Christian worship, like Christian ethics, is both a descriptive and a normative subject. Specific decisions have to be made locally in terms of people and places but I have tried to outline broad norms within which pastoral decisions can be made.

It is not easy to compress an entire discipline into the pages of a moderate-size book. Almost every paragraph represents material that could fill a book or several books. I have had to reduce books to paragraphs, chapters to sentences, allowing little space to qualify statements. This frustration has been alleviated slightly by listing related reading at the end of the book and in the notes. Many essential books are cited in notes, and references to these are not repeated in the bibliographies. I have had to concentrate on priorities of widest interest and to eliminate all others. A disproportionately small number of these pages discuss worship in the Eastern Orthodox churches since most of my readers represent Western Christianity and will be more interested in their own lineal ancestry than a collateral line. There is little herein about the bishop's liturgy, the concern of a small (and not oppressed) minority. And the particular concerns of monastic communities have received little attention.

I have concentrated on the practices and concepts of the church in the first four centuries. If one knows what decisions the church made in this period and why, all the rest is simple. Much of Christianity today is in a stage of recovery of early practices and concepts. Whether we have too easily romanticized the early period, future ages will judge. But in any case, knowledge of the decisions of the early period is essential in understanding all subsequent developments.

In order to make study easier, I have placed key names, terms, and a few dates in boldface type. Much of the introduction to any subject consists in becoming familiar with basic vocabulary. The words and phrases essential to liturgical studies are made more conspicuous so students can review by checking their familiarity with such terms.

We are more conscious today than ever before of how rapidly our language is changing. This is particularly apparent with regard to terms indicating sexual identity. The future resolution of these changes is still uncertain, and terms we use today still have a provisional character. Some of those I have adopted, such as "Godself," will undoubtedly seem unfamiliar and harsh. But infelicity is better than injustice, and only time will tell what reflexive pronoun comes to prevail with regard to God. I must ask my readers to be indulgent with provisional terms as English usage evolves.

This book represents the contributions of many people who have given of themselves to make it a better volume. I am indebted to Dr. Hoyt L. Hickman, Dr. Richard Eslinger, and

Preface

Elise Shoemaker of the Section on Worship of the United
Methodist Board of Discipleship; to my colleagues at Perkins
School of Theology, Professor H. Grady Hardin, Professor
Virgil P. Howard, and Dean Joseph D. Quillian, Jr.; to
Professor Don E. Saliers of Candler School of Theology; to
Arlo Duba of Princeton Techological Seminary; to Professor
William Crockett of Vancouver School of Theology; to Louise
Shown, and to Sister Nancy Swift of St. John's Seminary for
reading and commenting most helpfully on the manuscript. I
still am learning much from my seminary teacher Professor Paul
W. Hoon, who has continued to teach me by his comments and
corrections on these pages. Professor Decherd H. Turner, Jr.,
Director of Bridwell Library, has given much of himself to help
many others have scholarly careers. His constant generosity I
acknowledge by dedicating this book to him.

Bonnie Jordan has worked marvels, deciphering my
manuscript at a distance of nineteen hundred miles and
rendering it into clean and orderly copy. My wife and children
have suffered much neglect during these days when they
deserved more of the company I shared with the typewriter
alone. I ask their pardon and hope to become more human now
that these pages are done.

Passumpsic, Vermont
March 5, 1979
JAMES F. WHITE

Abbreviations

ANF   *Ante-Nicene Fathers.* New York: Scribner's, 1899. 10 vols.

BCP   *The Book of Common Prayer.* New York: Church Hymnal Corporation and Seabury Press, 1977. (Other editions noted by date.)

BoW   *The Book of Worship for Church and Home.* Nashville: The Methodist Publishing House, 1965.

CSL   *Constitution on the Sacred Liturgy.* Collegeville, Minn.: Liturgical Press, 1963.

HUCC   *The Hymnal of the United Church of Christ.* Philadelphia: United Church Press, 1974.

LBW   *Lutheran Book of Worship.* Minneapolis: Augsburg; and Philadelphia: Board of Publication, Lutheran Church in America, 1978. (Pew edition unless Ministers Desk Edition specified.)

NPNF   *Nicene and Post-Nicene Fathers.* New York: Scribner's, 1905–1907.

Rites   *The Rites of the Catholic Church as Revised by the Second Vatican Council.* New York: Pueblo Publishing Company, 1976.

Sac   *The Sacramentary.* Collegeville, Minn.: Liturgical Press, 1974.

SoC   *Services of the Church.* Philadelphia: United Church Press, 1969. Vols. 1-8.

SWR   *Supplemental Worship Resources.* Nashville: Abingdon Press or United Methodist Publishing House, 1972–80, vols. 1-10.

Wb   *The Worshipbook.* Philadelphia: Westminister Press, 1970.

I
What Do We Mean by "Christian Worship"?

In order to speak intelligently about "Christian worship," one must first decide just what this term means. It is not an easy expression to define. Yet until one reflects on what is distinctive about authentic Christian worship, it is all too easy to confuse such worship with accretions from present or past cultures in which Christians have worshiped.

First of all, "worship" itself is an exasperatingly difficult word to pin down. What distinguishes worship from other human activities, particularly those noted for their frequent repetition? Why is worship a different type of activity from doing daily chores or any habitual action? More specifically, how does worship differ from other recurring activities of the Christian community itself? What distinguishes worship from Christian education or works of charity, for instance?

And second, once we have made up our minds about what we mean by "worship," how do we determine what makes such worship "Christian"? Our culture is full of various other types of worship. A variety of Oriental sects have made their advent in many communities. Many practice worship, but obviously not Christian. What distinctive marks make worship Christian? Is all worship within the Christian community always Christian?

None of these is an easy question to resolve, but they all certainly need to be probed. And they are not simply speculative matters of theoretical interest alone. Defining what is distinctive about Christian worship is a vital practical tool for anyone who is responsible for planning, preparing for, or leading Christian worship. Recent years, with the sudden appearance of many new forms of worship, have made this type of basic analysis even more crucial for those charged with worship ministry. Such people are constantly involved in decision-making as they serve the Christian community through worship leadership. The more practical the decision, the more necessary the theoretical foundations often become. Is a certain act, such as the pledging of allegiance to a national flag, appropriate for Christian worship? Or is such an act out of place in Christian worship? Should some other acts that we have not been accustomed to thinking of as worship, such as the adoption of a child, find a place in the worship life of the church? Or is that, too, out of place in Christian worship? Only if one has a working definition of "Christian worship" can he or she cope with such problems.

I shall try three methods to help clarify what we mean by "Christian worship." First, I shall examine how several Protestant and Catholic thinkers define the term through their use of it. Then I shall explore some of the key words that Christians have chosen in various languages at differing times as most adequate to say what they meant by Christian worship. And then I shall quickly survey the enduring forms of Christian worship itself in order to discern constancy within diversity. It is my hope that these three exercises will help others clarify for themselves what they mean when speaking of "Christian worship."

I

Our purpose in looking at the various ways different Christian thinkers speak about Christian worship is not for comparative study but to stimulate reflection. The best way to grasp the meaning of any term is to observe it in use rather than to give a simple definition. So we shall look over the shoulders of three Protestant thinkers and three from Catholic backgrounds, and then explore two additional possibilities. None of these varying uses of the term excludes others. Frequently they overlap, but each use adds new insights and dimensions, thus complementing the rest. This effort to say what we mean and to mean what we say is a continuing one, subject to revision as one's understanding of Christian worship matures and deepens.

Professor Paul W. Hoon made a major contribution to liturgical studies in his important book, *The Integrity of Worship*. Writing from within the Methodist tradition, Hoon is concerned for "theological discrimination as well as sensitivity to cultures." Throughout, he emphasizes the christological center of Christian worship, which "by definition is Christological, and analysis of the meaning of worship likewise must be fundamentally Christological."[1] Such worship is profoundly incarnational in being governed by the whole event of Jesus Christ. Christian worship is bound directly to the events of salvation history. Every event in this worship is tied directly to time and history while bridging them and bringing them into our present. The "core of worship," Hoon says, "is God acting to give his life to man and to bring man to partake of that life." Hence all we do as individuals or as the church is affected by worship. The Christian life, Hoon asserts, is a liturgical life.

Hoon maintains that "Christian worship is God's revelation of himself in Jesus Christ and man's response" or a twofold action—that of "God toward the human soul in Jesus Christ and in man's responsive action through Jesus Christ." Through his Word, God "discloses and communicates his very being to man." The key words in Hoon's understanding of Christian worship seem to be "revelation" and "response." At the center of both is Jesus Christ, who reveals God to us and through whom we make our response. It is a reciprocal relationship: God takes the initiative in addressing us through Jesus Christ; and we respond through Jesus Christ, using a variety of emotions, words, and actions.

Peter Brunner, a Lutheran theologian who taught at the University of Heidelberg for many years, parallels Hoon's thinking in many ways but expresses himself in quite different terms in his major book, *Worship in the Name of Jesus*. Brunner has a distinct advantage in using the German word for worship, *Gottesdienst,* a word that carries a fine ambiguity reflecting both

God's service to humans and humans' service to God. Brunner capitalizes on this ambiguity and speaks of the "duality" of worship. The heart of the book is two chapters entitled "Worship as a Service of God to the Congregation" and "Worship as the Congregation's Service Before God." In this duality, we see similarities to Hoon's revelation and response; but again caution is necessary, for God is operative in both. First and last, God alone makes worship a possibility: "The gift of God evokes man's devotion to God."[2]

God gives Godself to us both in past historical events and in the present-day "word-reality of the event" in which even our human work of proclamation is actually God's doing. The same is true of the sacraments in which, through our actions, God works. Brunner quotes Luther about worship, "that nothing else be done in it than that our dear Lord Himself talk to us through His holy Word and that we, in turn, talk to Him in prayer and song of praise." Humans respond to God's acts of revelation by talking to God through prayer and hymns "as an act of the new obedience imparted by the Holy Spirit." Prayer, Brunner says, "is the permission which God accords His sons to join their voices in the discussion of His affairs." Thus the duality of worship, for Brunner, is overshadowed by a single focus, the activity of God in self-giving to us and in prompting our response to God's gifts.

Like our other thinkers, Professor Jean-Jacques von Allmen affirms the christological basis of Christian worship in his significant book, *Worship: Its Theology and Practice*. Writing from within the Reformed tradition, this professor at the University of Neuchâtel, in Switzerland, makes a strong case for understanding Christian worship as recapitulation of what God has already done. Worship, he says, "sums up and confirms ever afresh the process of saving history which has reached its culminating point in the intervention of Christ in human history, and through this summing-up and ever-repeated confirmation Christ pursues His saving work by the operation of the Holy Spirit."[3] Such worship is closely tied to the biblical chronicle of the saving events. It provides a fresh summing-up of what God has done and renewed anticipation of what is yet to be.

Von Allmen's description of the church's worship has other important aspects. Worship is the "epiphany of the Church," which, "because it sums up the history of salvation, enables the church to become itself, to become conscious of itself and to confess what it essentially is." The church gains its self-identity in worship as its real nature is made manifest and it is led to confess its own true being. But the world, too, is profoundly affected by Christian worship. Worship is both threat of judgment and promise of hope to the world itself, even though secular society professes indifference to what Christians do when they assemble. Christian worship challenges human righteousness and points to the day when all achievements and failures will be judged, yet offers hope and promise by affirming that, ultimately, all rests in God's hands. For von Allmen, Christian worship has three key dimensions: recapitulation, epiphany, and judgment.

Writing from the Anglo-Catholic tradition, Evelyn Underhill published her classic study, *Worship,* in 1936. She expressed earlier a number of the concepts we have already seen but provided some distinctive, sensitive insights. Her book begins with the words: "Worship, in all its grades and kinds, is the response of the creature to the Eternal." The ritual through which all public worship is expressed emerges, she says, "as a stylized religious emotion." Worship is characterized by "the worshiper's conception of God and his relation to God." Christian worship is distinguished by being "always conditioned by Christian belief; and especially belief about the Nature and Action of God, as summed up in the great dogmas of the Trinity and the Incarnation." Another hallmark of Christian worship is its "thoroughly social and organic character," which means it is never a solitary undertaking.

Far from being worship in general, "Christian worship," she asserts, is "a supernatural action, a supernatural life" involving "a distinct response to a distinct revelation." Christian worship has a concrete character, for it is only through the "movement of the abiding God towards His creature, that the incentive is given to man's deepest worship, and the appeal is made to his sacrificial love. . . . Prayer and . . . action, are ways in which he [man] replies to this utterance of the Word."[4]

In Roman Catholic circles, in recent years, it has been common to describe worship as "the glorification of God and the sanctification of humanity." This phrase comes from a landmark 1903 *motu proprio* on church music by Saint Pope Pius X, in which he spoke of worship as being for "the glory of God and the sanctification and edification of the faithful." Pope Pius XII repeated this expression in his 1947 encyclical on worship, *Mediator Dei*. The same definition appears frequently in the Vatican II *Constitution on the Sacred Liturgy*, which "in more than twenty places corrects the former definition of the liturgy and speaks first of the sanctification of man and then of the glorification of God."[5] That reversal of order asks much: Which takes precedence—the glorification of God or making people holy? Many of the debates about worship in recent years have revolved around that question, a question particularly pertinent for church musicians.

Should worship be the offering of our best talents and arts to God, even though unfamiliar or even incomprehensible to people? Or should it, rather, be in familiar language and styles so that the meaning is grasped by all, even though the result is less impressive artistically? Fortunately, these are false alternatives. Glorification and sanctification belong together. Irenaeus tells us "the glory of God is man fully alive." Nothing glorifies God more than a human's being made holy; nothing is more likely to make a person holy than the desire to glorify God. Glorification of God and sanctification of humans both characterize Christian worship. Apparent tensions between them are superficial. Hoon's use of revelation and response illuminates this: humans must be addressed in terms they can comprehend and must express their worship in forms that are authentic. Comprehensibility and authenticity are both part of worship. Furthermore, artistically naïve people have often created high art through their genuineness of expression.

Another way of speaking about Christian worship has become common in many Roman Catholic and Protestant circles in recent years. It is the tendency to describe Christian worship as "the Paschal mystery." Much of the popularity of this term is due to the writings of Dom Odo Casel, O.S.B., a German Benedictine monk who died in 1948, though its roots are as old as the church. The Paschal mystery is the risen Christ present and active in our worship. "Mystery" in this sense is God's self-disclosure of that which passes human understanding or the revelation of that hitherto hidden. The "Paschal" element is the central, redemptive act of Christ in his life, ministry, suffering, death, resurrection, and ascension. We can speak of the Paschal mystery as the Christian community sharing in Christ's redemptive acts as it worships.

Casel discusses the way that Christians live, "our own sacred history," through worship, in his *Mystery of Christian Worship*. As the church commemorates the events of salvation history, "Christ himself is present and acts through the church, his *ecclesia,* while she acts with him." Thus these very acts of Christ again become present with all their power to save. What Christ has done in the past is again given to the worshiper to experience and appropriate in present time. It is a way of living with the Lord. The church presents what Christ has done through the worshiping congregation's reenactment of these events. The worshiper can reexperience them for his or her own salvation.[6]

Two other definitions may be meaningful. The first is to speak of what happens in Christian worship: "called from the world, we come together, deliberately seeking to approach reality at its deepest level by encountering God in and through Jesus Christ and by responding to this awareness."[7] Several things need to be clarified in this definition. It underscores the corporate character, undoubtedly intended by the other definitions but not always specified in the sections cited. Underhill tells us that "the worshipping life of the Christian, whilst profoundly personal, is essentially that of a person who is also a member of a group. . . . The Christian as such cannot fulfill his spiritual obligations in solitude. . . . even his most lonely contemplations are not merely a private matter." Christian worship is a possibility only "in and through Jesus Christ." Though the definition includes the human context of the expectation that we bring to worship, it is meant to stress the activity of Jesus Christ in which we become united to Christ's eternal self-offering for us.

Three terms stand out in this approach: expectation, encounter, and response. Christian worship is not accidental; it involves deliberate seeking. The encounter that we seek in worship is not new discoveries of information but fresh vision of the basis of reality, God. And the gamut of responses is as wide as human expression can be. Deliberate communal expectation, encounter with the reality of God, and appropriate response would seem to be characteristic of all genuine Christian worship, no matter how varied its forms.

Second, I have developed a different type of definition, which may have some value at times. It is freer, less theological: "Christian worship is speaking and touching in God's name." This suggests a more personal and physical way to understand worship than an abstract intellectual definition provides. The meaning of this definition is that in worship we speak to God for people and to people for God. At the same time, our worship involves touching people in God's name, especially (but not entirely) in the sacraments.

The advantage of such a definition is that it reminds us that Christian worship is actual words and action and occurs in a specific time and place. It also reminds us that worship is not an abstract theological definition but something that one can only experience in the midst of a living, breathing congregation. As such, it needs to be experienced as well as defined. Definitions may make the experience more meaningful, but the experience of Christian worship in one's own life is absolutely necessary to understand the definitions.

Each of the eight definitions discussed above is only a way station on the reader's own journey toward an understanding of Christian worship. One must remain open to other definitions and to deeper understanding of these as he or she continues to experience and to reflect upon Christian worship.

II

Another useful way to clarify what we mean by "Christian worship" is to look at some of the key words the Christian community has chosen to use when speaking about its worship. Often such words were secular in origin but they were chosen as the least inadequate means of expressing what the assembled community experienced in worship.

There has been a rich variety of such words in past and current use. Each word adds shades of meaning that complement the others. A quick survey of the most widely used words relating to worship in several Western languages can show the realities being expressed.

We have already encountered one important word, the German term *Gottesdienst.* It is a word of which the English language could well be envious. Seven English words are needed to duplicate it: God's service and our service to God. The "God" part is obvious, but less familiar is *dienst,* which has no English cognate. Travelers will recognize it as the word identifying every service station in Germanic lands. **Service** is the nearest English equivalent, and it is interesting that we, too, use this word for services of worship just as commonly as we use it for gas stations. "Service" means something done for others whether we speak of a secretarial service, the Forest Service, or a catering service. It reflects work offered to the public even though usually for private profit. Ultimately it comes from the Latin word *servus,* a slave who was bound to serve others. The word **office,** from the Latin *officium,* service or duty, is also used to mean a service of worship. *Gottesdienst* reflects a God who "made himself nothing, assuming the nature of a slave" (Phil. 2:7) and our service to such a God.

It is only a short distance from this concept to that conveyed by our modern English word **liturgy.** Too often confused with smells and bells, "liturgy," like service, has a secular origin. Its origin is the Greek *leitourgía,* composed from words for work *(érgon)* and people *(laós).* In ancient Greece, a liturgy was a public work, something performed for the benefit of the city or state. Its principle was the same as that for paying taxes, but it could involve donated service as well as taxes. Paul speaks of the Roman authorities literally as "liturgists of God" (Rom. 13:6) and of himself as "a liturgist of Christ Jesus to the Gentiles" (Rom. 15:16).

Liturgy, then, is a work performed by the people for the

benefit of others. In other words, it is the quintessence of the priesthood of all believers in which the whole priestly community of Christians shares. To call a service "liturgical" is to indicate that it was conceived so that all worshipers take an active part in offering their worship together. This could apply equally well to a Quaker service and to a Roman Catholic mass, as long as the congregation participated fully in either one. But it could not accurately be applied to worship—whether a mass or a preaching service—in which the congregation was merely a passive audience. A related term is **paraliturgy,** usually a devotion or a service of instruction on the fringe of actual worship. In Eastern Orthodox churches, the word "liturgy" is used in the specific sense of the eucharist, but Western Christians use "liturgical" to apply to all forms of public worship of a participatory nature. Though in origin a secular word for a public work, "liturgy" has become a basic term in Christian worship. Liturgy is the essential outward form through which a community of faith expresses its public worship.

The concept of service, then, is fundamental in understanding worship. A somewhat different concept appears behind the common word in Latin and the Romance languages, a term reflected in our English word **cult.** In English, "cult" tends to suggest the bizarre or faddish, but it has an esteemed function in languages such as French and Italian. Its origin is the Latin *colere,* an agricultural term meaning to cultivate. Both the French *le culte* and the Italian *il culto* preserve this Latin word as the usual term for worship. It is a rich term—far richer than the English word "worship"—for it catches the mutuality of responsibility, as between farmer and land or animals. If I do not feed and water my chickens, I know there will be no eggs; unless I weed my garden, there will be no vegetables. It is a relationship of mutual dependence, a lifelong engagement of caring for and looking after land or animals, a relationship that becomes almost a part of the bone marrow of farmers, especially those whose families have farmed for several generations on the same land. It is a relationship of giving and receiving, certainly not in equal measure, but of being bound to each other. Unfortunately the English language does not readily make the obvious connection between cultivate and worship that we find in the Romance languages. We sometimes find more content in the words of other languages—such as the Italian *domenica* (Lord's day—Sunday), *Pasqua* (Passover—Easter), or *crisma* (Christ—anoint)—than in the English equivalents.

Our English word **worship** also has secular roots. It comes from the Old English word *weorthscipe*—literally *weorth* (worthy) and *-scipe* (-ship)— and signifies attributing worth, value, or respect to someone. It was and still is used to address various lord mayors in England, and the Anglican wedding service since 1549 has contained that wonderful pledge: "with my body I thee worship." The sense in this last case is to respect, esteem, or value another being with one's body. Unfortunately such frankness disturbs us, and this phrase has been banished from most modern wedding services. But the basic insight we gain is that worship means attributing value and esteem or abscribing worth to another being. The English words "revere," "venerate," and "adore" derive ultimately from Latin words for fear, love, and pray.

The New Testament uses a variety of terms for worship, most of them words that also bear other meanings. One of the more common is *latreía,* often translated service or worship. In Rom. 9:4 and Heb. 9:1 and 9:6, it suggests Jewish worship in the temple; or it can mean any religious duty, as in John 16:2. In Rom. 12:1, it is usually translated simply as "worship," and has a similar meaning in Phil. 3:3.

A fascinating insight appears in the word *proskuneîn* which has the explicit physical connotation of falling down to do obeisance or the act of prostration. In the temptation narrative (Matt. 4:10; Luke 4:8), Jesus tells Satan: "Scripture says, 'You shall do homage [*proskunéseis*] to the Lord your God and worship [*latreúseis*] him alone.' " In a famous passage (John 4:23), Jesus tells the Samaritan woman that the time has come when true "worshippers will worship the Father in spirit and in truth." *Proskuneîn* in various forms is used repeatedly throughout this passage. In a less familiar passage, Rev. 5:14, the twenty-four elders fell down and worshiped (*prosekúnesan*). The bodily reality of worship is underscored by this verb.

Two interesting words, *thusía* and *phosphorá,* are both

translated sacrifice or offering. *Thusía* is an important term in the New Testament and the early fathers, having been used for both pagan worship, e.g., "to demons" (I Cor. 10:20) and Christian, e.g., "a living sacrifice" (Rom. 12:1) or "sacrifice of praise" (Heb. 13:15). *Prosphorá* is literally the act of offering or bearing before. It is a favorite term in I Clement whether referring to Abraham's offering of Isaac or those of the clergy or of Christ "the high priest of our offerings" (36:1). Heb. 10:10 speaks of "the offering of the body of Jesus Christ once and for all." Both words play a significant, if controversial, role in the development of Christian eucharistic theology.

A much less prominent word in the New Testament literature is *threskeía,* a religious service or cult, as in Acts 26:5, Col. 2:18, and James 1:26. *Sébein* signifies "to worship" as in Matt. 15:9; Mark 7:7; and Acts 18:3 and 19:27. In Acts, another use of the verb designates God-fearers, Gentiles who attended synagogue worship (13:50; 16:14; 17:4, 17; and 18:7). One other term from the New Testament has important uses to describe worship. *Homologeîn* has a variety of meanings, such as to confess sins (I John 1:9) "if we confess our sins"; to declare or profess publicly (Rom. 10:9) "if on your lips is the confession, 'Jesus is Lord' "; or for the praise of God (Heb. 13:15) "the tribute of lips which acknowledge his name."

These terms from other languages can illuminate the one-dimensional English term "worship." All are worth pondering to give rich composite insights into what others have experienced at various times and places. A few English words related to worship need some clarification.

We need to make a clear distinction between two kinds of worship: common worship and personal devotions. The most obvious note of **common worship** is that it is the worship offered by the gathered congregation, the assembly of Christians. The importance of meeting or coming together can hardly be overstated. At times, the Jewish term "synagogue" (coming together) was also used for the Christian assembly (James 2:2), but the chief term for the Christian assembly is the church, the *ekklesía,* those who are called out from the world. This word for the assemblage, congregating, meeting, convening, or gathering is used repeatedly throughout the New Testament for the local or universal church. One of the most easily overlooked aspects of common worship is that it begins with the coming together in one place of scattered Christians to be the church at worship. We usually treat the act of assembling as merely a mechanical necessity, but it is itself an important part of common worship. We assemble to meet God and encounter our neighbors in so doing.

Personal devotions, on the other hand, usually occur apart from the physical presence of the rest of the body of Christ. By no means is this to say that they are not linked to the worship of other Christians. Indeed, personal devotions and common worship are both fully corporate since both share in the worship of the universal community of the body of Christ. But being alone, the individual engaging in personal devotions can determine his or her own pace and contents, even while following a widely used structure such as the liturgy of the hours. On the other hand, for common worship to be possible, there must be consensus on structure, words, and actions or else chaos would ensue. No such ground rules are necessary in devotions where the individual sets the discipline. ("Devotion" comes from a Latin word for vow.)

The relationship between common worship and personal devotions is important. Although the subject of this book is common worship and little will be said about personal devotions, it should be clear that common worship and personal devotions depend upon each other. As Evelyn Underhill tells us:

[Common] and personal worship, though in practice one commonly tends to take precedence of the other, should complete, reinforce, and check each other. Only where this happens, indeed, do we find in its perfection the normal and balanced life of full Christian devotion. . . . No one soul—not even the greatest saint—can fully apprehend all that this has to reveal and demand of us, or perfectly achieve this balanced richness of response. That response must be the work of the whole Church; within which souls in their infinite variety each play a part, and give that part to the total life of the Body.

Common worship needs to be supplemented by the individuality of personal devotions; personal devotions need the balance of common worship.

27

A widely used term in recent years is the word celebration. It is frequently used in secular contexts and seems to have developed a vagueness that makes it rather meaningless unless used with a specific object so that one knows what is being celebrated. If one speaks of celebration of the eucharist or celebration of Christmas, the content may be clear. Since the 1920s the word has been linked to such indefinite notions as celebration of life, joy, a new day, and other equally vacuous objects. It seems better to use it to describe Christian worship only when the object is clear and has a definiteness in content and form that the word "celebration" no longer implies. Christian worship is subject to pastoral, theological, and historical norms; celebration easily eludes all these.

Ritual is a basic term for Christian worship. It is a tricky term since it means different things to different people. To many people it often implies an empty ritual, a rut of meaningless repetitions. Anthropologists use the term in a more sophisticated way to describe repeated actions that are socially approved, such as a naturalization ceremony, a potlatch, or burial customs. Liturgists use the term to mean a book of rites. Rites are the actual words spoken or sung in a service of worship, though the term is often used to include all aspects of a service. Rites differ from actions or ceremonials, what is done in worship. Ceremonial is usually indicated in service books by rubrics, i.e., directions for carrying out the service. Rubrics are frequently printed in red, as the name indicates. Another essential is the basic structure for each service, called an ordo or order (of worship). Order, rite, and rubrics—i.e., structure, words, and directions—are the basic components of most service books. For Roman Catholics, the word "ritual" refers to the basic book of pastoral offices such as baptisms, weddings, and funerals. For Methodists, "ritual" has been used since 1848 for all the official services of the church including the eucharist and ordinal in addition to the pastoral offices.

III

The third and perhaps best means of making up our minds as to what we mean by "Christian worship" is through description of the outward and visible forms by which Christians worship. This approach looks at the whole phenomenon of Christian worship as it might appear to someone alien to Christianity. It means supplementing our definitions and word studies with observation of just what occurs, as far as the uninvolved observer can detect, when Christians gather to worship.

Such an effort has its complications, however. Christian worship is a fascinating mixture of **constancy** and **diversity**. Christian worship is practiced in almost every country in the world today and has accumulated almost twenty centuries of history in an enormous variety of cultures. It is not surprising, therefore, that one should encounter a diversity of forms used to express such worship. More surprising is the degree of constancy that we encounter despite such widespread variety of times and places. There are, it appears, certain givens in Christian worship that are capable of being adapted to an enormous variety of cultural circumstances. In trying to specify what these givens are, we must at the same time be fully aware of the diversity Christian worship has developed in two hundred countries and two thousand years.

One way to grasp the constancy in Christian worship is to look at the basic structures of worship and the books used for those structures. But peoples and places are equally important, and a quick survey of them can give us some idea of the diversity present in our subject. We shall try to do justice to both unity and multiplicity in the phenomenon of Christian worship.

The most noticeable instance of constancy in Christian worship is the persistent dominance of **four basic structures** of worship plus a more loosely defined collection of **rites of passage.** Most of this book will be a description of these five items, so there is no need to do more than list them here. They include, first, the understanding and use of time as a means of communication so that it shapes and organizes the other structures (chapter 2). Second, there are structures of worship centered in orderly daily instruction and praise and known by such names as the divine office or liturgy of the hours (chapter 4). Equally common are services of initiation, which mark the actions of the making of a Christian (chapter

6). And the most widespread structure of all is the Lord's Supper, or eucharist (chapters 4 and 7). There are also several widely recognized rites of passage that mark transitions in a person's or a community's life experience, such as marriage, ordination, sickness, and burial (chapter 8).

There are, of course, other forms of worship than these, though they are largely peripheral to the main body of Christian worship. One can think of occasional offices such as various blessings or consecrations of persons and objects, several types of prayer meetings, processions, revival services, hymn sings, and sacred concerts. There are also various paraliturgical events in which instructional efforts are made, such as a service without sermon or communion but with a commentary on each act of worship. These types of worship are subject to wide variety but are not the main diet of Christian worship. When all is said and done, it is remarkable how much constancy there is in the focus on time, liturgy of the hours, initiations, eucharist, and the various rites of passage. Most Christian communities center their worship life in this short list of basics.

Another way of glimpsing the constancy in Christian worship is by looking at the service books used. This demands caution; for it is tempting, and dangerous, to identify worship with books. Books are, indeed, used for much, if not most, worship; and they are certainly the easiest evidence of worship to study and to analyze. But much worship is based on **spontaneity,** the hardest element to study. Various types of worship contain differing degrees of both fixed formulas for word and action (such as are found in books) and spontaneity, which ebbs and flows as the spirit moves and is not subject to the medium of print. Though we shall say little about spontaneity, it is nevertheless an important ingredient in contemporary worship in all Western churches.

Where the neo-Pentecostal movement has reached people, among the classical Pentecostalists, and in many black churches, spontaneous exclamations are a vital part of worship. Quaker worship is spontaneity itself, though it exemplifies the need for a self-disciplined freedom for spontaneity to bear its best fruit. Spontaneity is not just turning people loose for individual introspection or speaking. It is the using of the various gifts of different people for the benefit of the whole gathered community. Paul's chapter on spontaneous worship immediately follows that on love (I Cor. 13) and aims at one purpose: building up the church (I Cor. 14:26). What gifts Christians have received are given to be shared in community, not kept in isolation.

Early Christian worship apparently involved some spontaneity. Most of it apparently had disappeared by the late fourth century only to spark up again in some Reformation traditions. Pentecostalist worship in the twentieth century has stressed the unexpected possibilities of spontaneous worship. The absence of service books or printed bulletins in some churches by no means ensures spontaneity. In many congregations, repetition has firmly established a structure of worship that is followed with little variation and no allowance for surprise. On the other hand, traditions that use service books increasingly today make place for elements of spontaneity within their structured service. These include responses to the sermon, intercessions, directed meditation, or statements about the concerns of the church.

If we say little in this book about spontaneity in worship, it is not because it is unimportant but simply because it is so exasperatingly difficult to chronicle since the evidence of it is so ephemeral. But it should be clear that worship and service books are by no means synonymous. Service books can only provide standard formulas. A healthy balance must remain between such formulas and the unwritten and unplanned elements that only spontaneity can provide.

With this caveat, let us look at what **service books** can tell us about constancy in Christian worship. Virtually all worship makes use of the Bible, which itself includes many portions written for cultic purposes. The Quakers are an exception to this statement, but biblical literacy among Quakers makes up for the lack of actual reading from the Bible in their public worship. Most Protestants and Roman Catholics also make use of a hymnal. In addition, worship in Roman Catholicism and several traditions of Protestantism frequently or always employs a service book. In short, at least one book is regarded as a necessity for worship in most of Christianity.

The books we shall survey are service books. They give a vivid glimpse of the constancy in Christian worship. Even though the books vary among themselves, their contents have remarkable similarities. Despite differences in traditions, common needs and similar resources to fill those needs are noticeable.

In the early church, a variety of books was used by a variety of people performing ministries of worship leadership within a single service. Both lay people and clergy had their recognized ministries to perform and proper books to enable them to take their distinctive parts in worship. The idea of everything in one book, and that book in the hands of the clergy only, is a medieval development that has little to recommend it. Currently there is a reversal of the single-book mentality and a return to various books for lectors, commentators, song leaders, and priests or ministers. There are, after all, a variety of ministerial roles in leading worship, roles that can be shared among a number of people when appropriate books are available.

The invention of printing, in the fifteenth century, brought about a new possibility—that of liturgical standardization. In the early sixteenth century there were some two hundred varieties of mass books in use in parishes and religious orders. (Five different uses are mentioned in the Preface to the 1549 *Book of Common Prayer*: those of Salisbury [Sarum], Hereford, Bangor, York, and Lincoln.) Both Roman Catholics and Protestants became convinced that liturgical uniformity was progress. And so the first Anglican prayerbook decreed that "from hencefurth, all the whole realme shall haue but one use." Effectively the same thing was done in standardizing the Roman Catholic books down to the last comma with exceptions allowed only for a few dioceses and religious orders.[8] Such a standardizing tendency in seventeenth-century Rome stifled a Chinese missal and other indigenous cultural adaptions that might have greatly strengthened the mission to China and drastically changed subsequent history.

Today, Protestants and Roman Catholics alike see standardization as a false goal. What may have been liberating in the sixteenth century now seems oppressive in the twentieth. We prefer instead to speak of **indigenization,** i.e., the adapting of universal rites to the cultures and customs of various peoples in diffcrent parts of the world or in different groups within the same society. Our times try to undo the medieval clericalization that compressed all liturgical books into clerical documents and the sixteenth-century standardization that made all books identical whether for clergy or laity. A variety of ministries in a variety of cultures demands a much more pluralistic approach to liturgical books. We may eventually see parallel service books put out by a single denomination, with several in effect at the same time. The notion that the advent of a new service book makes its predecessor obsolete should by now be an obsolete idea. We may see genuine liturgical pluralism with several alternative routes of equal authority available within the same denomination. The choice of books would be tailored to fit the worship to the people and situation involved rather than vice versa.

The basic book for the structure of time is, of course, the **calendar.** Its brevity should not conceal its importance. It governs those elements which change from day to day or from season to season in the daily round of services comprising the liturgy of the hours and the eucharist and appears in breviaries and missals. Somewhat similar is the **martyrology,** a book of the deeds of the martyrs and other saints arranged by calendar according to the day of their death.

The services revolving around the liturgy of the hours have entailed a whole collection of books, especially as developed in monastic worship. Various types of books originally allowed different people to perform their individual functions. The most important was the **psalter,** with psalms and canticles arranged in a variety of ways in different editions. Some were structured according to the weekly recital of the psalms, or to accord with feasts, or for each hour service. Musical portions appeared in the **antiphonary** and the **hymnal.** A lectionary eventually contained collections of the scripture readings for the night office of the liturgy of the hours.[9]

If it all sounds very complicated, it was; but each person had only to master certain parts, found in the appropriate book. All this changed in time, though not until eleven centuries had elapsed. Then efforts to collect this whole library of books for the daily services into a single book, the **breviary,** began to succeed. The advent of the Franciscan and Dominican orders in the thirteenth century—orders that were on the road constantly—brought about widespread use of the breviary, in which an isolated individual could read all of the daily services. Use of the breviary was also encouraged by the life-style of the Roman curia. But the breviary represents a tremendous loss in the variety of ministries and in worship as a community. The 1971 *Liturgy of the Hours,* which replaced the 1568 Roman breviary, seeks to return these services to both lay and clerical use.

The Reformation, in turn, compressed the breviary still further, into Luther's proposed two daily offices and those in the *Book of Common Prayer,* where psalter, calendar, lectionary, and morning and evening prayer had to share space with other types of worship. This development did make all types of worship available for the person in the pew, but it meant drastic reduction in the options provided.

The history of the books for initiation and the rites of passage is quite different. Originally, many of these rites occurred in the sacramentary, the priest's book for celebrating the eucharist and other sacraments. It contained all the appropriate prayers for various occasions and seasons. Baptism and confirmation, for example, occurred at the Easter vigil in the earliest books; ordinations tended to come during Lent. In the course of time, baptism and other rites were weened away from the sacramentaries, and separate books were developed for the various offices. The revolution in the practice of penance, for example, led to penitentials being compiled for the guidance of pastor and penitent. Benedictionals contained collections of various blessings of people and objects, some blessings being reserved for bishops only and others for priests. In time, these various rites of initiation and passage found their way into collections known variously as the *pastorale, manuale* (handbook), *sacramentale, agenda* or *rituale* (**ritual**). Litanies, hymns, prayers, and rubrics for processions found a place in the *processionale.* The Reformation simply incorporated much of the material into a simple service book. For example, the *Sarum Manuale* provided most of the 1549 BCP wedding service. Some churches still use the ancient terms, as in the *Pastor's Manual* published by the Church of the Brethren in 1978. The *Rituale Romanum* of 1614, was, in effect, a collection of ten separate books: general rules and rites, baptism, penance, administration of the eucharist, ministration to the sick and dying, funerals, matrimony, blessings, processions, and exorcisms. Since Vatican II, most of these rites have been revised and published as separate books. At present, there is no single-volume Roman ritual.

Nowhere else has the constancy of Christian worship been quite as readily apparent as in the pastoral offices found in the ritual. American Methodists still get married with almost the same vows as fourteenth-century English Catholics. The basic human needs to which the ritual ministers are common: birth, marriage, sickness, and death. Along the way we need to be forgiven and to have God's blessing invoked on people and things about us.

The history of the rites that concern the bishop is similar. Prayers for ordinations originally occurred in the sacramentaries and **ordines** (collections of instructions). Gradually, by a process not fully understood, the bishop's special rites became collected in a special volume, the **pontifical.** In the late thirteenth century, Bishop William **Durandus** of Mende, in southern France, edited a pontifical that has shaped all subsequent ones. Within it occurred the services for the blessing or consecration of various persons, such as confirmation, tonsure, ordinations; the blessings of abbots and abbesses; the consecration of virgins; the coronation of kings and queens, and so on. In addition, there were rites for the blessing or consecration of such objects as churches, an altar-table, vessels, vestments, bells, and cemeteries. And finally there was an assortment of rites for excommunication, reconciliation of penitents, blessing of holy oils, processions, and such. Some of this material, such as the ordination services, appears as the **ordinal** in most Protestant service books. Most of these books also retain rites for confirmation and the blessing and consecration of various persons and objects, such as offices for recognizing Sunday school teachers or for laying cornerstones. Most of the pontifical has been revised since Vatican II. No Protestant parallel exists for a late collection, the *Caeremoniale Episcoporum,* a 1600 compilation of rubrics and instructions on ceremonial for bishops. A new revision of this has yet to appear.

The other major collection of books is that dealing with the eucharist. We have already encountered the most important of these books, the **sacramentary,** which includes prayers for the priest's use appropriate to various seasons and events. The term "sacramentary" has been revived in recent years for the comprehensive volume used at the altar-table in Roman Catholic churches though it does not include materials now found in the pontifical or ritual as did early sacramentaries. But there are other ministries at the eucharist besides that of the celebrant. A **lectionary,** or *comes,* provided the lector, subdeacon, or deacon with lists of the beginnings and endings of lections read at mass. Eventually the lections were included in full.[10] Musicians depended upon the **graduale** for sung portions of the eucharist.[11] What we would call rubrics were supplied in early times in various *ordines,* which also dealt with the eucharist and with services now found in the pontifical or ritual. Forces were at work here similar to those influencing the breviary, the ritual, and the pontifical. By the late medieval period, the clergy got all the books, as the lections, musical portions, and rubrics were placed together in the **missal** so one priest could "say" mass by himself. From the end of the tenth century on, the missal simply echoed the clerical monopoly of worship that had already occurred through a variety of other forces. The sixteenth century standardized the missal except for a few dioceses or religious orders. The *Missale Romanum* of **1570** remained scarcely changed (except for new feasts) for exactly four hundred years—or until the Vatican II revision was published. Once again the lections have been relegated to a separate volume—the lectionary—and others besides the celebrant are again encouraged to exercise ministerial functions at mass.

The contents of the missal proved no less essential to the

Reformers. Most of them produced their own orders of mass and incorporated them into their service books, sometimes accompanied by collects and lessons appropriate to the various days of the church year. Even on the American frontier, the Methodists preserved an irreducible minimum of fixed forms for the eucharist. The contents found in the missal are as universal as any fixed rites in Christianity and provide a fascinating study of constancy.

Thus the contents of several of the liturgical books seem to witness to those constancies for which we are looking. The Reformation merely took to their final step the processes of compression and standardization already well under way in Roman Catholicism. Some of the Reformers managed to cram into a single volume calendar, breviary, ritual, processional, pontifical, and missal but found they could do quite well without the martyrology or the *Caeremoniale*. People and clergy shared the same books. The results, whether in the *Book of Common Prayer,* the *Book of Common Order,* John Wesley's *Sunday Service,* or various others are remarkably similar in their consensus as to the essentials of Christian worship. Gradually Protestants and Roman Catholics seem to be recognizing the values of a variety of ministries served by a variety of books, as seen in the several editions of the new *Lutheran Book of Worship* or the various United Methodist *Supplemental Worship Resources.*

Of course, there are many differences between all these books of the same type. The comparative study of rites is known as **liturgiology** and in the last hundred years has become a highly specialized science. But the striking fact remains the remarkable degree of consensus among these books from differing times and places as to what are deep human needs to be served and the ways to provide for them.

Much of this diversity is not due to disagreement over the needs to be served or the theological principles to be maintained. Rather the differences are reflections of the differences in peoples and places. The liturgical books provide parallel routes to cover the same journey. But they differ in style and details, just as different peoples in different places vary in the foods they prefer or the styles of clothing they wear.

It is now realized how important it is for Christian worship to reflect these national and ethnic differences. Therefore we cannot characterize Christian worship, even in sketchy fashion, without some indication of the varieties of peoples and places that have given it diversity.

Let us compare two passages with identical functions from the world's most widely used liturgies. The first is from the pre–Vatican II Roman Catholic mass, the common preface of the eucharistic prayer:

Just it is indeed and fitting, right, and for our lasting good, that we should always and everywhere give thanks to thee, Lord, holy Father, almighty and eternal God, through Christ our Lord.

The second is the same passage from the Liturgy of St. John Chrysostom:

It is fitting and right to sing to You, to bless You, to praise You, to give thanks to You, to worship You in every place of your dominion: for You are God, beyond description, beyond understanding, invisible, incomprehensible, always existing, always the same; You and your only-begotten Son and your Holy Spirit.

Both say the same thing, but the style and the spirit are quite different. The language of the first has been compared to the legalistic style of the Roman law court; the second, to the splendor of the court of the Byzantine emperors. Obviously we are dealing with two different styles of expression.

Liturgical scholars have sorted out the various ancient eucharistic liturgies into **seven classical liturgical families.** Like human families, they bear common features. Some belong to the Alexandrian family named after St. Mark and place the intercessions in the middle of the opening part of the eucharistic prayer. Others, such as the Roman rite, use characteristic words to introduce the words of institution—"who the day before he suffered"; while other families, such as that named after St. John Chrysostom, prefer the phrase: "on the night on which He was delivered up." Just as one may recognize a certain person's sons and daughters or brothers and sisters by

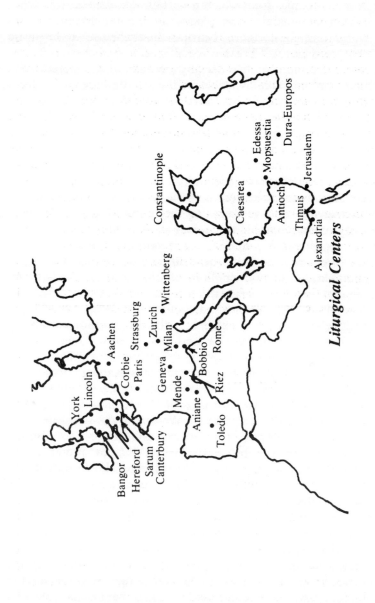

Liturgical Centers

Constantinople

Caesarea
Edessa
Mopsuestia
Dura-Europos
Jerusalem
Antioch
Thmuis
Alexandria

Aachen
Strassburg
Zurich
Wittenberg
Corbie
Paris
Milan
Bobbio
Rome
Geneva
Mende
Riez
York
Lincoln
Aniane
Toledo
Bangor
Hereford
Sarum
Canterbury

facial similarities, so too one can learn to recognize the liturgical family from which a certain text comes.

Different peoples and places around the Mediterranean world and in northern Europe gave their own linguistic characteristics to Christian worship. Some of these different features disappeared, especially because of the stereotyping that printing made available in the sixteenth century. But a wide variety still persists, particulary in Eastern Orthodoxy. There is variety even within Roman Catholicism, though confined to places such as Milan, Italy; Toledo, Spain; or in the Uniate churches. In these disparate rites, we have frank acknowledgment of the true catholicity, i.e., universality, of the church. What may seem like curious and quaint survivals are actually the voices of different peoples and places, adding their own distinctive voices to the praise of God.

It is common to identify seven areas of liturgical activity in the ancient world, though it is important to remember that survivors from each of these liturgical families still are in common use today by millions of Christians. These different families all use the same structures of worship, the same types of service books, but each shows individual peculiarities of style and expression. They exemplify diversity within constancy.

It is easiest to go around the Mediterranean world counterclockwise for a quick enumeration of these seven families. The first family is centered in **Alexandria,** Egypt, the most notable example being known as St. Mark. It has Coptic and Ethiopian survivors today in Egypt and Ethiopia. The second family is concentrated in **Western Syria,** which included the liturgical centers of Jerusalem and Antioch. A liturgy, probably conflating those used in these cities, preserves the traditional name of St. James, brother of the Lord and first bishop of Jerusalem. **Eastern Syria** around Edessa was the early center of the third family, a most distinctive one, of which the prime example is the rite named for Sts. Addai and Mari (Thaddeus and Marius). Caesarea, in Asia Minor, was the home of **St. Basil,** and the liturgy named after him (with an earlier Alexandrian version) derives from the western Syrian pattern. Also deriving from a western Syrian background is the fifth type, the so-called **Byzantine** liturgy, named after St. John

Chrysostom, fourth-century patriarch of Constantinople. From Constantinople this liturgy spread throughout much of the Byzantine empire and Russia. Only the **Roman rite,** at one time known as the rite of St. Peter, is in wider use. It is the dominant rite of Roman Catholicism. A large and mysterious family, the **Gallic,** comprises the seventh, the non-Roman Western clan. This family tree has four branches: the Ambrosian, the Mozarabic, the Celtic, and the Gallican. Relics of the Gallican rites appear in both Roman Catholic and Protestant liturgies today, such as the Anglican-Methodist collect for purity: "Almighty God, unto whom all hearts are open."

The persistence to this day of this diversity within the Orthodox and Catholic worlds, despite occasional efforts at suppression and standardization, is a triumph for ethnic and national differences. It represents the ability of people to preserve expressions and thought forms natural and dear to them. Today the importance of these diversities is cherished, and indigenization is a high priority for many churches. It seems likely that the next stage in liturgical development will be to encourage the survival and creation of more localisms and cultural diversities.

Diversity characterized Protestant worship from the start. By coincidence, most Protestant worship also falls into seven fairly distinct patterns. It is not as easy to distinguish these on the basis of eucharistic liturgies as the Roman Catholic and Orthodox liturgical families. Some groups, such as the Quakers, have no liturgies. But we can speak of distinct liturgical traditions, i.e., inherited habits and assumptions about worship as well as actual documents and practices. Some Protestant traditions, to be sure, can be easily defined in terms of service books. In each case, though, certain dominant characteristics have sufficient coherence to distinguish a distinct tradition.[12]

It is not easy to differentiate these traditions geographically since they overlap considerably. Free Church people, Anglicans, and Quakers lived side by side in seventeenth-century England, if not too happily. We can chart somewhat the dominant influences among the **seven Protestant liturgical traditions** thus:

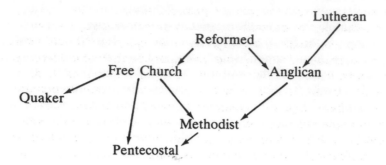

The chart moves downward from the sixteenth century to the twentieth and in a more conservative direction to the right.

Lutheran worship, originating in Wittenberg, thrived in the Germanic and Scandinavian countries in the sixteenth century and since has spread throughout the world. **Reformed** worship had its genesis in Switzerland (Geneva and Zurich) and France (Strassburg) but quickly spread throughout the Netherlands, France, Scotland, Hungary, and England. **Anglican** worship, as its name indicates, was that of the national church of England and represented many of the political compromises necessary for a national church. The **Free Church** tradition is the hardest to define. It, too, had its origins in Switzerland, but persecution drove the Anabaptists underground. They surfaced in the Netherlands and various Germanic lands. Under a different form, the Free Church tradition appeared in England among Independents (Congregationalists) and Baptists and found fertile soil in America, where it is the dominant worship tradition among Protestants. The Disciples of Christ, Churches of Christ, and many others stand in this tradition.

The most radical tradition was the seventeenth-century **Quaker** movement. The Quakers' silent waiting on God without the aid of sermons, songs, or scriptures made a clear break with the past. **Methodism,** in the eighteenth century, combined many strands, from both ancient and Reformation times, borrowing especially from the Anglican and Free Church traditions. America gave birth to the **Pentecostal** tradition in the

42

twentieth century, with blacks and women among the earliest leaders in developing this tradition.

Once again, we see in these seven traditions a constancy in basic structures of worship and types of service books (the Quakers being the chief exception) but considerable diversity in style. In eighteenth-century England, as today, those who felt too constrained by the BCP could hear the same types of services led extemporaneously in the Free Church tradition. And those who found such worship too clerical could find a different kind of freedom among the Quakers. Fervent hymnody and a warm sacramental life among early Methodists attracted others. Different people could match their diversities of expression by choosing the tradition that felt most natural to them. Yet at the same time, there was a high degree of constancy within them all.

This quick survey of definitions, key words, and overview of the phenomenon of Christian worship will, I hope, help the reader make up his or her mind as to what we mean by Christian worship. Further reading, experience of worship, and reflection can expand this understanding.

II
The Language of Time

The calendar is the foundation for most of Christian worship except the rites of passage. There is no better way to begin our investigation of the basic structures of worship than with an introduction to the way Christians use time as a language through which to speak in worship.

The centrality of time in Christian worship tells us a great deal both about Christianity itself and about Christian worship. It tells us that Christianity is a religion that takes time seriously. History is where God is made known. Without time, there is no knowledge of God. For it is through actual events happening in historical time that God is revealed. God chooses to make the divine nature and will known by events that take place within the same calendar that measures the daily lives of women and men. God's self-disclosure takes place within the same course of time as political events: "In the days of Herod king of Judaea" (Luke 1:5), or "It took place when Quirinius was governor of Syria" (Luke 2:2).

When we encounter one of the Eastern religions in which time is insignificant, we realize just how crucial time is to Christian faith. Much non-Western music also suggests a casual indifference to time, whereas Western music often seems possessed by a fierce urgency to get somewhere. Our music sweeps on toward climaxes and a finale. Christianity talks not of salvation in general but of salvation accomplished by specific actions of God at definite times and places. It speaks of climactic events and a finale to time. For Christianity, the ultimate meanings of life are revealed not by universal and timeless statements but by concrete acts of God. In the fullness of time, God invades our history, assumes our flesh, heals, teaches, and eats with sinners. There is a specific historical and spatial setting to it all. "It was winter, and the festival of the Dedication was being held in Jerusalem. Jesus was walking in the temple precincts, in Solomon's Cloister" (John 10:22-23). And when his work is done, Jesus is put to death on a specific day, related to the Passover festival of that particular year, and rises on the third day. It is the same time we inhabit, time measured by a spatial device, the calendar; the time in which we buy groceries, wash the car, and earn a living.

The centrality of time in Christianity is reflected in Christian worship. This worship, like the rest of life, is structured on recurring rhythms of the week, the day, and the year. Far from trying to escape time, Christian worship uses time as one of its basic structures. Our present time is used to place us in contact with God's acts in time past and future. Salvation, as we experience it in worship, is a reality based on temporal events through which God is given to us. Our use of time enables us to commemorate and reexperience those very acts on which salvation is grounded. Time is a language of communication in daily life (as when we are habitually late for unpleasant engagements). It is a form of communication used in varying ways with different meanings in every culture. Time is a language that Christian worship also speaks fluently.

In order to understand how the structures of Christian worship speak through the use of time, we need to explore the past experiences of Christians in structuring worship on the basis of time, the theological rationales for so doing, and the direction of current practice. Through study of these historical, theological, and pastoral dimensions, we can develop a functional understanding of how time provides the foundation for so much of Christian worship.

I

The way we use our time is a good indication of what we consider of prime importance in life. We can always be counted on to find time for those things we consider most important, though we may not always be willing to admit to others, or even to ourselves, what our real priorities are. Whether it be making money, political action, or family activities, we find the time for putting first those things which matter most to us. Time talks. When we give it to others, we are really giving ourselves. Not only does our use of time show what is important to us, but it also indicates who is most significant to our lives. Time, then, is a dead giveaway of our priorities. How we allocate this limited resource reveals what we value most.

The same is true of the church. The church shows what is most important to its life by the way it keeps time. Here again the use of time reveals priorities of faith and practice. One answer to "What do Christians profess?" could be "Look at how they keep time!" How have Christians kept time?

The earliest portions of the New Testament are imbued with a sense of time as *kairos,* the right or proper time present in which God has accomplished a new dimension to reality: "The time has come; the kingdom of God is upon you" (Mark 1:15). Yet already within the New Testament itself we see the beginning of a tendency to look back, to recall the time past in which things had happened. The eschatological hope, i.e., the belief that the last times were at hand, seems to be slackening by the time Luke writes his Gospel and church history begins with the book of Acts. Remembering comes to be almost as important as anticipating before the first century is done.

The priorities of the early church's faith are disclosed by the way Christians of the second, third, and fourth centuries organized time. This was not by a systematic or even a planned method but the church's spontaneous response to "the events that have happened among us" (Luke 1:1). The same type of response, the keeping alive of memories, had also prompted the writing of the Gospels so that others might be able to follow "the traditions handed down to us by the original eyewitnesses and servants of the Gospel" (Luke 1:2). The use of time was not as systematic as the Evangelists' efforts "to write a connected narrative" (Luke 1:3) but has had almost as consistent an influence in shaping Christian memories as the written Gospels. Thus, for Christians, Easter is an annual *event* just as much as it is a narrative in writing. Even today Christmas is far more a yearly *occurrence* than a nativity story for most people.

What was the faith of the church of the first four centuries, as witnessed to by the church's use of time? It was, above all else, faith in the resurrection of Jesus Christ. Second, it was trust in the abiding presence of the Holy Spirit, known and experienced in the holy church. And it was belief that witnessed to those signs by which God had become manifest among us in Jesus Christ. This may not be a systematic summation of Christian belief, but it gives a clear indication of the heart of the faith of the early church, a faith revealed by how the church kept time.

There even was an implicitly trinitarian structure: belief in the Father made manifest, the Son risen, and the Holy Spirit indwelling the church. This, however, should not be pushed too far since it is far from explicit. But the priorities are clear. Nothing can be more practical for us than probing deeper into the history of how the early church kept time so that we may compare its practices with ours. We may find reasons to readjust our priorities in light of those of the heroic age of Christianity.

The evidence begins not with the church year but with the **church week,** particularly with the testimony of **Sunday.** And our story really begins with the first day of creation when "God said, 'Let there be light,' and there was light. . . . So evening came, and morning came, the first day" (Gen. 1:3-5). The four Gospels are all careful to state that it was on the morning of the first day, i.e., the day on which creation began and God "separated light from darkness," that the empty tomb was discovered.

In at least three places the New Testament indicates a special time for worship, probably Sunday. Paul told the Christians in Corinth to set aside money for the collection on the first day of the week (I Cor. 16:2). At Troas, after talking until midnight on Saturday, Paul broke bread (presumably the eucharist) and remained in conversation with Christians there until Sunday dawned (Acts 20:7, 11). John tells us he "was caught up by the Spirit" and "it was on the Lord's day" (Rev. 1:10). The term "Lord's day" had become a Christian term for the first day of the week by the end of the first century. **Ignatius** wrote about A.D. 115 to the Christians in Magnesia and spoke of those who "ceased to keep the [Jewish seventh-day] Sabbath and lived by the Lord's Day, on which our life as well as theirs shone forth, thanks to Him and his death."[1] The *Didache,* written sometime in the late first or early second century, reminds Christians literally, "on the Lord's day of the Lord come together, break bread and hold eucharist."[2] And even pagans noticed that "on an appointed day they [Christians] had been accustomed to meet before daybreak"; though Pliny, the Roman administrator who wrote those words, hardly understood this to mean a meeting for the Lord's Supper.[3]

Another term appeared by the middle of the second century. **Justin Martyr** told his pagan audience about A.D. 155 that "we all hold this common gathering on Sunday since it is the first day, on which God transforming darkness and matter made the universe, and Jesus Christ our Savior rose from the dead on the same day."[4] Christians soon adopted the newly coined pagan term "Sunday" and compared Christ rising from the dead to the rising sun. Even today, the English and German word is "Sunday," while French and Italian refer to the "Lord's Day." The Epistle of Barnabas called Sunday "an eighth day, that is the beginning of another world . . . in which Jesus also rose from the dead."[5] The themes of a new creation and light are important dimensions in the Christian celebration of Sunday as the day of the resurrection.

Sunday was a day of worship for Christians but not yet of rest. It was made such by the Emperor Constantine in A.D. 321. "All judges, city people, and craftsmen shall rest on the venerable day of the Sun. But countrymen may without hindrance attend to agriculture."[6]

The week had still more contour to it for the early church. Luke tells of the Pharisee who said, "I fast twice a week" (18:12). But the *Didache,* in all seriousness, told Christians: "Your fasts must not be identical with those of the hypocrites. They fast on Mondays and Thursdays; but you should fast on Wednesdays and Fridays."[7] Commemorative reasons had appeared for this by the time of writing of a late fourth-century document, *The Apostolic Constitutions:* "Fast . . . on the fourth day of the week, . . . Judas then promising to betray Him for money; and . . . on [Friday] because on that day the Lord suffered the death of the cross."[8] There is evidence that some early Christians also held a certain regard for Saturday as "the memorial of the creation" from which work God rested on the seventh day. **Tertullian** tells us there were "some few who abstain from kneeling on the Sabbath." All these other days were inferior in importance to Sunday.

Sunday stood out because it was the weekly anniversary of the resurrection. In the early church, Sunday also commemorated the Lord's passion and death but it was, above all else, the day on which the Savior rose from the dead. Even today, Sunday takes precedence over most other observances. Every Sunday witnesses to the risen Lord. It is the Lord's Day, the day of the sun risen from darkness, the start of the new creation. Tertullian tells us Christians did not kneel on Sunday, "the day of the Lord's resurrection." Sundays in Advent and Lent remain days of joy though within penitential seasons. Each Sunday testifies to the resurrection faith. Every Sunday is a weekly little Easter, or rather every Easter is a yearly great Sunday. The primacy of Sunday and the resurrection is clear.

Even the ordinary **day** itself became for the early church a structure of praise. The *Didache* instructed Christians to pray the Lord's Prayer "three times a day." Psalm 55:17 spoke of calling upon God "evening and morning and at noon." Another psalm declared: "Seven times a day I praise thee for the justice of thy decrees" (119:164) and, "At midnight I rise to give thee thanks" (62). By the early third century, Tertullian could speak of the third, sixth, and ninth hours of the day as times of "special solemnity in divine prayers" because of actions of the apostles at those times.

Hippolytus, a Roman Christian in the early third century, could speak of seven daily occasions for prayer. For him, nine o'clock in the morning, noon, and three in the afternoon, respectively, recalled the moments at which Christ was nailed to the cross, "there was a great darkness," and he died. Each day memorialized the crucifixion in this way. Hippolytus saw midnight as a time of prayer, for the bridegroom comes at midnight (Matt. 25:6) and we must be prepared to meet him. Prayer is needed at cockcrow, for at this moment Christ was denied (Matt. 26:75). Prayer is also advocated upon rising and retiring. Monasticism later developed the hours of the day into a daily eightfold cycle of prayer. Late in the fourth century, Chrysostom urged each newly baptized Christian to begin the day's work with prayer for strength to do God's will and to end the day by rendering "an account to the Master of his whole day, and beg forgiveness for his falls."[9] The Christian day, then, early became a cycle of remembering Christ throughout one's daily labors in the midst of worldly concerns. Christians adopted the Jewish sense of the liturgical day beginning at nightfall. Hence the **eve** of a festival (e.g., Christmas Eve, Easter Eve, and Halloween) is a part of the day that continues at daybreak.

Just as the week and the day witnessed to Jesus Christ, so too the early church saw the **year** as a structure for commemorating its Lord. Just as Sunday was the center of the week, so too the year focused on the **Pascha** (Passover-Easter) happenings as its central feature. The Pascha had been the center of the Jewish year; it was no less so for Christians. Paul deliberately took over the language of the Jewish Feast of Unleavened Bread (the Pascha):

The old leaven of corruption is working among you. Purge it out, and then you will be bread of a new baking. As Christians you are unleavened Passover bread; for indeed our Passover has begun; the sacrifice is offered—Christ himself. So we who observe the festival must not use the old leaven, the leaven of corruption and wickedness, but only the unleavened bread which is sincerity and truth. (I Cor. 5:7-8)

This passage is the chief evidence of the keeping of Easter by the New Testament church. The old Jewish commemoration of deliverance was now made completely new in Jesus Christ. Slavery and redemption were rehearsed but in a new sense, through release from sin and death by what Christ had done.

The second- and third-century church kept the Pascha with services signifying the making of new Christians through the acts of baptism, confirmation, and first communion. Just as the Pascha commemorated the escape from slavery by passage through the Red Sea, so too the church saw baptism as a burial with Christ in which "we were buried with him, and lay dead, in order that, as Christ was raised from the dead . . . we shall also be one with him in a resurrection like his" (Rom. 6:4-5). In the first three centuries, Christ's passion, death, and resurrection were commemorated together at the Pascha. Tertullian tells us that "the Passover affords a more than usually solemn day for baptism; when, withal, the Lord's passion in which we are baptized, was completed."[10] Hippolytus tells us that those to be baptized fasted on Friday and Saturday and then began an all-night vigil Saturday evening. At cockcrow, at the hour of the resurrection on Easter morning, they were baptized beneath the waters and rose with Christ as from the dead.

Early in the fourth century the church finally agreed that, unlike the Jewish Passover which could come on any day of the week, the Pascha must always be celebrated on a Sunday. The **Quartodeciman** controversy involved a long debate over whether to follow the Jewish dating or not. The resolution of this controversy clearly recognizes the symbolic meaning of Sunday: "Never on any day other than the Lord's Day should the mystery of the Lord's resurrection from the dead be celebrated. . . . On that day alone we should observe the end of the Paschal fast."[11] Thus the weekly and yearly cycles of resurrection reinforced each other.

In the course of the fourth century, the ancient unitive Pascha, which commemorated all the events of the last days of Jesus in Jerusalem, was divided into distinct commemorations. The dissolution apparently first occurred in **Jerusalem,** where time and space came together at the sites of Jesus' life and ministry. A need was felt to hold separate commemorations for each event at the holy places in order to serve the throngs of pilgrims who were arriving from all over the world. Scripture itself was mined for evidence as to time and place of all the events of Christ's last week in Jerusalem. We have a good example of what had developed by about A.D. 384 as chronicled in the writings of a Spanish woman named **Egeria.** Her notes, apparently written down so she could give talks when she got back home, have survived and give us a clear insight as to how late-fourth-century Jerusalem had developed its way of keeping time.

Egeria tells us that what recent revisions have reunited as Palm/Passion Sunday, or the beginning of Holy Week, was "the beginning of the Easter Week, or, as they call it here, 'The Great Week.' . . . All the people go before him [the bishop] with psalms and antiphons, all the time repeating, 'Blessed is he that cometh in the name of the Lord.' "[12] There were minor services on the next three days, except that on Wednesday the presbyter read about Judas' plot to betray Jesus and "the people groan and lament at this reading." On Thursday, after everyone had received communion, all "conduct the bishop to Gethsemane." And on Friday, services occurred on Golgotha, where fragments of the wood of the cross were adored by all the people. They marched past the cross and kissed it. By the end of the fourth century, the historicizing process was complete, and Augustine stated as accepted fact that "it is clear from the Gospel on what days the Lord was crucified and rested in the tomb and rose again" and that the church has "a requirement of retaining those same days."[13] The ancient unitive Pascha had been broken into separate commemorations: Maundy Thursday, Good Friday, Holy Saturday, and the Easter Vigil, plus Palm/Passion Sunday and the three lesser days of Holy Week. And this is how Christians have kept it ever since. This gives us Holy Week, beginning with Palm/Passion Sunday, Monday, Tuesday, (Spy) Wednesday, Maundy Thursday, Good Friday, Holy Saturday, and Easter (Eve and Day). The English term "Easter" comes from the Old English *eastre,* a pagan spring festival; Romance languages use forms of "Pascha."

Closely connected with Easter are two seasons: Lent and the Season of Easter. **Lent** began as an intensive final period of preparation for those catechumens (converts under training) who had been set apart, after considerable preparation, to be baptized at the Easter Vigil. The Council of Nicaea, A.D. 325, first referred to Lent as "forty days." About A.D. 348, Bishop Cyril of Jerusalem told those to be baptized, "You have a long period of grace, forty days for repentence."[14] By the time of **Augustine,** Lent had become a time of preparation for all Christians, baptized or not, in the "part of the year . . . adjoining . . . and touching on the Lord's passion." It begins on **Ash Wednesday;** the Sundays in Lent are not counted as part of the forty days.

Far more important was the **Season of Easter,** the fifty days extending the celebration of Easter through the Day of Pentecost. The great fifty-day season (originally called "the Pentecost") was far more important than the forty days of Lent. It is perplexing why modern Christians concentrate on Lent, the season of sorrow, rather than on the Season of Easter, the season of joy. Augustine tells us: "These days after the Lord's Resurrection form a period, not of labor, but of peace and joy. That is why there is no fasting and we pray standing, which is a sign of resurrection. This practice is observed at the altar on all Sundays, and the Alleluia is sung, to indicate that our future occupation is to be no other than the praise of God."[15] The resurrection was and is commemorated by a day of the week, a day of the year, and a season. There can be no doubt as to the centrality of the resurrection in the life and faith of the early church.

The most significant development in the fourth-century calendar was the elaboration of **Holy Week** (beginning with Palm/Passion Sunday) and Easter Week (beginning with Easter Day). Much of this elaboration occurred in Jerusalem, very likely under the leadership of **Cyril of Jerusalem,** bishop from 349 to 386. Egeria gives us a full report of what was being done in Jerusalem shortly before Cyril's death. Eventually the Jerusalem practices became common throughout Christianity and represent some of the church's oldest liturgical treasures. The Holy Week rites commemorate the climactic moments of Jesus' ministry and death in Jerusalem. They use the most dramatic forms of Christian worship. Indeed, medieval drama sprang from Easter Day worship but eventually became too complicated to remain in the chancels. It was natural that Jerusalem should be the place where such dramatic rites developed, for the actual settings of the events leading up to and following Jesus' death were at hand. Ever since Constantine made Christianity respectable, pilgrims had been flocking to see those places for themselves. All that was needed for liturgical realism was to match the times and places mentioned in scripture with appropriate ceremonies. Jerusalem fused these elements together in the fourth century, and they have shaped Christian worship ever since. Revived in fuller form in 1955 under Pius XII, the rites of Holy Week were reformed after Vatican II and appear in the *Sacramentary* (pp. 196-231). Similar rites have found increasingly enthusiastic responses in recent years among Protestants, despite general unfamiliarity of Protestants with these rites (cf. BCP, 270-95; LBW—Ministers Desk Edition only—134-53; and SWR #8).

The fully developed rites include on **Palm/Passion Sunday** an opening procession with palms and a dramatic reading (usually with several readers) of one of the passion narratives from the Gospels. **Maundy Thursday** begins in Roman Catholic cathedrals with the Chrism mass, in which are consecrated the three oils used sacramentally in parish churches during the year. The unity of all the priests of the diocese with their bishop is stressed in this manner. The **Easter Triduum** (three days) begins at sunset Thursday, as the most holy part of the Christian year commences. The evening is marked in most churches by a eucharist commemorating Christ's gift in giving us this sacrament as at this time and the events of his passion. Often **foot washing** is included (John 13:3-17), and at the conclusion of the service the altar-table is stripped and all crosses and images removed or covered until Easter Eve.

Traditionally the Lord's Supper is not celebrated on **Good Friday** or **Holy Saturday,** the Netherlands Reformed Church being an exception. The ancient Good Friday rite includes the liturgy of the word with extensive intercessions, **veneration of the cross** (kneeling before it or kissing it), the singing of the **reproaches** (Lam. 1:12), and possibly the giving of communion with elements consecrated on Maundy Thursday. A seventeenth-century rite from Peru, the **Three Hours,** is based on the seven last words of Jesus from the cross. The service of **tenebrae** (darkness) may occur on any or all of the last three days of Holy Week with the reading of fifteen psalms plus lessons and the gradual extinguishing of the fifteen candles on a special large candlestick.

Easter Eve climaxes the whole year with the **Easter Vigil** as the church gathers in darkness to celebrate the resurrection. Traditionally it includes the kindling of new fire and lighting of the **Paschal candle;** the singing of the Easter *exsultet;* the reading of nine lessons, mostly from the Old Testament; the blessing of water, and baptism or renewal of baptismal vows; and the celebration of the Easter eucharist.

In ancient times, **Easter week** was devoted to instruction of the newly baptized in the meaning of the sacraments, the so-called **mystagogical catechesis.** Fourth-century collections of these catechetical lectures survive, attributed to Cyril of Jerusalem, Ambrose, Chrysostom, and Theodore of Mopsuestia. They are very important documents for recovering both the practices of various Christian centers and the differing interpretations given of these practices. On the Sunday following Easter, the new Christians doffed their white robes as fully initiated and instructed members of the body of Christ.

Second in importance in early centuries was the celebration of another event, the **Day of Pentecost.** Like the Pascha, it was also a Jewish feast: "The day after the seventh sabbath will make fifty days, and then you shall present to the Lord a grain-offering from the new crop" (Lev. 23:16). Sometime during the first century A.D., the Day of Pentecost came to reflect for Jews the giving of the law at Mt. Sinai. Paul contrasts this with the giving of the Spirit: "The law, then, engraved letter by letter upon stone, dispensed death, and yet it was inaugurated with divine splendour. . . . Must not even greater splendour rest upon the divine dispensation of the Spirit?" (II Cor. 3:7-8). For Christians, the Day of Pentecost commemorated the birthday of the church, when, with the noise of a wind, tongues of flame rested on the disciples and they began to talk in other tongues (Acts 2:1-41). The book of Acts is a chronicle of the work of the Spirit-filled church in its earliest years.

The Day of Pentecost began as a unitive feast, too, originally including commemoration of the **Ascension.** Tertullian suggests that Christ has ascended into heaven at Pentecost.[16] And in the first half of the fourth century, Eusebius speaks of "the august and holy solemnity of Pentecost [i.e., the fifty days], which is distinguished by a period of seven weeks, and sealed with that one day on which the holy Scriptures attest the ascension of our common Savior into heaven, and the descent of the Holy Spirit."[17] In other words, for almost four centuries the Day of Pentecost commemorated both the ascension of Christ and the descent of the Holy Spirit. By the end of the fourth century, these two commemorations had been separated. The *Apostolic Constitutions* describes forty days after Easter as the proper time to "celebrate the feast of the ascension of the Lord." Once again, the biblical witness has been historicized by being interpreted as a means of dating past events in time. In this case Acts 1:3, with its mention of "a period of forty days" during which Jesus taught his disciples, seems to have been the source of pinpointing the date of the ascension. Where there had been one feast, by the late fourth century there were two: Ascension Day and the Day of Pentecost. Christ was in heaven, and the Holy Spirit dwelt in the holy church on earth. It was a daily reality the church could experience, not an abstraction.

The third chief event in the calendar by the fourth century was the **Epiphany.** Its origins are more obscure; they were certainly not Jewish but probably were Egyptian. The date, January 6, took the place of a pagan feast at the Egyptian winter solstice. The Epiphany signified several things, all of which had to do with the beginnings of Jesus Christ's work of manifesting God. This feast referred to the birth of Christ (with which two Gospels begin), to the baptism of Jesus (with which the other Gospels begin), and to the first miracle, of which John's Gospel says: "This deed at Cana-in-Galilee is the first of the signs by which Jesus revealed [*ephanérosen*] his glory and led his disciples to believe in him" (2:11). The common theme of all these events is Jesus Christ manifesting God to humans. Appropriately, the early church often called this day the Theophany (manifestation of God), and some Eastern Orthodox churches still do. The prologue to the Fourth Gospel sets the theme: "God's only Son, he who is nearest to the Father's heart, he has made him known" (1:18).

Epiphany underwent a split in the first half of the fourth century, probably beginning in Rome. Our earliest mention of the new feast, **Christmas,** occurs in a Roman document from A.D. 354, which reflects the custom of about A.D. 336. It lists December 25 as *"natus Christus in Betleem Iudeae."* Apparently this date was chosen to replace a pagan festival of the Unconquered Sun as the sun begins to wax again at the winter solstice. (By the fourth century A.D., the Julian calendar was off by four days.) Gradually, the new festival of Christmas took over part of the commemorations of the Epiphany. Chrysostom told a congregation in Antioch on Christmas Day, A.D. 386: "This day . . . has now been brought to us, not many years ago, has developed so quickly and borne such fruit."[18] The following Epiphany Day he explained: "For this is the day on which he was baptized, and made holy the nature of the waters. . . . Why then is this day called Epiphany? Because it was not when he was born that he became manifest to all, but when he was baptized; for up to this day he was unknown to the multitudes."[19] Epiphany, in the West, came to commemorate chiefly the visit of the wise men.

The Epiphany, then, is older than Christmas and has a deeper meaning. For instead of simply being an anniversary of the birth of Christ, it testifies to the whole purpose of the incarnation: the manifestation of God in Jesus Christ, beginning both with his birth and with the beginning of his ministry (the baptism when he is proclaimed "My Son, my Beloved"). And the mighty signs and teachings, narrated in the Gospels as Jesus accomplished this manifestation, give the opportunity to use the **Season after the Epiphany** for commemoration of Jesus' works and teachings up to the final events in Jerusalem.

A council in Spain in A.D. 380 decreed that "from December 17 until the day of Epiphany which is January 6 no one is permitted to be absent from Church."[20] This was a precedent for **Advent** at a time when Christmas itself was as yet unknown in Spain. By the fifth century, a forty-day season of preparation for the Epiphany was being practiced in Gaul. (This paralleled Lent and began about when Advent now begins.) Rome eventually adopted a four-week Advent before Christmas.

A process similar to that which had splintered the Pascha into a series of commemorations also operated with Christmas. As a Jewish boy, Jesus would likely have been circumcised and named on the eighth day after his birth. Luke tells us: "Eight days later the time came to circumcise him, and he was given the name Jesus" (2:21). Accordingly, the commemoration on January 1 became known as the Feast of the **Circumcision** or the **Name of Jesus.** Roman Catholics now keep this as the Solemnity of Mary, Mother of God. Luke 2:22-40 gives the story of the **Presentation in the Temple,** an event that would have occurred forty days after his birth, or February 2. It was discerned that the **Annunciation** mentioned in Luke 1:26-38 would have happened nine months before Christmas, or March 25. Elizabeth was then six months pregnant, and Mary's subsequent **Visitation** to Elizabeth (recorded in verses 39-56) was fixed at May 31, or just before the birth of John the Baptist, identified as June 24 (three months after the Annunciation). John's birth came at the summer solstice, when the sun wanes until the birth of Christ: "As he grows greater, I must grow less" (John 3:30). All these developments are combinations of Luke 1 and 2 and obstetrics.

The Christian year, especially the **temporal cycle** (movable dates plus the Christmas cycle), was basically complete by the end of the fourth century. The subsequent history is that of development of the **sanctoral cycle** (those fixed dates commemorating the deaths of saints aside from dates based on Christmas). These began early; the "Martyrdom of Polycarp" mentions commemoration of a second-century martyr. Basically these were commemorations of local heroes and heroines of the faith. Tertullian tells us: "As often as the anniversary comes round, we make offerings for the dead as birthday honours."[21] After all, one's birth into eternity (death) was far more important than his or her birth into time. The temporal cycle increasingly became obscured with commemorations of saints, especially after relics of saints began to be moved from place to place. The days of local saints eventually were supplemented by those of saints from other regions.

Only two significant additions occurred after the fourth century: Trinity Sunday and All Saints' Day. **Trinity Sunday,** the Sunday after the Day of Pentecost, was introduced about A.D. 1000. Unlike other feasts, it represents a theological doctrine unrelated to an historical event. The ninth century saw the designation of November 1 as **All Saints' Day.** It had earlier, springtime precedents, but the Gallican placement of it in the harvest season was accepted by Rome about A.D. 835.

Let us recapitulate. **John Chrysostom,** in a sermon preached in A.D. 386, effectively sums up the liturgical year: "For if Christ had not been born into flesh, he would not have been baptized, which is the Theophany [Epiphany], he would not have been crucified [some texts add: and risen], which is the Pascha, he would not have sent down the spirit, which is the Pentecost."[22] In the fourth century, the three great primitive feasts—the Epiphany, the Pascha, and the Day of Pentecost—had split from them related days—Christmas, Good Friday, and Ascension, plus some lesser days. Gregory Dix interpreted these developments as a sign that the fourth-century church was becoming "reconciled to *time*" and was losing its fervent expectation of the end of time.[23] But this reconciliation to time was an inevitable process, as those of us who have lived through a national bicentennial can attest. People want to know, to visualize, to experience for themselves, a very normal human desire. Worship builds on our humanity, after all. And so what happened in the fourth century was that the church developed a more dramatic way of expressing the central realities Christians experienced—manifestation, resurrection, and the indwelling Spirit. Eschatological fervor certainly slackened with the peace of the church after Constantine, if not long before. But the imagination of Christians directed backward in time was no less fruitful and intensified their perception of the incarnation. The success of these fourth-century changes is shown by their vivid presence among us even today. Obviously they have rung true to both Christian faith and human experience.

All in all, the church year is a very satisfactory reflection of the life and faith of the early church and has remained in use with little change ever since. Modern efforts to systematize and tidy it up have never been satisfactory. Granted the ancient church year leaves large gaps in time, especially after the Day of Pentecost; but its strength lies in its firm grasp of the core of the Christian experience and in its ability to reflect in a vivid way that Christ has made God manifest, that Christ has risen from the dead, and that Christ has sent the Holy Spirit to dwell in the holy church.

The sixteenth-century Reformers took various approaches to the calendar. **Martin Luther** purified it of saints' days by seeking "to celebrate only on Lord's Days and on Festivals of the Lord, abrogating completely the festivals of all the saints. . . . We regard the Festivals of the Purification [Presentation] and of the Annunciation as Festivals of Christ, like the Epiphany and the Circumcision."[24] The Church of England originally only retained materials to commemorate saints mentioned in the Bible plus All Saints' Day. The Church of Scotland was more radical. Its 1560 *Book of Discipline* condemned all "feasts (as they term them) of Apostles, Martyrs, Virgins, of Christmas, Circumcision, Epiphany, Purification, and other fond feasts of our Lady. Which things, because in God's scriptures they neither have commandment nor assurance, we judge utterly to be abolished from this Realm; affirming further, that the obstinate maintainers and teachers of such abominations ought not to escape the punishment of the Civil Magistrate.[25] **John Wesley,** always the pragmatist, abolished "most of the holy-days . . . as at present answering no valuable end."[26] His calendar included the four Sundays of Advent, Christmas Day, up to fifteen Sundays after Christmas, the Sunday next before Easter, Good Friday, Easter Day, five Sundays after Easter, Ascension Day, the Sunday after Ascension Day, Whitsunday, Trinity Sunday, and up to twenty-five Sundays after Trinity. Wesley's journals reveal a personal fondness for All Saints' Day. Both Wesley's calendar and lections were soon lost among American Methodists.

Renewed interest in the church year among American Protestants occurred in the 1920s and 1930s, a period in which an aesthetic approach to worship tended to be prominent. An effort to rearrange the year was advanced in the form of a new season, **Kingdomtide.** It seems to have been promoted largely by Professor Fred Winslow Adams of Boston University School of Theology. Kingdomtide originally appeared in a Federal Council of Churches publication, *The Christian Year,* published in 1937 and 1940. The first edition suggested observing Kingdomtide for the last six months of the church year; in 1940 this time was divided between Whitsuntide and Kingdomtide.[27] Eventually only Methodists were left observing Kingdomtide, and the United Methodist Alternate Calendar (SWR #3 and #6) omits it. A somewhat similar experiment was briefly tried by American Presbyterians. They experimented with a suggestion made in 1956 by Allan McArthur, a Scottish pastor, of having a season of "God the Father"[28] in the fall. After four years of trial use, this, too, was abandoned.

Since Vatican II, a profound new interest in the calendar has emerged and a deep new appreciation has developed of how our way of keeping time shapes and reflects our lives as Christians. The first landmark was the new *Roman Calendar,* which went into effect among Roman Catholics on the first day of the 1970s. It is the fruit of the most careful scrutiny of the way Christians use time. Most of its reforms have been adopted by the major Protestant bodies in this country: Lutherans,

Episcopalians, Presbyterians, the United Church of Christ, the Christian Church (Disciples of Christ), the Consultation on Church Union (COCU), and (as an alternative) United Methodists (*Seasons of the Gospel,* SWR #6).

The most radical Roman Catholic change, that of not treating the weeks after the Epiphany or after the Day of Pentecost as distinct seasons but only as parts of the "season of the year" (*per annum*) or **Ordinary Time,** has not been adopted by Protestants. Certainly it is a realistic approach to these seasons of little distinctive character. But other basic changes have been accepted including keeping the Sunday after the Epiphany as the Baptism of the Lord and the last Sunday of the year as Christ the King. The Lutheran practice of commemorating the Sunday before Ash Wednesday as the Sunday of the Transfiguration of the Lord has been adopted by Episcopalians, COCU, and United Methodists. Roman Catholics have observed the Transfiguration on August 6 since the fifteenth century. For the first time in four hundred years, an ecumenical calendar in basic outlines is being followed by Protestants and Roman Catholics around the world. There is agreement on many of what Roman Catholics now call "solemnities"; there is less agreement on the lesser "feasts" and "memorials." The newest calendar is the result of a careful attempt to recapture the structure and meaning of the oldest calendar, that filled out in the fourth century. The calendar can prove a strong witness to the priorities of Christian faith, as did the oldest Christian calendars.

II

How the church kept time in early centuries has been discussed in detail because, as so often happens in Christian worship, if we understand well the experiences of the church's first four centuries, we have gained the heart of the matter. It will be worthwhile, though, to reflect a bit on the meaning of this.

It is revealing to compare the keeping of time in the early church with current practice. We may see a shocking contrast. The average congregation today finds its time occupied with various promotions, much like the yearly cycle of a department store. Instead of a white sale or a Washington's birthday sale, we have our own array of loyalty Sundays, bishops' fund Sundays, rally days, student recognition Sundays, and such. Even the seasons have been misinterpreted. For many, the Season after the Epiphany was used to focus on human efforts in missionizing. Some hymnals list the topic of "missions" under the Season after the Epiphany with such hymns as "Heralds of Christ" or "We've a Story to Tell to the Nations." And Kingdomtide, at worst, carried the suggestion that the kingdom of God would be brought in by the expanding of greater effort on our part. The hymn "Turn Back, O Man" reflects this optimism in resolute human effort.

All these aspects of the modern *de facto* calendar betray one great difference from that of the early church. *Our de facto calendar stresses human agency; that of the early church centered upon what God had done and continues to do through the Holy Spirit.* Our keeping of time has a strongly humanistic tint. We cannot quite let God do it all for us. Yet the point of the church's year is that all *is* done for us. All we have to do is to accept what God has done. Then we really are free to act. The church's liturgical year both accepts the futility of our efforts and yet exults in God's victories for us.

In short, the church year is a constant reminder of gifts that we cannot create but can only accept. Pius Parsch called it "the church's year of grace."[29] Throughout the year, the various seasons and days remind us that salvation is a gift offered to us in all its different aspects. Humanizing the year by making it a recital of our own activities misses the point altogether. Focusing on particular promotional causes instead of God's actions is a constant pressure that has to be resisted. Yet, unfortunately, the promotional level seems to be the favorite way of keeping time for many congregations. If our *de facto* calendar truly witnesses to our faith, it is an impoverished faith indeed that we manifest. It suggests that our faith is in our own efforts and activities rather than in God's. Certainly our activity is important, but it can be promoted in other, less conspicuous ways than by taking over the church year.

Recovery of the church year can help us determine our real priorities. Keeping time with the rhythms of the early church can be a source of renewal for us today in sorting out our own priorities.

In briefest terms, the church's year of grace functions to show forth Jesus Christ until he comes again and to testify to God the Holy Spirit indwelling the church in the meantime. The church year is both proclamation and thanksgiving. In much the same way as Jewish and Christian prayer recites what we give thanks for, so the Christian year proclaims and thanks God for God's marvelous actions. Christians and Jews praise God, not in abstract terms, but by reciting the marvelous works of God. It is a think/thank process by which we glorify God through recalling what God has done. Thus the liturgical year reflects the very nature of Christian prayer and our relationship to God. Much of its power, as with daily prayer, comes through reiteration. Year after year, week after week, hour by hour, the acts of God are commemorated and our apprehension of them deepened. These cycles save us from a false spirituality, based on ourselves, by showing forth God's works instead.

Keeping time, of course, can also become an idolatrous gimmick like anything else that is good. Time can be used simply to dress up our services and to make them look fashionable. Keeping the church year for the wrong reasons is worse than useless, for we can end up worshiping our own gimmicks rather than God. But when we do use the structures of time to bring us closer to God, they can serve that purpose exceedingly well by helping us to encounter the wholeness of the gospel.

How does time bring us closer to God? The church year is a means by which we relive for ourselves all that really matters of salvation history. When we recall the past events of salvation, they come alive in their present power to save. The doing of acts of remembrance brings the original events back to us with all their meaning. And so we continue to "proclaim the death of the Lord, until he comes" (I Cor. 11:26). The various acts of rehearsing salvation history give us anew the benefits of what God has done for us in these past events. Christ's birth, baptism, death, and resurrection are all given to us for our own appropriation through corporate reenactment of them. These events then are no longer simply detached data from the past, but become part of our own personal history as we relive salvation history through rehearsing it in our worship. Thus Christ dies again for our salvation every Good Friday. And every Easter and every Lord's Day we are witnesses to the resurrection.

The Christian year becomes a vital and refreshing means through which God is given to us. It is a giving that is never exhausted. Each time the year, week, and day push us a bit deeper into encounter with God. We perceive one aspect of Christ submitting to baptism this year, another next year, but never do we touch bottom. So the liturgical year is a constant means of grace through which we receive God's gifts to us.

The year of grace is about what God does for us, not our efforts. The whole structure calls attention to God's work, not ours. And God's work is made known in different ways through the changing events and needs of every time and place where Christians worship.

Advent is both a time of thanks for the gift of Christ to us in the past and a time of anticipation of his second coming. It contains both threat and promise. Christmas rehearses God's self-giving in the birth of Jesus Christ. The **Christmas Season** continues this commemoration through the Epiphany.

The **Season after the Epiphany** (or Ordinary Time) has been neglected. The whole season can stress the various ways in which Jesus Christ has made God manifest to us by making the Father known through mighty signs and teachings. These begin with the **Baptism of the Lord** (when Jesus' Sonship is declared and his ministry begins). The Sundays after the Epiphany continue with readings about the signs and teachings by which Jesus made his glory known through manifesting God. The season ends with the Last Sunday after the Epiphany, or the **Transfiguration of the Lord,** in which Jesus is once again proclaimed "My Son, my Beloved."

Lent is the season in which we anticipate that final trip to Jerusalem and the self-giving nature of love shown in Christ's passion and death. All is changed as Christ gives himself to us as the resurrected One at Easter. The **Season of Easter** begins with Easter Eve and concludes on the Day of Pentecost. Ascension Day commemorates the ending of Christ's historical visibility and the beginning of his sacramental visibility.

The **Season after Pentecost** (or Ordinary Time) signals the long interim of the new-covenant church until Christ comes in glory. Both Old Testament and New remind us of God's continuing saving works. The Last Sunday after Pentecost, or **Christ the King,** pushes us to anticipate the consummation of all things, when Christ comes in glory as King of all and all human failures and achievements are, at last, made of no account, a most comforting doctrine. And then, the following week, we are once again into Advent, and the year starts over afresh.

The **minor christological feasts** have evangelical values that we are just beginning to discover. The Name of Jesus, Presentation, Annunciation, and Visitation are christological and call attention to Christ's full humanity and his identification with human social patterns. All Saints' Day is christological, too; it dwells not on the virtues of the saints but on the love of Christ, who works in people throughout time to accomplish God's purposes. The chief value of commemorating the saints is recognition through them of Christ, who never leaves us without a witness. If commemoration of individual saints could help us realize this, such piety could once again serve a "valuable end."

III

Every service of Christian worship is composed of two kinds of acts of worship: the ordinary and the propers. The **ordinary** is those elements which remain the same from week to week: the basic structure of the service and such items as the Lord's Prayer, the offering, the Creed, and a doxology. The **propers** are those elements which change from week to week. We read different lessons, sing varied hymns, pray a variety of prayers, and (we hope!) hear a somewhat different sermon whenever we gather for worship.

The importance of the propers in Christian worship is that they supply variety and interest. While the ordinary parts provide a necessary constancy, Christian worship without the proper parts would be deadly dull, a repetition of exactly the same thing week after week. Without the constants that the ordinary parts provide, Christian worship would be chaos.

Variety is an important ingredient in Christian worship. The good news of the gospel is much too wide and deep to be encompassed by a single service or season. Every time a congregation gathers for worship is a different event. Never before and never again will exactly the same people be assembled for worship. But the uniqueness of each gathering goes beyond that. The life of the local community, as well as that of the national and global communities, is never the same from week to week. Christian worship reflects this in its acknowledgment that every Sunday or special day is a different occasion. Christmas is not Easter, nor is the Sunday after Easter the same as the Sunday before Labor Day, though the attendance may be about the same. A wedding is not a funeral, though the flowers may be similar. Nor is a Sunday evening service the same occasion as that morning's service, for the people may (or may not) be in a more relaxed mood in the evening. In a similar way, no two family meals are identical. Each occasion for worship is unique.

Variety, then, is an important characteristic of Christian worship as worship relates both to the eternal gospel and to our ongoing daily life. One of the sharpest criticisms of Christian worship in recent years has been that of dullness. Yet this criticism is apt only when Christian worship has been unfaithful to its own nature. The surest way to avoid the boredom of constant repetition is to revel in the rich variety inherent in Christian worship. And the best way to ensure dullness is to ignore this same variety.

Nothing is a better source for variety and interest in Christian worship than careful following of the church year. The structure of the year provides an orderly pegboard on which to hang all our best ideas and is a real creative stimulus of the imagination. The first question to raise when planning any service ought to be: When does it occur in the church year? The answer should be the first and best clue for providing ideas. The church year divides the fullness of the gospel into digestible fragments so we have enough to savor afresh each week of the year.

The **calendar,** as we have said, is the foundation of most Christian worship. The reader will probably want to refer to it frequently while reading what follows. The calendar opposite reflects the revisions now in use by most major churches in North America (e.g., *We Gather Together,* SWR #10).

The Calendar

Seasons	*Festivals*
ADVENT	
First Sunday in Advent . . .	
to Fourth Sunday in Advent	
CHRISTMAS SEASON	Christmas Eve and Day
	(December 25)
First Sunday after Christmas . . .	The Epiphany, or the Manifesta-
to [Second Sunday after	tion of God in Jesus Christ
Christmas]	(January 6)
SEASON AFTER THE	First Sunday after the Epiphany,
EPIPHANY*	or the Baptism of the Lord
Second Sunday after the	Last Sunday after the Epiphany,
Epiphany . . .	or the Transfiguration of the
to [Eighth Sunday after the	Lord
Epiphany]	
LENT	Ash Wednesday
First Sunday in Lent . . .	Holy Week
to Fifth Sunday in Lent	Palm/Passion Sunday
	Monday, Tuesday, Wednesday
	Maundy Thursday
	Good Friday
	Holy Saturday
SEASON OF EASTER	Easter Eve and Day
Second Sunday of Easter . . .	Ascension Day (Sixth Thursday
to Sixth Sunday of Easter	of Easter)
Seventh Sunday of Easter	The Day of Pentecost, or the
	Descent of the Holy Spirit
SEASON AFTER	First Sunday after Pentecost, or
PENTECOST*	Trinity Sunday
Second Sunday after	All Saints' Day (November 1)
Pentecost . . . to [Twenty-	Last Sunday after Pentecost, or
seventh Sunday after Pentecost]	Christ the King

*or Ordinary Time (Sundays in)

How does the calendar work? It consists of six seasons: Advent, Christmas Season, the Season after the Epiphany, Lent, the Season of Easter, and the Season after Pentecost. The number of Sundays in Advent, Lent, and the Easter Season is constant. Rarely are all the Sundays after the Epiphany or after Pentecost used. The final Sunday of the post-Epiphany Season (that just prior to Ash Wednesday) is always the Last Sunday after the Epiphany, or the Transfiguration of the Lord. The same is true after Pentecost; the Sunday before the beginning of Advent is always the Last Sunday after Pentecost, or Christ the King.

It may help to remember that as far as Sundays and festivals are concerned, each season except Advent begins and ends with a special day. The Christmas Season extends from Christmas Eve and Day through the Epiphany; the Season after the Epiphany, from the Baptism of the Lord through the Transfiguration of the Lord; Lent, from Ash Wednesday through Holy Saturday; the Season of Easter, from Easter Eve and Day through the Day of Pentecost; and the Season after Pentecost, from Trinity Sunday through Christ the King. White vestments and hangings usually are used on all these special days, except for Ash Wednesday, Holy Saturday, and the Day of Pentecost.

A few other dates may be unfamiliar or have special problems. In some churches, Epiphany Day may be celebrated on the first Sunday of January, combined with the First Sunday after Christmas, or with the Baptism of the Lord. The **Baptism of the Lord** is a new festival for Western Christians, though closely associated with Epiphany. The Baptism of the Lord comes on the first Sunday after January 6 (the Epiphany). Palm/Passion Sunday is now observed as one and the same, since this is when the passion narrative is usually read. The Easter Vigil ought to be celebrated the eve or night before Easter Day. And Ascension Day may be commemorated on the Seventh Sunday of Easter, if deemed advisable. The Day of Pentecost has recovered its earlier place as the fiftieth day and last Sunday of the Easter Season, the entire season once having been known as "Pentecost." All Saints' Day may be observed on the first Sunday of November when

November 1 is not a Sunday. Reformation Sunday, the last in October, has now been dropped in many churches as an ecumenical gesture. Instead, it seems more appropriate to commemorate our common inheritance in All Saints' Day, rather than something divisive.

It will be necessary to exercise discretion with regard to promotional, patriotic, and other topical occasions. Never should Mothers' Day, for instance, take precedence over the Day of Pentecost, though one can make discreet references to motherhood (and fatherhood) on Pentecost or any other day, if considered necessary. Thanksgiving Day certainly has religious overtones. Though not listed in the calendar, it is often observed with ecumenical and inter-religious services.

For those who would like to keep the minor christological feasts, there are other possibilities. The color for each is usually white. The Name of Jesus (January 1) calls to mind Jesus' humanity and his full identification with human society (cf. Luke 2:15-21). The Presentation (February 2) traditionally was called Purification or Candlemas, since the candles to be used that year were blessed on this occasion. It can call attention to the aged in our society, who, Luke tells us, were the first to proclaim the Lord (Anna and Simeon) (cf. Luke 2:22-40). Annunciation—Lady Day in some countries (March 25)—calls attention to the power of the humblest person when fulfilling God's will (cf. Luke 1:26-38). Visitation (May 31), with its dialogue between two women, calls attention to the incarnation and contains Mary's Song, the socially radical *Magnificat,* in essence the social creed of Christianity (cf. Luke 1:39-56). Roman Catholics also keep other **solemnities:** Mary, Mother of God (January 1); Joseph, Husband of Mary (March 19); Corpus Christi; Sacred Heart; Birth of John the Baptist (June 24); Peter and Paul, Apostles (June 29); Assumption of Mary (August 15); and Immaculate Conception (December 8). The course of the normal Sunday readings ought rarely to be broken for special observances without good reason, since the lessons are usually constructed to cover scripture in a comprehensive way.

If the calendar is the foundation of Christian worship, the first floor is certainly the lectionary, or list of lections (scripture lessons) based on the Christian year. One of the most significant changes in Protestant worship in recent years has been the widespread adoption of a lectionary and the use of it in worship as the basis of preaching in thousands of congregations. All too often, previous haphazard methods of choosing scripture had, in fact, eliminated major portions of God's word and reshaped scripture in the preacher's own image. Social activists might be partial to passages in the prophetic books, and conservatives to the more rigid passages in the Pastoral Epistles. Yet both, in choosing passages they found congenial, were, in effect, rewriting scripture. Liberals and conservatives were equally guilty of revising God's word in accord with personal preferences.

One of the most useful developments of the post–Vatican II era has been the **ecumenical lectionary.** Begun after Vatican II by the Roman Catholic Church, it was brought to its present form by several years' work by a full-time staff and eight hundred consultants—Protestants, Catholics, and Jews. Published as *The Lectionary,* it went into effect for Roman Catholics with the beginning of the 1970 liturgical year on November 30, 1969. It is the most carefully prepared lectionary in all Christian history. Episcopalians (BCP, 888-931), Lutherans (LBW, 13-41), and Presbyterians (Wb, 167-75) made their own versions of it. In 1974, the Consultation on Church Union prepared a consensus of the Roman Catholic, Episcopalian, Presbyterian, and Lutheran versions. This was adopted as an alternative version by United Methodists (SWR #3, 50-57, and SWR #6) and the United Church of Canada. The United Church of Christ (HUCC, 444-51) and the Christian Church (Disciples of Christ) have used the Presbyterian version, but now both have opted for the COCU-United Methodist version.

How does it work? The new lectionary is a three-year lectionary, the years designated as A, B, and C. Year C is a year, such as 1980, evenly divisible by the number 3. Year A follows (1981, 1984) and year B (1982, 1985). The church year begins between November 27 and December 3 of the preceding civil year so that Advent in civil year December 1979 is part of the church year 1980, and hence is the beginning of year C.

For each Sunday, three lessons are appointed: first (usually Old Testament), second (usually an Epistle), and Gospel. During the Easter Season the first lesson is from the book of Acts as the story of the new creation begins with the resurrection. Chrysostom explains that the book of Acts is "the demonstration of the Resurrection," and hence it is read during the Season after Easter, a custom that Augustine also notes in Africa. Occasionally readings from Revelation take the place of the Epistle. In the course of three years, most of the New Testament and large portions of the Old Testament are read when all three lessons are used. Two principles are in operation here. The Gospels reflect the church year, with the first lessons more or less dependent upon them. The greatest single weakness of the new lectionary is that this christological approach to the Old Testament frequently does an injustice to the Old Testament lessons by presenting them in a foreign context. The second lessons, on the other hand, are usually read in order (*lectio continua*) from each book from beginning to end. First Corinthians, for example, is read chiefly during the Season after the Epiphany. Year A is devoted to reading the Gospel of Matthew; year B to Mark; and year C to Luke. Portions in all three years are filled in from the Fourth Gospel. The new lectionary provides the most comprehensive method now available for reading the entire Bible that can be accomplished in three years. After that, it is time to start over again. There are two exceptional dates: On Palm/Passion Sunday the full passion narrative may be read, especially in dramatic fashion. For the Easter Vigil, the traditional scheme of nine or more lessons with marvelously rich Old Testament passages is suggested.

More than any single item, the lectionary guides the choices appropriate for any given Sunday. It is reflected in the opening prayer, the psalm, the hymns, the choral and instrumental music, the sermon, and the visual materials used. The second question to ask in planning any service is: "What does the lectionary provide?" The use of a lectionary makes it possible to plan actual services months or even years in advance. This makes it especially useful for musicians and artists who need much advance preparation. Since the lectionary shapes other choices, it is important that we examine briefly its effect on them in turn.

An **opening prayer** sometimes is an effective way to articulate the general thrust of the lessons for the day and to alert the congregation to the event. The Roman Catholic *Sacramentary* provides opening prayers (and alternatives) for Sundays and special occasions. Episcopalians retain the ancient term "collects" and provide them in traditional and contemporary language (BCP, 158-261). "Prayer of the day" is the Lutheran term (LBW, 13-41), and "collect for the day," the Presbyterian (Wb, 135-63). All these churches provide them for all Sundays and major festivals. United Methodists provide seasonal, festival, and special occasion opening prayers (SWR #6).

Psalms are used in worship as responses to or commentaries on the lessons. Roman Catholics, Episcopalians, Lutherans, and United Methodists now provide lists of psalms chosen deliberately to relate to the lessons in the lectionary. A psalm is a response and does not function as a lesson, but it does need to be matched carefully to the lessons.

Appropriate **hymns** are indicated in almost all denominational hymnals for seasons, festivals, and special occasions. United Methodists also have a hymn lectionary that suggests hymns suitable for the dates and lections of the year (SWR #6).

No one has ever questioned that J. S. Bach wrote some of the greatest of all **choral music** and **instrumental music** while following the guidance of the lectionary and calendar. When well planned, choral music can mesh successfully with the ministry of the Word by providing a musical commentary on the lessons. Frequently, anthems with texts unrelated to the occasion blunder into the otherwise carefully planned sequence of the service. This is not at all necessary. Careful use of the calendar and lectionary can be a tremendous boon to church musicians, since it gives them lead time to order and rehearse appropriate music.

Nothing is as thoroughly and obviously affected by the lessons as is the **sermon.** Or at least we would hope so. There seem to be three main results from the widespread use of the new lectionary. First, it has made it financially feasible to publish a number of top quality aids to biblical study in the form of commentaries and other resources to improve our use of the Bible.[30] Second, the lectionary has forced many preachers to preach on a much wider selection of scripture than most of them ever did. That does not mean that one should preach on all three lessons at one time. Sometimes the lessons relate to one another well; more often than not, the second lesson goes its own separate way. But to preach on any one of these texts will force the preacher to study and ponder many portions of God's word that are unfamiliar. And third, anyone who really follows the year and the lessons carefully finds himself or herself probing deeper into Christology. One simply cannot preach on the Baptism of the Lord, The Transfiguration, Palm/Passion Sunday, Ascension Day, All Saints' Day, Christ the King, and others without being forced to make up one's mind about who one says Jesus Christ is. Without such discipline, it is amazing how long one can jump around that vital question. Many preachers have agreed that preaching from the lectionary improves the content of their preaching. And many have been amazed how relevant assigned passages often are for their congregation's time and place.

Finally, we must say a word on the **visual aspects** of the lectionary and calendar. Protestants have largely been blind to these matters. One could go to a church week after week, and it would look as if all times and occasions for worship were identical. But now our eyes have been opened. We have realized that the gospel can be seen as well as heard. One church used a banner showing a tow-headed boy blowing a whistle and the words: "God so loved the world . . . well, you would hardly believe it!" How many sermons have we heard—and forgotten—about John 3:16? But the memory of such a banner message may remain with us for years.

Ideally we ought to have a different building each Sunday. The amazing thing is that that is possible to a certain extent. With the use of textiles, graphics, and other art forms, we can have a new church setting each Sunday. And where projections are possible, a wall can be whatever we want to project on it. "Okay, we'll have the Sistine Chapel this week, but for next week's lessons Big Sur would work better." We are limited only by the horizons of our imaginations.

Some of the things we have learned about worship in the last few years seem irrevocable. In 1966 few, if any, churches had ever used a banner. By now, few have not. If the gospel can be proclaimed visually, why shouldn't it be? Each new dimension we add to our perception of the good news seems to be clear gain.

How do we do it? The simplest concept is just to use pure **color.** Color helps form general expectations for any occasion. We do not wear flamboyant colors to a funeral. Traditionally, purples, grays, and blues have been used for seasons of a penitential character, such as Advent and Lent, though dark, earth colors could be used, too. White has been used for events or seasons with a strong christological flavor, such as the Baptism of the Lord or the Season of Easter. Yellows and golds are also possibilities at such times. Red has been reserved for occasions relating to the Holy Spirit (such as the Day of Pentecost) or to commemorations of martyrs. Green has been used for seasons of less pronounced character, such as the Season after the Epiphany or the Season after Pentecost. These longer seasons need not stagnate in a single color or hue any more than nature retains a monotonous green as the delicate shades of spring progress to the deeper hues of fall. The absence of any color from Maundy Thursday to the Easter Vigil is striking.

Much may be done with pure color. However, we are coming to realize the need to be equally sensitive to hues and **textures.** A purple silk might be less preferable for Lent than a rough-textured blue or gray. And a splendid tightly woven gold might be better for Easter than a rough white material.

Colors and textures can be used most effectively in textiles for hangings on pulpits, lecterns (if any), the stoles worn by ordained ministers, or ministerial vestments. Sometimes bolts of cloth may simply be hung as giant abstract banners. It is better not to hide the altar-table with cloth hangings, since a white tablecloth expresses its function better.

Banners can be hung almost anywhere in the church. Increasingly we see a move to large-scale banners, fifteen feet or so in length. They ought to be changed frequently as the year turns. The Easter church building ought to be quite different from the church in Lent.

74

Posters, bulletins, placards, and other **graphics** can express the gospel in forceful ways. Photographs may be blown up cheaply. A few words of press type—"Lord, when was it that we saw you?" (Matt. 25:37) or "Is it of no concern to you who pass by?" (Lam. 1:12)—lettered on them may be a powerful message. Try to discover key words for any occasion—"Peace on earth," "My Son," "He is risen"—and use them. Visit a local art-supply store to see how many possibilities churches have neglected. Many posters and bulletins will not soon be forgotten, especially when created locally.

Certain **objects** communicate at different seasons, such as an Advent wreath with four candles, a Lenten veil, palm branches, and a Paschal candle. Symbols pertain to different occasions too: a star, a crown of thorns, tongues of flame, and so forth. The lack of things is also a powerful form of communication. The absence of any flowers and candles during Holy Week can say much.

A word of caution is necessary. None of these colors, textures, images, or objects is a decoration or an ornament. If they are used as such, they are trivialities not worth the time or effort they consume. But if used to add one more dimension to our perception of the good news, they can well be worth considerable effort and expense. Much work goes into a sermon, meant to be preached only once. Work from a broader segment of the community can well go into visual forms of presenting the gospel, even though these forms, like the sermon, may be disposable.

All in all, Christians are called to proclaim the gospel of salvation by every means available. The church's year of grace and the lectionary based on it are two vital resources in doing this. If keeping time with the church can make better Christians, it is well worth exploring all the possibilities such a discipline can offer.

III
The Language of Space

It should not surprise us that a religion whose fundamental doctrine is the incarnation should take space seriously in its worship. Not only did Christ enter our time, but he also came to dwell among us, occupying a specific and definite place on earth in Judea. The New Testament is full of place names; Jesus was at Jerusalem, Bethany, the Sea of Galilee, the River Jordan, and so on.

The same is true of the rest of salvation history. The Jewish and Christian God is made known by events that occur among men and women, not off on Mount Olympus or in Valhalla. It is space on earth that is made holy, not because of the place itself but because of what God does for humans there. The saving events usually happen at some ordinary field, well, or village street. Today it would be as commonplace as a McDonald's or Woolworth's. The location is indifferent; the event is crucial.

Of course, after the event, the place becomes significant as a bearer of meaning: the place where something happened. Jacob had a dream at an insignificant place and woke to exclaim that it was a fearsome place, the house of God, the gate of heaven (Gen. 28:17). His dream provoked him to erect a pillar and give the place a new name, house of God, that all might know the event. We have already seen how fourth-century Jerusalem shaped all subsequent Christian worship by commemorations at the times and places where climactic events in Christ's life and death occurred. Fourth-century pilgrims were

76

shown the sycamore tree Zacchaeus had climbed to see Jesus—an ordinary tree but a holy place. Europe eventually became dotted with pilgrimage places where an event had made a spot significant. All these testify to the eloquence of the language of space. A religion of the incarnation has to have its feet planted firmly on the ground. God and humanity meet *somewhere,* be it as casual as a desert bush or as magnificent as the Jerusalem temple.

Any Christian community needs a place for worship of the Incarnate One. It can be anywhere, but it has to be somewhere designated, so the body of Christ knows where to assemble. Early missionaries in the British Isles simply set up a cross, but it determined *the* place for worship. Eventually such places were roofed and walled, and the spaces thus sheltered were organized for the convenience and comfort of the worshipers. The organization of space we call "architecture." Today we are so accustomed to the use of architecture that, in many languages, the word "church" refers to a building just as much as to the body of believers.

The relationships between architecture and what Christians do when they worship are complex. Church architecture both reflects the ways Christians worship and shapes worship—and, not uncommonly, misshapes it. Architecture reflects Christian worship by providing the setting and shelter needed for a community to do its worship together. This is perhaps obvious; not even a football crowd would sit still in below-zero weather. But, at the same time architecture is accommodating worship, it is also in a subtle and inconspicuous way shaping that same worship. In the first place, the building helps define the meaning of worship for those gathered inside it. Try to preach against triumphalism in a baroque church! Try to teach the priesthood of all believers from a deep gothic chancel never occupied by any but ordained ministers! Second, the building dictates the possibilities open to us in our forms and styles of worship. We may want good congregational song, but do the acoustics swallow up each sound so all seem mute? Or do we have to give up any hope of movement by the congregation because everyone is neatly filed away in pews? We soon realize that architecture presents both opportunities and limiting

77

factors; some possibilities are opened and others closed. We could worship only with difficulty without buildings; often we worship with difficulty because of them.

The way space is organized reflects and shapes Christian worship so much that we must examine why and how space speaks a language that is so important for worship. In this case, it works best to interpret theory first; then to survey the history and draw practical conclusions from the history of church architecture; and finally to note how space affects church music and the visual arts.

I

How does the way space is organized reflect what happens in Christian worship? To answer this, we need to return to one of the definitions for Christian worship suggested in chapter 1: "Christian worship is speaking and touching in God's name." Another way of saying the same thing is that in worship we speak for God, speak to God, and touch others for God. This is unquestionably a drastic oversimplification of what happens in Christian worship, but it does provide a method to analyze the spatial requirements of worship. It also makes clear that Christian worship is action that requires space, and that is a crucial insight not apparent in some of the more abstract definitions.

Let us begin, then, by asserting that in worship God gives Godself to us through human words and by human hands and we give ourselves to God through our words and hands. All that happens in worship depends upon God, but it occurs through the instrumentality of human speech and the human body.

How does God give Godself to us through words? God speaks God's Word to us through the mouths of humans. That seems a strange way to reach people; it displays a far greater trust in humans than most of us would ever have. But it is God's way, as scripture repeatedly testifies: "I put my words into your mouth" (Jer. 1:9) or to tongue-tied brothers: "I will help both of you to speak" (Exod. 4:15). There can be no doubt in biblical faith that God calls men and women to speak God's Word.

Now there are few, very few, necessities required for one

human being to speak to others. One is that, in order to communicate best, one ought to be able to see those to whom one is talking, with the possibility of sustaining eye contact. One speaks best to those one can look in the eye, not to those off to one side, behind one, or listening on a tape. Eye contact is part of reaching out in love to others and is an important part of speech. Mark tells us "Jesus looked straight at" the rich young man "and his heart warmed to him" (Mark 10:21). Looking is part of loving.

Spatially this implies a straight line between the speaker and hearer. The speaker may need to be elevated a few inches, so the heads of others do not interfere with sight lines; but too great an elevation becomes a visual barrier, a moat of height. Pillars, partitions, and other barriers must not intervene. The audience and speaker must meet face to face. The best space for face-to-face encounter is organized along a horizontal axis, as if there were a straight line from the speaker to the person in the middle of the audience. What this creates, of course, is a synagogue form where people come together to hear God's Word read and expounded or a meetinghouse where Christians assemble to hear the gospel.

God gives Godself through speech to people gathered along a horizontal axis from human speaker to human hearer. If that were all, the planning of worship space would indeed be simple. But God not only places God's Word in our mouths but puts Godself into our hands. And this is where organizing space for Christian worship gets complicated. For we must provide not only for receiving the Word but also for receiving the sacraments. God gives Godself to us in both ways. All good church architecture is a compromise in providing for both types of divine activity. The whole history of church building is the history of compromises between arrangements best for speaking in God's name and those best for touching in God's name.

If the path of the speaking voice is a horizontal axis, the locus of the outstretched hand is on a vertical axis. God has created each of us small enough so that we can reach out only about a yard. Others have to come to us, and they come best in a circle gathered about us. The image this projects is of people gathered in concentric circles around a vertical axis. On that vertical axis may be an altar-table, a font, or simply a person. From there we can reach out—God can reach out through our hands—to the standing-around community.

In other terms, we need both a synagogue and an upper room for Christian worship. We need space in which we can both project our voices and reach out our hands, whether they be hands baptizing a new Christian, hands giving the Lord's body at the eucharist, hands laid on a head, hands uniting the hands of a couple, hands blessing or reconciling, or hands sprinkling a coffin. Not only do we speak for God but we also touch others for God. And we have to be close enough really to touch them. A woman touched the hem of Jesus' garment, and power passed to her. We touch others' heads, lips, or hands, and power passes to them. But our reach is limited by arms that, unlike our voice, no microphone can stretch. We need intimate, concentric space when God places Godself in our hands.

How do we reconcile space organized along a horizontal axis with that around a vertical axis? There is something of a paradigm of worship itself in that problem, the God-to-human relationship represented by the vertical, the human-to-human represented by the horizontal. We shall trace different ways this tension has been resolved shortly.

But what also of the words people offer to God? There seem to be few spatial requirements for this; prayer and praise can be offered anywhere that people can assemble. Above all else, a church building is a place for people to come together. In Quaker terms, where many candles are brought together there is more light. Christians can speak to God wherever they can assemble for worship. Spatial requirements for this act are minimal. Older churches tended to suggest that God was high and lifted up—maybe in the dim recesses of the rafters or at the end of the chancel. Today we are more inclined to suggest that God is in the midst of the worshipers, not in a remote holy spot.

Of course, we cannot touch God, but each of us can touch others in God's name. In recent years, the passing of the peace has been a prominent act of reconciliation and love. Other possibilities occur, such as pronouncing God's forgiveness after a prayer of confession, an act that can be done with the hands even better than the voice (a sign of the cross traced on one's neighbor's forehead, for example). Footwashing is a dramatic occasional act. And in services of reconciliation, touching others for God may occur. All that seems necessary for these aspects of worship is accessibility to one another.

We can break down more specifically the components of space for speaking and touching in God's name. Christian worship usually necessitates **five liturgical spaces** and **three or four liturgical centers** or items of church furnishings. It is amazing how few and how simple are the physical necessities for Christian worship. But since we never encounter them in isolation from one another, we may not be aware of them individually. If a church building can be compared to a complete sentence, it is time for a moment to look at the individual words that compose that sentence.

The first component of liturgical space is **congregational space.** Basically a church is a people place. The pagan temple was the reverse; they kept the money on the inside and the people on the outside. We use the money for the world outside, and we serve the people inside. Quaker meetinghouses consist entirely of congregational space and make it manifest that God's presence is known in the midst of God's people. In an important passage, Vatican II's *Constitution on the Sacred Liturgy* lists as one of the ways Christ is present in the Church's liturgical celebrations: "He is present, lastly, when the Church prays and sings, for he promised: 'Where two or three are gathered together in my name, there am I in the midst of them' (Matthew 18:20)" (paragraph 7).

The second type of space is **movement space.** Christian worship demands considerable movement. Revivalists in the nineteenth century and charismatics today remind us that to move people spiritually we have to move them physically, too. Christians seem to be a restless pilgrim people. Every service begins with the people gathering and ends with scattering. Processions, weddings, funerals, baptisms, offerings, and receiving communion are all actions built upon movement. And these are important actions, not just incidentals. We come together to "discern the Body" of the Lord, and we scatter to serve the Lord's world. Rarely do we think through when we

81

design a church just how people best interact as they gather to be the church or as they go forth to serve the world.

Choir space may be the most difficult space to deal with, especially when there is uncertainty about the function of a choir in worship. Such space may also need to accommodate instrumentalists or dancers. The chief function or functions assigned to the choir should determine the location and design of this type of space.

We are accustomed to speaking of baptism in terms of a font or baptismal tank; less often do we think of it in terms of **baptismal space.** At worst, baptism has been a private ceremony tucked off in a remote corner of the church. Yet every baptism is an act of the whole community, not just because it adds to the body's number but because it witnesses again and again to the fact that we are those who have gone through the waters of death and resurrection and been united to Christ. Like the wedding service, baptism involves both the whole church community and the more intimate circle of family and sponsors gathered as a special focus of love about the one being baptized. In terms of space, this necessitates space and access for the candidates and baptismal party without blocking the sense of participation by the whole congregation. Baptismal space is people space in concentric circles. About the font or baptismal tank gather, first of all, the candidates and ministers, then family and sponsors, and finally the whole congregation.

Sanctuary space is the space about the altar-table. Usually it is the most conspicuous space in the building, often blinding us to the fact that its role is to serve, not to dominate. Thus we need to avoid such barriers as excessive height, the glare of too much direct light, overscaled furnishings, enclosures, and other ways of making this space seem a remote and detached holy spot. Strangely enough, in many denominations with little eucharistic piety, this is the one spot in the church never approached by the people. It remains more aloft and aloof than in those denominations where people gather around it weekly.

There are also three or four liturgical centers essential to Christian worship. Again, their use reflects ways we perceive the presence of Christ in our worship. A **baptismal font** or **baptismal tank** is a necessity for the sheer physical fact that water demands a container. It can be a recess in the floor (as the earliest surviving baptistry buildings indicate) or a basin mounted on a pillar. The one necessity—that it can contain water—seems more concealed than revealed in most designs. The *Didache* called for cold running water where possible. The Vatican II *Constitution* reminds us: "By his power he [Christ] is present in the sacraments, so that when someone baptizes it is really Christ himself who baptizes." Without a container for water, we cannot baptize or experience this form of Christ's presence.

Christ is also "present in his word, since it is he himself who speaks when the holy scriptures are read in the Church" (CSL, 7). One could argue that in a strict sense a **pulpit** or **ambo** is not a necessity but a convenience. Yet if we do believe that the reading and preaching of God's word is a fresh theophany each time the people of God gather, then we ought to provide physical testimony to that belief in the form of a pulpit that adequately displays the Bible when it is not being read and holds it so the reader's and preacher's hands are free when they read or preach. The visual aspects of this form of Christ's presence are not to be minimized. This also means that bookbinding must again become a major art form for the church.[1]

There is no need to emphasize the importance of the **altar-table** for Christian worship, but we do need to be reminded that it is not present as the architectural focus of the building or even as a symbol of Christ. It is there because it is used; in short, just as fonts hold water and pulpits hold Bibles, so do altar-tables hold communion vessels. The altar-tables depicted in early Christian art seem hardly larger than card tables. They were ministerial altar-tables, quite adequate to hold what was put on them but not monuments to fill space or to create an architectural focus or religious symbol. It would be very inconvenient in Western culture to have to put the communion vessels on the floor, so an altar-table comes close to being a necessity.

In the early church, until late in the fourth century, the presider's **chair** was the center from which much of the service was conducted and the place for preaching. There has been a revival in the importance of the presidential chair since Vatican II in Roman Catholic circles. Many Protestants are still recoiling from the ugliness of the inevitable three pulpit chairs representing that trinity (not always holy) of preacher, song leader, and guest preacher which the nineteenth century deemed necessary. One could argue that the minister's place ought to be a seat with the congregation except when he or she needs to be on his or her feet. The *Constitution* does speak of Christ's presence "in the person of the minister." It is questionable, however, how much a living person is identified with a chair in the way we associate water with a font, the Bible with the pulpit, or communion elements with the altar-table. A chair does not function in quite the same way, since Christ's presence in a person does not need a furnishing to make it visible. Certainly the presidential chair is a convenience, but it ought to be designed and located with reticence.

Well, that is all it takes. There is a certain sense of poverty or economy of means about Christian worship, although too often we gild the lily. Other spaces, other furnishings (lecterns, prayer desks, communion rails) are not necessary and may confuse us by concealing those that are. If we stick to the essentials, we soon discover that restraint and understatement are the most powerful forms of statement. Only the essential spaces and centers can reveal what is vital in Christian worship. Recognizing them is like planning the essentials for a backpacking expedition as contrasted to cramming everything into the station wagon for an afternoon's outing.

II

A look at how Christians have arranged these liturgical spaces and centers over the course of history can teach us much. The relative prominence or reticence of various spaces or centers, their relation to one another, and the design of the liturgical centers themselves all give us a clear indication of shifts in practice and theological perspective. This variety indicates the diversity inherent in Christian worship. Yet the persistence of the same five spaces and three or four centers is a clear witness to the degree of constancy in Christian worship. We can give only a rapid survey of this diversity and constancy here, but will suggest the great variety of liturgical arrangements that others have found useful.[2]

The early church had to live in makeshift quarters during periods of persecution; yet we know buildings of some magnificence were occasionally built even while Christianity was an illicit religion. We have very little documentary or architectural evidence of the architectural setting of Christian worship before Constantine. Apparently, early Christians often met in private homes, usually those of the more well-to-do members of the community. During periods of persecution, there was always the danger that Christians could be put to death for the crime of assembling for worship or be the victims of mobs who considered such assemblies unpatriotic or irreligious. Thus it was probably wise to use regular family furniture and rooms for such worship and to return them to their places immediately after.

The domesticity of such locations in private homes gave a sense of hospitality and intimacy that was lost when Christian worship went public. Yet the advantages of such intimate space recur again and again whenever Christians are persecuted or an impoverished minority: the Quakers, the Anabaptists, the Amish, Christians in communist countries today. We probably fool ourselves if we think this same domestic feeling of hospitality and intimacy can be easily imitated in public buildings; yet we are equally deceived if we forget the need to seek these qualities in good church architecture. Obviously these qualities shape the style of worship offered within such settings.

We do have an astonishingly well-preserved example of a house-church in **Dura-Europos** on the Euphrates River. This is a home that was adapted on a permanent basis for Christian worship early in the third century and destroyed about A.D. 256. The ruins indicate that a wall had been removed and two rooms joined to provide space for the eucharistic assembly (Figure 1).[3] At one end appears a small platform, possibly for the altar-table and bishop's throne. A room at the opposite side of the house was probably used as a baptistery. It has a font covered by a canopy, and walls ornamented with frescoes. Thus early there appears an explicit allocation of spaces for different liturgical functions, a pattern reflected in almost all subsequent church buildings.

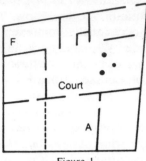

Figure 1

In the fourth century, Christianity became not only legal and respectable but was espoused by the emperor Constantine, who showered magnificent gifts on the church: nine new churches in Rome, and others in Jerusalem, Bethlehem, and Constantinople. The worship in these magnificent new buildings matched all the sumptuousness of the imperial court, a far cry from the persecuted Christians huddled together in secret meetings. The emperor's architects simply adapted a well-developed building type, the **basilica,** or Roman law court. The civil basilica served much the same functions as the county courthouse and high-school auditorium do in American towns. Basically it was a rectangular building with a semicircular apse at one end. In

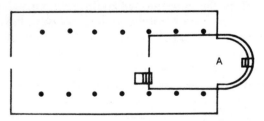

Figure 2

this apse there was a platform with a throne for the judge, who might be flanked by scribes. It was basically a **longitudinal building** organized along a horizontal axis. This building type the church made its own in the fourth century (Figure 2). The bishop's throne replaced that of the judge, and the presbyters sat on either side of him. A platform for the singers extended out into the nave (congregational space). The altar-table usually appeared near the junction of apse and nave, and an ambo (pulpit) stood on the end or side of the platform. Preaching, at first, was from the bishop's throne, and the eucharistic prayer was offered facing the people across the altar-table. The rest of the building was unencumbered by seating, the mobile congregation moving wherever they could best hear and see.

From an early time, there has also been a tradition of **centralized buildings** organized around a vertical axis in the center of the building. A separate type of building for baptism, the **baptistery,** was often designed on this basis, as was the **martyrium,** or chapel over the grave or relics of a martyr. Both of them were based on the mausoleum. New technology for building domes over square naves led to the gradual adoption of centralized buildings among Eastern Orthodox churches, instead of the elongated basilicas favored in the West. Frequently three apses appear walled off by an **iconostasis** (icon screen) from the centralized congregational space, which is frequently covered by a dome (Figure 3). The people are shielded from the awe and mystery of the service surrounding

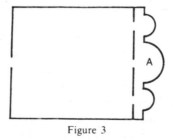

Figure 3

the altar-table by the iconostasis. This creates in Eastern Orthodox churches the appearance of two simultaneous services, in the congregational space and in the sanctuary. Images of the saints (**icons**) surround the congregation, reminding them that they worship amidst the whole company of heaven.

In the West, churches tended to develop in a longitudinal direction, partly because of technology. (Maximum width of gothic vaulting was about eighty feet, but by repeating bays a church could be extended lengthwise.) But it was also a result of complex developments in the forms of worship and the specialization of priests and lesser clergy plus those in religious orders. These influences can be seen most dramatically in the retreat of the altar-table from proximity to the congregational space until the sanctuary space becomes located at the furthest extremity of the building from congregational space.

The Middle Ages saw the development of highly specialized types of churches: pilgrimage churches, churches for

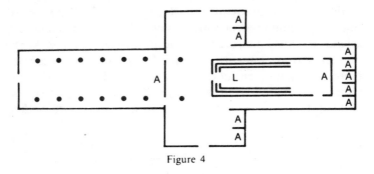

Figure 4

monastic communities, collegiate churches, cathedrals, preaching churches, and ordinary parish churches. The pacesetters, though, always seem to have been the **monastic churches.** A large part of the time of these communities revolved around saying and singing the seven daily offices and the night office. Since large communities could include as many as a thousand members, it is not surprising that a magnificently functional type of building evolved, specifically designed to accommodate monastic worship. The most important space came to be the choir stalls (for all the community was a choir) arranged in two parallel sections so psalms could be sung antiphonally (back and forth). In effect, these elongated choirs provided a church within a church, often sectioned off from the nave by screens (Figure 4). For a monastic community, it was a functional arrangement. A high altar-table in the sanctuary served for mass, and other altar-tables were scattered throughout the building for private masses. Various other arrangements were tried for monastic communities: a choir in the western apse in Germany, a walled-in space in the middle of the nave in Spain. Cathedral churches followed similar patterns, often subdividing the interior space into more specialized compartments for chantry chapels, where mass was said for the repose of the dead.

It should not surprise us that these highly specialized churches had a disproportionate effect on **parish churches** where most people worshiped in their villages (Figure 5). These buildings, too, sprouted large screened chancels, spaces used only by the local clergy and the family of the lord of the manor. But the congregation was not monks or clergy but lay people, relegated to the nave, from which they could glimpse mass being said at the altar-table at the other end of the chancel. The nave contained a pulpit about which they could stand.

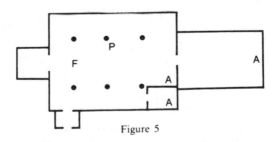

Figure 5

Unlike the monastic church, each parish church contained a font. The services of baptism and marriage, by the late Middle

Ages, began in a porch, just outside. And the whole nave was decorated by a vast array of sculpture, painting, and stained glass meant to instruct and to stimulate devotions. Until the fourteenth century, the nave was clear of chairs and pews. A mobile congregation moved where they could see and hear best. The introduction of pews meant sitting down on the job and a congregation no longer mobile. The peoples' time had come to be spent in personal devotions. So divorced had clergy and people become that a sixteenth-century Roman Catholic bishop could write: "The people in the church [nave] took small heed what the priest and clerks did in the chancel. . . . It was never meant that the people should indeed hear the Matins or hear the Mass, but be present there and pray themselves in silence."[4]

The division between nave and chancel, so functional in a monastic church, was a disaster in parish churches but nevertheless was imitated with zeal. The medieval parish church had become an excellent place for personal devotions (which was really how it had come to be used primarily) but a very poor place for genuinely liturgical worship with that "full, conscious, and active participation in liturgical celebrations which is demanded by the very nature of the liturgy" (CSL, 14).

Another medieval development was that of attributing symbolic meanings to every bit of space, furnishings, and the actions of worship, a fanciful development that often betrayed the loss of comprehension of items once functional and obvious in purpose.

The Reformation and Counter-Reformation saw drastic changes in the arrangements. The Jesuits, who had no need for choir space to say the daily office together, led the way among Roman Catholics in building sumptuous churches where the mass could be a dazzling spectacle. The altar-table once again became conspicuous without the intervening space of a deep choir, and ornate pulpits vied for attention with it.

It is hard to generalize about the **Protestant experiments** in liturgical architecture, so richly varied were they in trying to leapfrog over medieval developments to achieve what they, rightly or wrongly, considered to be primitive (early church) patterns in building. It was difficult, if not impossible, to teach the priesthood of all believers in a building rigidly divided into clerical chancel and lay nave. Medieval buildings were adapted by bringing all the communicants into the chancel for communion or by moving the whole service out into the nave. Often the chancel was simply walled off or demolished.

When Protestants began building numerous new buildings in the seventeenth and eighteenth centuries, the variety of shapes they experimented with was extraordinary, though many were of a centralized type. Figure 6 shows several patterns drawn from German, Dutch, and Scottish examples (left to right).

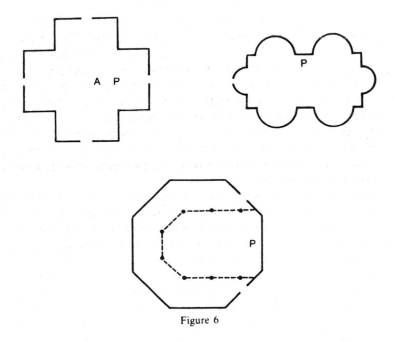

Figure 6

The same variety of experimentation continued in eighteenth-century America. Figure 7 shows (left to right) a typical Congregational meetinghouse, one of the at least six different arrangements tried by Anglicans, and a Quaker meetinghouse with a movable partition between men's and women's meetings.

91

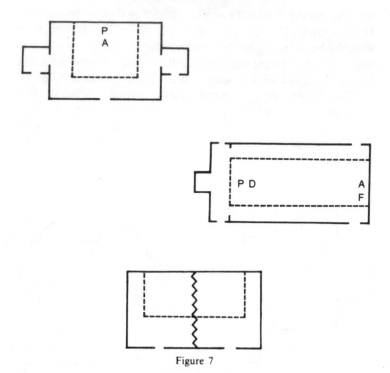

Figure 7

What do these have in common, if anything? None has a chancel; it virtually disappeared from Protestant buildings for a quarter of a millennium. Instead, congregational space has been magnified, and choir and sanctuary space have shrunk or disappeared. The Quaker building is entirely congregational space. A characteristic Protestant addition was a balcony to enable speakers to be heard by a large number of people. Balconies also helped bring the total community together about the pulpit and Lord's table, though movement was difficult.

The nineteenth century saw a strange reversal. The romanticism of the **Cambridge Movement** led many churches in the English-speaking world to see the Middle Ages by moonlight and to clamor for a return to a neo-medieval type of building (Figure 8; compare with Figure 5). Revivalism, on the other hand, emphasizing pulpit personalities and massed choirs, developed the **concert stage arrangement** (Figure 9). Roman Catholic churches of this period tended to be versions of Figure 9 with the altar-table at C, a font near the door, and only a diminutive pulpit off to the side of the chancel.

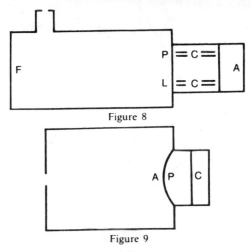

Figure 8

Figure 9

Recent years have seen drastic changes, especially since Vatican II. In common, many of these represent a move to a centralized plan, though with compromises necessary to make the spoken word function well and yet allow concentric arrangements of people. Try to guess which traditions are represented in Figure 10.

They are (left to right) Reformed, Roman Catholic, and Anglican. Each of them is unique, but they do represent common features: directional space for preaching with the congregation nevertheless gathered about the altar-table. None is them is completely successful; yet all try to balance the requisites for effective speaking and touching in God's name.

Some of the most pronounced characteristics of current church building are the result of economic necessity and new construction methods. But others, such as low profile buildings, nondirectional interior space, and flexible seating, show deliberate attempts to recover some of the hospitality and intimacy of the homes in which early Christians worshiped.

What practical conclusions for our times can we draw from

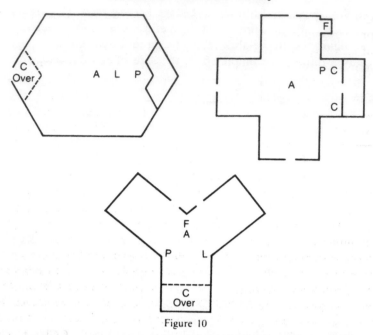

Figure 10

this rapid survey of the Christian experience with liturgical space? Obviously there is enough diversity here to make generalizations of any type difficult. Yet when we look at these experiences with a critical eye, there is much to admire, much to deplore. Obviously our time has different standards of judgment than had other ages; but if we accept the limitation that we are speaking from a late–twentieth-century viewpoint, we can develop some criteria of practical relevance for those who build or remodel space for Christian worship today.

Our first criterion is that of **utility.** Just how well does a building function to be used—not admired, but used—by worshipers? The question can be resolved only by seeing how adequately it serves our speaking and touching in God's name. If speaking cannot be heard because of atrocious acoustics, even though the space functions well for the sacraments, it can hardly be considered adequate. Or, if speaking functions well but the congregation is fractured into inaccessible balconies so that giving communion is difficult, the design again flunks.

Obviously there must be compromises between an ideal preaching church and a perfect sacrament church. The criterion of utility covers all uses. Churches are built to be used, not as monuments for tourists to admire or art historians to chronicle.

Much of the success of the most usefully organized space for Christian worship is the result of devotion to **simplicity.** Only when our mind is clear as to what is basic and essential in our worship can we build well for it. Restraint and discipline are crucial. Too many churches have been ruined by too much money and effort expended on nonessentials and too little concern directed to basics. Attention to the five essential liturgical spaces and three or four liturgical centers gives the core of our discipline of simplicity. Knowing when to stop is all-important. One must talk worship before one talks architecture. Church building committees are notoriously poor clients because they do not do their homework and make up their minds about what the church is and does in its worship. Without such information, even the best architects cannot produce an adequate building for worship although they can erect a most attractive facade.

Our survey has shown that the circumstances of Christian worship and the needs perceived are subject to change. The events of the last few years, especially, have also taught us the importance of **flexibility.** Despite the constancy in Christian worship, there are strong forces shaping and changing the outward forms through which these constants are expressed. The most difficult churches to deal with today are those built a short while ago, when we had not yet come to accept the reality of change in worship. A most important new element today in our thinking about church architecture is the frank acceptance of change. John Ruskin's romantic "when we build, let us think that we build for ever" belongs to another age.[5] Rather we should say today, "When we build, let us not tie knots in the future." For we know it will be different, maybe even in a very short time. Immovable pews, massive pulpits, fixed choir stalls all belong to an age that could not accept the possibility of change. But both history and recent experience have taught us that what seems so true and obvious in one period of time may not be so in the next. Let us not try to impose our will irrevocably in concrete on those who come after us. They deserve a voice, too.

An elusive strand throughout our historical survey has been the need for buildings that foster a sense of **intimacy**. This was certainly true in the early church, recovered again in many Reformation traditions, and now ardently sought in building today. The sense of intimacy is important as we emphasize participation by the entire worshiping community. Current revulsion against monument-type buildings is a healthy sign that a servant people has learned that architecture is meant to serve the community, not dominate it. This means smaller-scale and less expensive buildings that make each worshiper feel he or she is on stage and playing an important role in worship rather than being a lonely spectator lost in the audience.

Utility, simplicity, flexibility, and intimacy seem to be the criteria by which we can best judge how adequately liturgical architecture serves the church today. These are obviously not the standards by which the great cathedrals of the thirteenth century were built, or even the city churches of the 1920s, though we can earn much from both. But the directness and honesty sought in our time can indicate new directions to add to the varied legacy of the past.

Those who have the responsibility of building or rearranging space for a worshiping congregation have a wonderful opportunity to renew the life of their community. A building project can be the catalyst that makes church renewal possible. It also can be sheer hell. The process (of planning to build) can be more important than the final product (the building). After all, the church is people, not a building. But planning for a building can often help the people discover or rediscover what it means to be the community of God's favor. Much depends upon the leadership given in guiding the planning process and the willingness to take the time needed to prepare adequately.

But the building is not unimportant, either. For after it is built it will continue to shape worship in its image for generations. Although it is not completely true that the building will always prevail, at least we must recognize in it a powerful ally and formidable foe. Its witness will outlast most of us. The more carefully we study and reflect on our worship, the better equipped we will be to help plan a building that will be a valuable tool in helping us to speak and touch in God's name.

III

Space determines many things about worship, but one of the most easily and tragically overlooked is how it affects sound. Each church building forms an **acoustical environment.** Every one is unique. And few things affect worship more profoundly than the way sound behaves in space. Sound, of course, exists in time, too, and it could well have been treated in the previous chapter. But the relation of sound to space needs emphasis, especially since this is so frequently overlooked when liturgical space is planned. Churches are built to be used. They usually are photographed empty of people, but a church functions chiefly when peopled by a congregation. The very act of people assembling is a sound event, often commencing with bells calling them out of the world.

Sound exists in space, then, as well as in time. Our concern here is with all the sounds that exist within a church building and the way those sounds act in that space to shape and determine the nature of the worship offered therein. A few examples may be helpful. The large dimensions and hard surfaces of medieval stone buildings necessitated the practice of chanting prose recitations in melodic form in order to ensure audibility. The psalms were usually chanted in unison to plainsong melodies, a practice well adapted to an acoustical environment where sound lingers. On the other hand, it is no accident that congregational song in England developed in the small meetinghouses of dissenters rather than in stately, medieval parish churches. Hymnody was picked up in time by Anglicans, but Congregationalists and Methodists took the lead. Their small, intimate meetinghouses encouraged congregational song by making everyone feel "onstage." It would be hard to imagine the silent waiting on God of Quaker worship in any place where sound is as resonant as in a large stone cathedral. In a small, domestic-type space, it is natural; in vastness it is lost.

Worship involves a wide gamut of sounds. How do people interact as they gather? There is sound of feet, voices, moving

97

chairs mixed into our worship. Babies cry, and children whine. These are not sounds to be suppressed but are the natural and welcome sounds of forming the body. But there may be annoying sounds from outside that need to be subdued, or internal mechanical hums from lighting, heating, or air conditioning that ought to be absorbed.

Still more crucial is the spoken voice. If there is an echo bouncing off hard or curved surfaces preaching may be difficult. Hearing the Word of God ought not to be prevented by echoes. There are also similar problems with too absorbent an environment, which makes each person think she or he is singing solo and so each one usually stops. Too much absorption can make organ music lose much of its brilliance. Bad acoustics can frustrate both the speaker and the musician, although their requirements are not the same. The speaker wants no echo, while the organist relishes a bit of reverberation. Compromises between the two are usually necessary.

Our chief concerns are the spoken voice and music, though we must realize there are many other audible components of worship. Much will be said about both the spoken voice and music under each topic in this book. But it may be useful to say a few words at this point about church music in general, especially as it is affected by space. Just as architecture is the organization of space, so music is the organization of sound.

The chief function of **church music** is to add a deeper dimension of involvement to worship. By now almost every choir room in America must have a sign quoting words frequently attributed to Augustine to the effect that the one who sings prays twice, though Augustine's fears about the over-attractiveness of music never seem displayed. There is much truth to the statement about praying twice, though. One must be even more fully aware and conscious of what one is doing when singing. Dancing would add yet a further layer of consciousness. Singing a text requires more concentration than just reciting something, though over-familiarity can make singing threadbare at times. When there is music, usually a deeper level of performing or listening is involved than when there is no music. Music, then, gives an added dimension to any event. Sometimes one has to experience the absence of music from a familiar service to realize just how greatly music enhances participation.

One of the reasons music aids worship is that it is a more expressive medium than ordinary speech. Music enables us to express an intensity of feeling through variety of tempo, pitch, volume, melody, harmony, and rhythm. Thus one has a greater range for expressiveness when singing than when speaking. Music can and often does convey a greater intensity of feeling than would be expressed in its absence.

Music also aids worship through its beauty. We must be cautious here because the creation of beauty is not the purpose of worship (or of some music either), though beauty may be of considerable value in worship. Much music with pretty minimal aesthetic qualities nevertheless functions as a satisfactory vehicle for some individuals to express their worship. One cannot criticize a church service by the same standards one would apply to a concert. Many who have been educated to know what is "good" church music for sophisticated people fail to recognize that they should also learn what is "good for-ness" in terms of people and circumstances when music is used. At every level of cultural sophistication, there are many different possibilities, some much more adequate than others for each situation. Discrimination thus occurs within a cultural and situational context.

One function of music, then, is the offering of something we consider to be beautiful, no matter how meager our own musical accomplishments may be. And this is why actually singing oneself involves more participation than listening to someone else singing, no matter how superior the other's musical attainments may be. Fortunately we do not often have to choose between the two; we can have both choral music and congregational song in the same service. But congregational song does have the distinct advantage of giving everyone the opportunity to offer to God the best sound he or she can create. This effort cannot be replaced by someone else's doing it for us.

Church music, then, is essential in adding further dimensions of feeling and beauty to our worship. If music is so important to worship, the effects of the building on music are crucial. In worship the whole church building itself becomes a musical instrument. Sound bounces around in it or is sucked up inside of it, just as in any other musical instrument. Some new concert halls are actually built to be "tunable" with adjustable louvres so that the walls can absorb or reflect more sound. To a certain extent, this adjustment happens in church buildings too. The acoustics change as more people assemble and more sound is absorbed. As a musical instrument, the church building functions in a variety of ways to affect different types of music. It can enhance or deaden every kind of church music.

The needs of **instrumental music** vary somewhat according to the instrument or combination of instruments used. Usually a bright, lively sound is desired and some reverberation preferred, but not enough to create an echo that would interfere with speaking. The increasing use of instruments other than the piano or organ demands provision of space. Usually this is part of choir space. It is best to have singers and instrumentalists adjacent to each other, since it is difficult to sing to accompaniment from afar. This flexibility is especially important for choir space. It is difficult to wedge a cello between choir stalls, hard to lug a piano up stairs. But the whole interior of the building must be carefully planned so that sound will not be expected to turn a right angle to emerge from a chancel or so that a hundred-thousand-dollar pipe organ is not buried in a transept. The effects of surfaces and materials throughout the building will have major impact on the quality of instrumental music heard, no matter how talented the performance.

Space has other effects on **choral music.** Indeed, the sound of this type of music will be largely conditioned by the space provided for it. Before we build, we must ask: What is the function of choral music? Unfortunately we usually get a whole chorus of confused voices for an answer. Most congregations devote far more time and energy to building bigger and better choirs than to examining how they conceive choirs to function in worship. But what we consider to be a choir's chief functions will certainly determine the organization of choir space and its location with regard to the other four liturgical spaces.

If the chief function of the choir is conceived to be a sharing in the ministry of the Word—singing *to* the congregation—this may indicate a location facing the congregation. A choir is meant to be heard rather than seen. Clergy should not have to vie with the choir for the congregation's attention, especially during preaching. On the other hand, if a choir is considered necessary chiefly for the offering of beauty—singing *for the congregation—a less conspicuous location could serve just as well. Increasingly it is realized that one of the prime functions of a choir is leading congregational song—singing with* the congregation. This is particularly true in introducing new hymns or in leading difficult music. In this case, the choir ought to be as close to the congregation as possible, maybe mingled with it. The old basilican arrangement (with the choir in the front of the nave and surrounded by the congregation on three sides) has much to commend it today for all three of these functions. Finally, choirs sometimes are used to provide a musical background, reducing church music to entertainment. In these cases both choir and choir space might be better omitted altogether.

But wherever the choir is located its place will determine with what sense and meaning choir and congregation hear what is sung. Thus the location of the choir is probably the most vexing single problem in organizing space for worship today. Ideally, since the function of a choir can change from week to week, choir space ought to be treated as mobile space. On some occasions, such as Good Friday, it might be omitted entirely. Some congregations, after much thought, use a choir only for special occasions and sacred concerts. In any case, choir space ought to be related closely to congregational space, so that choir and congregation readily identify with each other rather than the one appearing to be performers and the others listeners. In worship, all are performers.

Most important of all is **congregational song.** In this type of music, all those present have an opportunity to express themselves. The prime criterion here is not beauty but adequacy of expressiveness. Congregational song must pass the test of expressing the innermost feelings and thoughts of the worshipers. When it succeeds in so doing, it frequently is also (but secondarily) of great beauty.

Congregational song is divided into hymnody and service

101

music. Augustine called a hymn "the praise of God in song," but in a narrower sense most **hymns** are metrical poetry set to melodies. These vary tremendously in form and content. The **gospel song** is an informal and highly individualistic type. Fanny Crosby's "Pass Me Not, O Gentle Savior" and "Blessed Assurance, Jesus Is Mine" are popular examples. The **office hymn** consists of music and text for use in the liturgy of the hours and often ends in a doxological stanza addressing the Trinity. "Awake My Soul, and with the Sun" and "All Praise to Thee, My God, This Night" are well-known examples written in English. Many others were translated from Latin by John Mason Neale. **Service music** is music to a fixed set of words in the liturgy, such as the *Gloria Patri* or the *Sanctus*. Usually many musical settings are available for such texts in a variety of styles.

The importance of congregational song does not always prevent it from neglect. Carlton R. Young has said that we tend to treat the choir as if it were the congregation, whereas we ought instead to treat the congregation as if it were the choir. The choir is always and only a supplement to the congregation except at sacred concerts. The choir exists only to do what the congregation cannot do or to help the congregation do its singing better. Choral music is not a substitute for congregational song.

Much of the effectiveness of congregational song is dependent upon acoustics. A building full of carpeting and drapes may be too spongy and soak up sound, so that every member of the congregation sounds alone and is embarrassed out of singing. Hard surfaces in flooring and walls can be of major help for singing. Nor should the congregation be divided into separate transepts or balconies unless necessary. Such arrangements may be good for **antiphonal singing** (i.e., with responsive alternation between sections), but such a method is infrequent outside of monastic communities.

Music is a body art. Our inhibitions may keep us from acknowledging it, but music calls the whole body into motion. Children, unfortunately, learn *not* to dance. Younger children frequently break out dancing at the sound of music, but age stills them. At times Christians have used dance as a major part of worship: Clement of Alexandria, in the second century, spoke of prayer as involving hands and feet. The Shakers in the late eighteenth century and throughout most of the nineteenth century made dance a major part of their worship. They gave it up only when advancing age made it difficult for all members of their community to participate. Some Christians in Africa find drumming and dancing natural ways to worship with hands and feet. Most American Protestants are only a generation or two removed from ancestors who did understand hand-clapping and foot-tapping as part and parcel of church music. In many Eastern Orthodox churches the whole congregation is still as mobile today as were Western Christians until the introduction of pews.

The whole body participates in worship through various **postures** (kneeling, standing, sitting); **gestures** (embrace, breaking of bread, making the sign of the cross); and **movement** (to the communion rail, assembling, offerings). In recent years, the ancient **procession** (or Christian demonstration, to use secular terms) of the whole congregation has been rediscovered as a stirring form of witness, especially when accompanied by appropriate hymnody. Even our **clothing** is an important part of worship. It testifies to our understanding of the occasion and our role in it as well as facilitating or constraining meaningful movement.

Liturgical dance has become more common in recent years. In many respects it is comparable to choral music, with the trained and skilled performers providing leadership. When possible, the congregation ought to be active participants, too, just as with music. Where the congregational space is packed full of immovable pews, the possibilities of congregational dance are greatly limited. Once again, the building is hard to fight.

Silence, too, is an important part of worship. The absence of sound can often communicate much. The Quakers can teach all Christians about silence. Best use of silence depends upon discipline; silence comes to be fully corporate when it is directed silence, in which all worshipers are together, as in confessing sin, reflecting on a lesson just read, or offering intercession. Directed silence can be intensely communal, while undisciplined wool-gathering can be anything but. Uninterrupted silence may necessitate shielding space from outside noise, or subduing mechanical sounds within the building. Even in silence, space is all-important.

IV

Space also provides the setting for another important component of Christian worship, the **visual arts.** Ralph Adams Cram, the famous architect, was fond of referring to architecture as the "nexus of the arts." To a large degree this is true; architecture provides shelter not only for music and dance but also for sculpture, painting, and a variety of visual arts and crafts. But architecture does far more than just shelter the other arts; it adds to or subtracts from their effectiveness in helping Christians express their relationship to God.

What function do the various visual arts play in Christian worship? Some traditions have avoided them altogether. At times, in the early church and during the Reformation, there were violent outbursts against them, though these various outbreaks of **iconoclasm** (image smashing) were in themselves strong testimony to the power of visual images. The other extreme is the use of such arts in a purely decorative way, simply to ornament space. Thus tamed and innocuous, they have little potency for contributing to worship and merely provide a visual Muzak.

We must distinguish between religious art in general and **liturgical art** (sometimes called cultic art, especially when non-Christian examples are being considered). Most briefly stated, liturgical art is art used in worship. "Religious art" is a much broader category and, by some definitions, includes illustrations in Sunday school literature, Van Gogh's landscapes, and some abstract art. Paul Tillich was willing to apply the term "religious" to any art that had a dimension of depth, penetrating beyond superficial observation.[6] Liturgical art, by contrast, is defined more by its use, though its subject matter is usually the divine or those through whom God has worked.

The prime function of liturgical art is to bring us to awareness of the **presence of the holy,** to make visible that which cannot be seen by ordinary eyes. Liturgical art does not make God present, but it does bring God's presence to our consciousness. Somewhat as a photograph brings to mind loved ones who may be absent from us, so liturgical art opens our eyes to the unseen presence of God. There is a difference, of course; liturgical art makes us aware of a presence, not an absence.

Really adequate liturgical art has a tremendous potency because of its **religious power**.[7] This is the power to penetrate beneath the obvious and to convey the divine. Much of the art placed in churches in recent centuries was profoundly deficient in this respect. Liturgical art has to use the objects of this world to represent the immaterial. But when painting and sculpture simply reflect naturalistic reproductions of the appearance of persons or objects, they fail to penetrate beneath the surface, no matter how skillful the artist. Many popular paintings of the head of Christ represent only the human nature of Jesus and never lead us beyond the obvious. Rouault, on the other hand, could treat the head of Christ with such sensitivity that we know we stand before a suffering God. The far less skilled makers of *santos* of nineteenth- and early–twentieth-century New Mexico and Colorado created a liturgical art of extraordinary religious power, just as their contemporaries the Shakers did for liturgical dance. Primitive and crude their images are, but no one can contemplate them without being called to worship. They let loose numinous power in a piece of wood or canvas by relying on conviction and insight far more than on academic artistic skills. Our inner eye is addressed by such art, and we discover how close seeing is to believing.

Those who destroyed liturgical art in the past recognized clearly its religious power, but they feared ignorant people might confuse the mirror with what it reflected. This is probably the least dangerous form of idolatry we face today. Indeed, when liturgical art calls us from indulging in egocentric satisfying of our emotions and self-centered lives, it can break down a far worse form of idolatry.

Another characteristic of good liturgical art is its **communal nature**. What is projected is not the individual experience of the artist but the insights of the total community. Good liturgical art is noted not for originality in subject matter but for capturing the experience of a community. This does not mean that the artist must even be Christian; from the ancient catacombs to contemporary France, successful liturgical art has often been done by non-Christian artists working under the careful guidance of the Christian community. And many believers have failed to produce satisfactory liturgical art because their muse called them to a personal vision rather than a communal one. No more can an architect design a good church without understanding the life of the community that will use it than an artist can produce good liturgical art without comprehending the same life.

The community whose life together such art is meant to serve is not just one generation old. It is a community of traditions. Those reflect the way other generations have experienced and rejoiced in God's actions. They have found some adequate ways to reflect these realities in visual form. Past experience is always our point of departure in creating liturgical art for today. That is not to say liturgical art is unchanging; historical research can easily chronicle the introduction of new styles and contents. But beneath all its diversity, there is an underlying strong current of constancy in returning again and again to the same basic contents just as we still prefer many of the same words and acts that link us to other Christians in different ages.

Part of the inherited vocabulary of the past takes the form of **visual symbols.** Every mass movement creates its own visual symbols. Think of those of the Vietnam war, the ecology movement, or the Equal Rights Amendment cause. Each symbol is an instantaneous way of recalling shared beliefs. The church has long used the same kind of visual shorthand. A crown of thorns, a manger, tongues of flame—all these and many more convey shared beliefs and have done so for centuries. But symbols are mortal. Where now is the World War II "V" for victory? To how many Christians now does a pomegranate or a peacock speak of resurrection? Nor is it easy intentionally to create new symbols afresh. They sneak up on us spontaneously. Probably thousands simultaneously thought of the aptness of the mathematical equal sign for expressing the justice of equality for women and men. We can await the appearance of new symbols and bury those that have died. For a symbol has died when it becomes an esoteric code. Symbols are meant to be used because they reflect realities of compelling importance for the lives of those experiencing them. They can be visual (images), audible (words), and kinetic (movement), but in all cases they must refer us to realities we experience.

We shall speak briefly of nine art forms commonly used as liturgical arts. The visual arts function in worship in two ways. Some are fixed and permanent; others are for seasonal or occasional use only. Both the commonness and the uniqueness of each event can be underscored by different liturgical arts illustrating continuity and change.

One of the most important of the fixed and permanent art media used in worship is **sculpture.** It has been greatly mistrusted in the Eastern Orthodox churches, which generally forbid sculpture in favor of two-dimensional representations. Until recently, most Reformation traditions also avoided three-dimensional forms as too tangible. It is hard, though, to doubt the religious power that sculpture can have after seeing the work of Henry Moore or Jacob Epstein in churches.

Painting seemed dangerous to some of the Reformers, but it must be remembered that each medieval church was itself a whole catechism, painted from floor to roof with sacred history past and future. Some of the images (God the Father with a long beard) proved offensive to Roman Catholics as well, and a great deal of such art was obliterated. It was easier to print new catechisms—far less imaginative, no doubt, but far more explicit in teaching correct doctrine in any age of religious controversy. Today Rouault and Sunderland have shown us how much painting can contribute to knowing the object of our worship in ways that transcend most verbal categories.

Much that was said of painting applies equally well to colored light, i.e., **stained glass.** Few human creations are more beautiful or more changing than the warm splash of colored light on cold stone or plaster. We have misunderstood the medium too often by trying to make it explicitly pictorial. Its nature is closer to instrumental music, an abstraction that says something words and pictures cannot. There is no denying the emotive factors present in all worship, and stained glass seems to make an almost universal appeal to these.

Every church makes use of **basketry, glassblowing, ceramics,** or **metalsmithing** for communion and baptismal vessels. These art forms provide opportunity for expressing the community's joy in its Creator. Good baskets, glassware, ceramics, and silverware are available commercially in most areas. Almost every community college in the country has a studio art department that would welcome a chance to produce or help a congregation acquire these vessels.

Bookbinding, too, is a neglected but necessary art that deserves much more cultivation by the church today.[8] If we regard the contents of Bibles and service books as vital, there ought to be outward and visible testimony to this.

Liturgical arts for seasonal or occasional use include many possibilities, especially textiles, graphic arts, and the new electronic media. There has been an explosion of interest in **textile arts** in recent years, though their use is as old as the church itself. Undeniably, part of the attraction of textiles is their impermanence.[9] They can be removed, even discarded, after a single occasion or season. The variety of uses that textiles serve is impressive. **Antependia** or **paraments** can hang as falls on pulpit and lectern, or as **frontals** on altar-tables (though the preference today is not to conceal the form of the altar-table). Seasonal colors and symbols are often used. **Banners** may be carried in processions or suspended where air currents will give them movement.

More controversial are **vestments,** which are really testimony to the conservatism of the clergy.[10] When barbarians swarmed down from northern Europe in the fifth century and introduced men's trousers to Rome, the clergy kept the sartorial faith by continuing to wear the everyday garb of imperial Rome: the **chasuble,** a kind of poncho-like outer covering; the **alb,** a white tunic worn by men and women alike; the **stole,** a scarf-like badge of public office (comparable to a police badge); and the **cope,** a cloak. Derived from the tunic are the **dalmatic** with wide sleeves and slit sides, and the **surplice** with full sleeves, often worn over a long black outer garment, the **cassock.** Special garments are worn by bishops in some churches. Protestant clergy, academics, and judges continued to wear the black medieval gown, occasionally continuing the use of two small white **bands** or **tabs,** predecessors of the necktie. The vestment growing most rapidly in popularity these days is the alb, now used as an outer garment. Stoles provide a variety of colors, textures, and designs to whatever other garments are worn under (or over) them. Clothing is a means of communication, and whatever the clergy wear says something, desirable or not.

The **graphic arts** take as many forms as textiles. One's first impression of worship is often a printed bulletin thrust into one's hand upon entering the building. And then one picks up a hymnal or other service book. Gradually we are coming to see that how a page looks is almost as important as what is printed on it. Liturgical graphics have moved in recent years from depressingly drab to halfway exciting, although good examples are still all too rare.[11] Perhaps there are posters in the church or entrance. Obviously some buildings are more adaptable to the display of banners and posters than others, but suitable lighting and places to hang changeable art forms ought to be considered requisite in all designs for new churches.

This is especially true when we consider the most recent varieties of art forms, those utilizing the **electronic media.** Motion picture films are too disruptive to employ in most worship services, but still images may be projected with sensitivity provided the building allows for this. Where there are adequate control of lighting, flat reflective surfaces, and electrical outlets, projections can add a new dimension to worship by opening possibilities no other generation has known. Today a wall can be anything we want to project on it. It is power that must be used with care so as not to overwhelm but to supplement and underscore the rest of the service. Like good liturgical music, it must be carefully coordinated with the rest of the service.

In all these art forms, we are heavily dependent upon what the space will allow. It can greatly enhance the effectiveness of the various liturgical arts, or it can hamper them greatly. For better or for worse, the influence of the space in which we worship is crucial. How could it be otherwise in a religion focused on the incarnation?

IV
The Spoken Word

We have seen, in the two previous chapters, how important both time and space are as vehicles of communication in Christian worship. Indeed, it is quite possible that non-Christians gain most of their impressions of Christian worship by noticing the holy days their Christian neighbors keep and the buildings Christians frequent on such days. The impressions many Christians have of Jewish worship are largely founded on such observations. If time and space communicate even to those who never enter a church for worship, they work still better as communication vehicles for those who congregate there.

But the community gathered for Christian worship relies even more heavily on two other forms of communication: the spoken word and the acted sign. We shall examine these in turn in this and the next chapter. The importance for worship of these two communication vehicles should not surprise us: they are also the primary ways people relate to one another. Saying and doing are as vital in our relating to God through worship as they are basic for communicating with other humans. Our Creator knows us best and communicates with us through words and actions, through our speaking and our touching. Our concern in this chapter is with how the spoken word by itself forms the basis for much of Christian worship. In following chapters, we shall explore how words joined to actions form the basis of sacraments.

So important is the term "word" as a symbol of presenting

oneself that the Fourth Gospel uses it (*Lógos*) for Christ himself (John 1:1, 14). Though frequent, references to "the hand of God" are only half as numerous in scripture as "the Word of God." The "Word of God" became a prominent symbol in Reformation and subsequent theology as a term referring to Jesus Christ, the Bible, and the event of communication of God through human speech. It is with the last of these that we are concerned at present. The ambiguity of God, book, and speech implied by "the Word" simply underscores the complexity and importance of this image for Christian life.

Throughout Christian history, two structures of worship have been built on the spoken or sung word, with actions playing only an insignificant role. We must deal with complicated and confusing developments in trying to sort out these two types of worship. Not all these developments are as yet known or understood. Both structures have parallel historical evolutions; both exist side by side in the church today.

Our task is made even more difficult because of lack of consensus as to names for these two structures of worship. Christians have not agreed on standard terms for their normal Sunday and weekday services. My choice of terms—"the liturgy of the hours," or simply "the hours," and "the ministry of the Word"—admittedly is arbitrary and may be unfamiliar to some.

The observance of "hours" is a type of worship evolving from private and public worship in the early church and reaching high development among monastic communities. It often is also called "the divine office," "the daily and night office," "the choir offices," "the *opus dei*," or "the canonical hours." Anglicans recognize the hours as "morning prayer" and "evening prayer"; Lutherans use the terms "matins" and "vespers." This structure certainly had impact on the Free Church, Reformed, and Methodist "Sunday service," "Service for the Lord's Day," "preaching service," "divine worship," "morning order," or plain "eleven o'clock."

The other structure of worship, based just as heavily on the spoken word, has been linked to the service of actions about the table in the Lord's Supper ever since the second century. In this context, as a normal portion of the Lord's Supper, it has been known as "*synaxis*," "*pro-anaphora*," "mass of the catechumens," "Ante-Communion," "liturgy of the Word," and "fore-mass." "Ministry of the Word," the term we shall use here, is the earliest distinctive term, first suggested by Tertullian.

In order to understand how both structures function, we need to look at their common heritage and separate development. By no means is this simple, but we shall limit ourselves to broad outlines. Only by surveying these histories can we then specify the theological priorities in the function of each structure. On the basis of these priorities, we shall suggest the grounds for pastoral decisions in planning and preparing for such worship today.

I

We shall begin our discussion of both the liturgy of the hours and the ministry of the Word with a glimpse at the worship of the Jewish **synagogue.** We have already seen that the church adopted much of the Jewish rhythm of time and the mentality that made such rhythm a means of remembering. And we shall see again and again that both Jewish structures of worship and underlying mentalities made Christian worship possible.

The Jewish synagogue service and its mentality underlie our two structures under consideration. So we must ask what function did the synagogue service fulfill? Strangely enough, it seems to have originated to fulfill a nationalistic function, the survival of Israel while in exile in Babylon. Although we lack clear information on the origins of the synagogue service, it appears to have originated sometime in the sixth century B.C. while the Jews were in captivity in Babylon. The Jerusalem temple lay in ruins, and the nationalized worship centered there had come to an abrupt halt. There was no way to pick up elsewhere the temple cult of sacrifice, which by that time had become identified exclusively with Jerusalem. A new beginning had to be made for Israel to survive.

The synagogue apparently originated as a survival agency, just as many emigrant groups in this country have established nationalistic clubs. Israel kept its identity by remembering. It remembered what God had done for God's chosen people whose history made them unique. In answer to the pitiful question, "How could we sing the Lord's song in a foreign land?" (Ps. 137:4), Israel invented the syngagogue service. Survival, for Israel, meant the ability to remember God's actions that had made them a distinctive people. And the best ways to remember, it turned out, were through instruction and prayer together. It is difficult to tell whether synagogue worship began primarily for cultic purposes or for educational ones, just as it is difficult to tell if some television is for education or entertainment. Recalling what God had done and rejoicing in those memories—is that worship or education? It does not much matter, the result is the same. Israel could survive through worship, though countless other kingdoms were obliterated by the sword or by absorption. But the power to remember, reinforced generation after generation by worship, was too powerful even for the tyranny of Babylonia.

It was soon realized that putting the corporate memories of God's actions into writing was highly useful for recalling what God had done to make the Jews a unique people. Teaching these writings through synagogue classes was useful. But the memories really came alive when they were read aloud, reflected upon, and rejoiced in by the gathered community. Maybe this was not intended as worship at first, but worship it became and still is: the synagogue service. Homesick Jewish exiles gathered to read, reflect on, and rejoice in what God had done for their people. And every time they did these things, their self-identity was renewed.

No temple was needed for this kind of instruction or worship, nor were priests needed. It was a type of worship that lay people could lead; anywhere ten Jewish men could gather, a synagogue could be formed. All that was needed was a book and people. The lay character of such worship cannot be overemphasized; it is equally true of the Christian hours even to this day.

The synagogue service focused on what God had done. Jews celebrated God's actions not only in the record of their history (scripture) but also in songs rejoicing in this history (psalms), in prayer blessing God for that history, and in reflection on that history (sermons). Eventually, the prayers that recalled what God had done also began to anticipate what God yet promised to do. This took the form of supplication for God to act, a natural development in prayer. Stylized in time, the prayers eventually came to function as creeds as well as praise and supplication. Reading of the law and the prophets became standard practice as Jews recalled God's gift of the law and God's speaking to them through the prophets.

Worship thus became a way of teaching and transmitting the corporate memories of a people with whom God had covenanted. Survival came through remembering. But it was not just a dead, detached past that was recalled, but a living God who was made known through past events as well as encountered in present worship. As past events were recited they became present reality through which God's power to save could be experienced again and again. Through worship, people could relive for themselves the whole history of salvation. Individual lives were changed by sharing in the recital of common memories, just as an adolescent is helped to gain individual identity by looking through the family photograph album with the rest of the family. The core of synagogue worship is identification with the community's corporate memories of what God has done for God's people. And the spoken word is the medium through which this occurs.

Such was the worship familiar to the earliest Christians. We glimpse this worship in the Nazareth synagogue in Luke 4:16-28. Jesus read the lesson from the prophet Isaiah and sat down to preach. At the synagogue in Pisidian Antioch "after the readings from the Law and the prophets, the officials of the synagogue" invited Paul and his companions to speak (Acts 13:15). It was a style of worship thoroughly familiar to the earliest Christians; their Lord had sanctioned it by regular attendance (Luke 4:16), and the apostles had utilized it to the fullest. Christians could feel at home in such worship until an alarmed Judaism thrust them out.

Thus far the liturgy of the hours and the ministry of the Word share a common inheritance in nonsacrificial worship based on instruction and prayer. The synagogue service and its underlying assumptions made both possible. But additional factors come into the picture early in the Christian era. Rather than trying to ride two horses simultaneously, we shall concentrate on the **liturgy of the hours** and return to the ministry of the Word later.

The gradual evolution of discipline of **personal devotions** for individual Christians was a second ingredient in the development of the hours. Late in the first century or early in the second, the *Didache* advised Christians to pray the Lord's Prayer three times a day.[1] Others sought disciplines in the Bible itself as ways to make practical the scriptural injunction to "pray continually" (I Thess. 5:17). Psalm 55:17 had suggested "evening and morning and at noon," while Daniel had prayed three times a day (Dan. 6:10). Sacrifices had been offered in the temple daily, a lamb in the morning and another at evening (Exod. 29:38-39), and devout Jews prayed daily at these hours. Psalm 119:164 had mentioned "seven times a day I praise thee for the justice of thy decrees," and in verse 62, "at midnight I rise to give thee thanks."

The proper times per day for prayer concerned many early Christian writers, though Clement of Alexandria felt the true Christian "prays throughout his whole life."[2] Tertullian, Origen, and Cyprian[3] all called for prayer thrice during the day, referring to Daniel's example and to various acts of the apostles at the third, sixth, and ninth hours mentioned in the Bible. This threefold discipline is a "sacrament of the Trinity," according to Cyprian. Tertullian also insists on prayer at both dawn and evening.

Hippolytus was a presbyter of the church in Rome, a staunch conservative who resisted liturgical innovation. Despairing because of novelties in the Roman Church, he was chosen an antipope. He died while suffering for his faith and is the only antipope to be canonized. Sometime about A.D. 217 he wrote the *Apostolic Tradition*.[4] It gives details of worship in Rome, probably as remembered from the late second century. The *Apostolic Tradition* includes the earliest surviving liturgical texts for several types of worship and is the most important third-century document on worship. This book has been the source of many a liturgical reform of recent years.

One of the many insights Hippolytus gives us of Roman

practice of his time appears in his description of seven daily hours of private prayer, presumably followed by the more devout. The day began with prayer, after which all were encouraged to participate in public instruction "in the word" if any was held that day. At nine, prayer was enjoined, "for in this hour Christ was seen nailed upon the tree"[5]; at noon, when "it became darkness"; at three, when Christ died; before one goes to sleep, at midnight, for "in this hour every creature hushes for a brief moment to praise the Lord; stars and plants and waters stand still in that instant"; and again at cockcrow, when Peter denied Christ. It was a rigorous pattern, which structured the day around the passion and death of Christ.

Perhaps even more important than the hour of private prayer is Hippolytus' note of a daily gathering for instruction and prayer. Particular emphasis is placed on the attendance of the deacons. "When all have assembled they shall instruct those who are in the assembly and having also prayed, let each one go."[6] Hippolytus may be indicating the beginnings of an almost lost tradition, the so-called ecclesiastical or **cathedral office.** These were daily services in the chief church of a city for instruction in the Word, praise of God, and common prayer by all Christians. Evidence of these cathedral services, attended daily by the clergy and laity of a city, mounts as we look to the fourth century A.D. and the growing respectability of Christianity after persecution ceased. The cathedral office points to what may be the biggest gap in Roman Catholic liturgical life today, an alternative to eucharistic worship engaged in daily by the laity. In the West, the cathedral office became submerged in a few centuries, much to the loss of Christianity. The liturgy of the hours became an almost exclusively clerical and monastic tradition within Roman Catholicism for many centuries.

We get some fleeting views of the cathedral office during the fourth century. Eusebius of Caesarea mentions that "throughout the whole world in the churches of God, hymns, praises, and true divine delights are arranged for God at morning sunrise and in the evening. . . . These 'delights' are the hymns which are sent forth in his church everywhere in the world in the morning and evening hours."[7] Late in the fourth century, the *Apostolic Constitutions* instructed Christians: "Assemble yourselves together every day, morning and evening, singing psalms and praying in the Lord's house."[8] In a latter book, the same document tells us: "When it is evening, thou, O bishop, shall assemble the church; and after the repetition of the psalm at the lighting up the lights, the deacon shall bid prayers for the catechumens. . . . But after the dismission of these, the deacon shall say: 'So many as are of the faithful, let us pray to the Lord.' " A bidding prayer, other prayers, a blessing, and dismissal follow. The morning pattern is similar without the lighting of the lights. Chrysostom told newly baptized Christians they ought to gather "in the church at dawn to make your prayers and confessions to the God of all things, and to thank him for the gifts He has already given"; and then each one "at evening . . . should return here to the church, render an account to the Master of his whole day, and beg forgiveness for his falls."[9]

Egeria took careful notes of the daily round of worship in fourth-century Jerusalem. She indicated that three groups participated in daily worship at the Church of the Holy Sepulchre: monks and virgins, lay people, and clergy and bishop. The worship of the monks and virgins was more extended, with hymns, psalms, antiphons, and prayers occupying much of the day and night. Some laity joined them, but the laity and clergy mostly shared in the "Morning Hymns" at daybreak; again at lesser or **apostolic hours**—nine in the morning (in Lent only), noon, three in the afternoon—and in the evening at the lighting of the lamp (which she calls *lucernare*). There were psalms, antiphons, hymns, prayer for all and commemoration of individuals by name, blessing of both catechumens and faithful, and dismissal.[10] On "the Lord's Day," the whole multitude assembled before cockcrow for an early morning vigil with psalmody, prayer, a reading of the resurrection narrative, a procession to Golgotha with singing, a psalm, a prayer, blessing, and dismissal. At daybreak on Sunday came the eucharist, with many sermons and "a thanksgiving" afterward. To be sure, Jerusalem as a pilgrimage center was not typical, but daily gatherings of the devout for instruction and prayer before and after the day's work seem to have been common in the chief church of most cities by the late fourth century.

The demise of the cathedral office was a slow process. Eventually it was supplanted in the West by the **monastic office.** This process we have just seen anticipated in Jerusalem, where the monks and virgins pursued a course, the *cursus,* of reciting the psalms. Egeria was impressed by how "suitable, appropriate, and relevant" these were, but most of the laity and clergy did not attend for much of the psalmody. Increasingly the monastic office dominated nonsacramental worship until the cathedral office disappeared in the West, leaving only remnants such as tenebrae and certain services in Milan and Toledo.

Monasticism originated as a revolt against deadened sensitivity in the church and was basically a lay movement in its origins. In the fifth century, Cassian reported that the early Egyptian monks observed "a prescribed system of prayers . . . in their evening assemblies and nocturnal vigils,"[11] i.e., at the end of the day and the night. He tells of an angelic visitant who departed after the twelfth psalm, thus establishing that a dozen psalms at matins were enough for angel or monk. In addition to psalmody and prayer, the Egyptian monks read an Old Testament and a New Testament lesson on weekdays and an Epistle and a Gospel lesson on Sundays and in the Easter Season.

In Eastern regions, the development of monasticism brought refinement of a daily cycle of worship. Basil, in his fourth-century *Long Rules,* cites various precedents of the apostles for prayer at the minor hours and at midnight plus prayer "early in the morning, so that the first movements of the soul and mind may be consecrated to God," and "when the day's work is ended, thanksgiving should be offered for what has been granted us . . . and confession made."[12] "At nightfall, we must ask that our rest be sinless and untroubled by dreams," and early in the morning "we must anticipate the dawn by prayer." He summarizes: "None of these [eight] hours for prayer should be unobserved by those who have chosen a life devoted to the glory of God and His Christ."

Chrysostom tells us of another scheme in religious communities where, "having divided the day into four parts, . . . at the conclusion of each they honor God with psalms and hymns" and the day begins and ends with worship.[13] In the *Institutes,*

Cassian tells us of the addition of another morning service in Jerusalem monasteries so that the seven services "clearly makes up according to the letter that number which the blessed David indicates . . . 'Seven times a day . . .' [Ps. 119:164]."[14]

The cycle was completed in the West by adoption of the existing seven, plus an office of compline on going to bed. St. Benedict, in the early sixth century, set up the definitive Western pattern (slightly different from that of the Eastern churches), which operated until shortly after Vatican II. The scheme of daily and nocturnal prayer is:

Vespers (at the end of the working day)
Compline (before bedtime)
Nocturns or **Vigil** or **Matins** (middle of the night)
Lauds (at daybreak)
Prime (shortly thereafter)
Terce (middle of the morning)
Sext (at noon)
None (middle of afternoon)

It called for a strenuous but not exhausting daily and nightly cycle of work, prayer, and rest. Benedict equated both work and worship as service to God: "That in all things God may be glorified."[15]

Monasticism and the choir offices evolved together, being virtually identified with each other. Increasingly the divine office moved away from identification with the secular life of the laity. Monasticism set the tone for this type of worship, and it was imitated by parochial clergy who said the offices daily in the chancels of their empty churches. Even the chancels, as we have seen, were copies of monastic choirs and the music sung reflected monastic chant. Secular and religious life-styles produced only one kind of daily worship, the monastic office. Clergy were obliged to follow it; laity were free to ignore it. And ignore it they did, so that "the Offices ceased to be in practice, if not in theory, the common prayer of the Christian people."[16]

If the hours served the people poorly, they did succeed magnificently in digging a deep channel for the liturgical life of religious communities. In distinction from the cathedral office's selective use of psalms, Benedict had provided for systematic

weekly recital of the entire psalter. Psalmody, sung antiphonally back and forth across the monastic choir with appropriate
antiphons, was the heart of the monastic office. Weekly
recitation of the psalms throughout a lifetime of stable
community life shaped the lives of thousands of men and
women for centuries. The monastic office also used a
continuous reading of scripture, almost an athletic discipline,
rather than reading edifying portions of it as had the cathedral
office. A wide assortment of office hymns developed from the
fourth century onward. Fragments of patristic sermons and
expositions, legends of the saints and martyrs, a rich collection
of prayers, and reponsories and invitatories filled out the
monastic hours.

Change continued during the Middle Ages. Increased
mobility of the clergy, the development of universities, and less
time for saying the hours led to widespread adoption in the
twelfth century of the *modernum officium* used in the papal
church. It featured an abbreviated lectionary, more hymns, and
a modified calendar. The advent of the Franciscans in the
following century brought further pressures for brevity and an
office that could be said while traveling. Structurally the office
underwent a change: further reduction in the amount of
scripture read and more festivals of saints. The office became
more and more a succession of festival days rather than the
orderly recitation of the psalter and scripture week in and week
out. Even more important than change in structure was change
in practice. The office had developed until the thirteenth
century as a **choral office,** said and sung in choir by religious
communities and (in parish churches) by priests and minor
clergy. New conditions of travel and study brought about
private and individual recitation from a portable breviary,
certainly a convenience but also a subversion of the whole
principle of worship together in choir. But so firmly did this
revolutionary development assert itself that in the sixteenth
century a new order, the Jesuits, was dispensed from the
obligation for choral recitation altogether, a fact underscored
by their choirless church buildings.

The wild tangle of festivals and complicated rules led to
attempts at reform, the most successful being those of Cardinal

Francisco de **Quiñones** in 1535, revised in 1536.[17] After sudden popularity, it was suppressed in 1558 and supplanted by the Roman Breviary of 1568. All other breviaries less than two hundred years old were superseded, leaving a few in use such as the *Monastic Breviary*. But for the overwhelming majority, strict uniformity was imposed; and, except for relatively minor changes, the 1568 breviary endured until the 1970s.

Vatican II mandated a thorough reform of the liturgy of the hours. Morning and evening prayer were declared the "two hinges on which the daily office turns; hence they are to be considered as the chief hours. . . . Matins . . . may be recited at any hour. . . . Prime is to be suppressed. . . . Outside of choir it will be lawful to select any one of these three [apostolic hours]" (CSL, 89). Not only was the daily schedule rearranged, but the psalms were distributed over a period of four weeks instead of one. "Readings from sacred scripture" were provided "in more abundant measure," readings from the Fathers "better selected," and saints' legends chosen "to accord with the facts of history" (CSL, 92). The *Constitution* did not anticipate the subsequent widespread abandonment of saying the office in Latin, but it did encourage laity "to recite the divine office" (CSL, 100).

The result has been the publication, in the early 1970s, of *The Liturgy of the Hours* with the day hinging on the old offices of lauds and vespers, familiar to both cathedral and monastic offices. An **office of readings,** centering in scriptures and the Fathers or hagiography, can take place at any time during the day. One may select one of the apostolic hours "so as to preserve the tradition of praying in the middle of the day's work."[18] And Compline is provided for the end of the day. The revised liturgy of the hours is meant to be used by clergy and laity, by people in religious communities and in parishes. How much success it will have is yet to be seen. It remains debatable whether such stylized common worship and devotion, even with various options allowed, can now be imposed from above on clergy and religious communities, many of whom adopted a more pragmatic approach to daily worship by drawing up their own disciplines after Vatican II.

Only one unquestioned success in popularizing the hours has

occurred since early times. That was in the Church of England in the sixteenth century. Apparently Archibishop **Thomas Cranmer** was familiar with both the Lutheran reforms of the hours and those of Cardinal Quiñones, and he prepared schemes on the basis of both. In 1523 and 1525 Martin Luther had proposed a return to two daily services: Matins and Vespers on ferial days (weekdays not feasts), comprising lessons, psalms, canticles, hymns, the Lord's Prayer, collects, the Creed, with the addition of preaching.[19] Though they were intended for lay people, Luther seems to have had in mind especially the use of Matins and Vespers in schools and universities. The role of the hours in Lutheranism is relatively minor; they never competed with the Sunday eucharist. In the 1978 *Lutheran Book of Worship* appear "Morning Prayer: Matins," "Evening Prayer: Vespers," and "Prayer at the Close of the Day: Compline" (pp. 131-60). A musical setting is printed for each. Morning Prayer includes psalmody, canticles, lessons, hymnody, prayers, and provision for an optional sermon and offering and a Paschal blessing (on Sundays). Evening Prayer may begin with a service of light and contains psalmody, hymnody, canticles, lessons, a litany, and an optional sermon and offering. Prayer at the Close of the Day includes confession, psalmody, a brief lesson, a responsory, hymnody, prayers, a canticle, and a benediction. Provisions are also made for two services of Responsive Prayer, the Litany, Propers for Daily Prayer, Psalms for Daily Prayer, and a Daily Lectionary (LBW, 161-92).

Whatever Cranmer's sources, there is no question that he did a masterful job in fusing materials from five offices in the **Sarum** breviary (that used most widely in southern England). Matins, Lauds, and Prime became his Matins, while Vespers and Compline were mined for Evensong in the **1549 Book of Common Prayer.** In the **1552** second edition, the names became **Morning Prayer** and **Evening Prayer.** The apostolic hours disappeared altogether. Cranmer made his purpose clear in the Preface, occasionally even following Quiñones' words. Cranmer hoped "that the people (by daily hearyng of holy scripture read in the Churche) should continuallye profite more and more in the knowledge of God, and bee the more inflamed with the loue of his true religion."[20] Believing (wrongly) that the "auncient fathers" had provided systematic daily reading to cover the "whole Bible (or the greatest part thereof)" each year for the people, Cranmer eliminated all "Anthemes, Respondes, Inuitatories, and suche like thynges as did breake the continuall course of the readyng of the scripture."[21] "The rules," he claims were "fewe and easy," and only the prayer book and Bible were necessary for conduct of services. National uniformity would be secured since "all the whole realme shall haue but one use."

The scheme is simple enough; the Psalms are "red through once euery Moneth," several each day at morning and evening prayer, starting afresh at the beginning of the month. The Bible is read through in course (*lectio continua*), starting with Genesis, Matthew, and Romans (Old Testament lection and Gospel at Matins, Old Testament and Epistle at Evensong). The rest of the service consists of a masterful blend of the elements of the Sarum offices. These include the Lord's Prayer, versicles, psalms with *Gloria Patri,* two lessons, canticles, Kyrie, Creed, Lord's Prayer, versicles, and three closing collects. A change came in 1552 with the addition of a penitential prelude consisting of penitential sentences from scripture, a call to confession, a general confession, and absolution. Precedent for this manner of beginning is found in both Quiñones (at Matins) and in the continental Reformers. Unfortunately this has been the most widely imitated part of morning and evening prayer among the Free Churches and Methodists, often giving a penitential cast to an entire service by coming so early. In the **1662 BCP,** additional prayers and provision for an anthem were added at the end of the services.

There can be no question of Cranmer's success. Indeed his hours were too successful, for they did what no one desired or expected: they ousted the eucharist as the normal Sunday service for four hundred years, as well as supplying the normal weekday services. The litany and the ministry of the Word from the Lord's Supper were usually joined to morning prayer on Sundays until well into the nineteenth century, causing a bit of redundancy. But eucharistic piety and frequent communion in England had to wait until the Methodists in the eighteenth century and the Tractarians in the nineteenth. The widespread popularity of morning and evening prayer is quite understandable. Both services have a large amount of scripture and considerable congregational participation, especially when psalms and canticles are sung. The hours are indeed deficient in their lack of hymns. Cranmer bemoaned the lack of suitable poets to translate the medieval office hymns. As these were daily services, intended to be supplemented on Sunday by the eucharist, no provision for a sermon or an offering was included. Cranmer's morning and evening prayer became the well-beloved worship of the English people for centuries and nurtured a rich biblical piety instead of a sacramental one. No doubt part of the offices' enduring popularity was due to the state of the English language in 1549 and Cranmer's skill in using the spoken language of his time in carefully balanced cadences.

Much of the quality of Cranmer's work is reflected by the fact that only minor changes have occurred in the two offices. The new American Episcopal *Book of Common Prayer* shows, at long last, considerable development in the daily office, including 110 pages of materials (BCP, 36-146). The most important change is frank recognition that this is an age of pluralism in worship as in society. Diversity within the church is recognized in the printing of both traditional and contemporary wording of the same services. Many options appear for the first time in an American BCP: a short noonday service; "An Order of Worship for the Evening," structured around the lighting of candles and lamps; Compline; and daily devotions for individuals and families. A two-year daily lectionary, based on the church year, provides the lessons (BCP, 934-1001). But aside from providing more options for opening sentences, antiphons, canticles and collects, the basic pattern has changed remarkably little since Cranmer put down his pen in 1552. Further proof of the BCP's appeal is found in the propensity of Free Church people and Methodists to imitate its structure. The 1965 Methodist Order of Worship is basically Anglican morning prayer shorn of the canticles but with hymns, pastoral prayer, offering, and sermon added (BoW, 4-6). Versions of the liturgy of the hours for daily use are being developed by

United Methodists and the Commission on Worship of the Consultation on Church Union.

The history of the liturgy of the hours is a mixed one of loss and gain, involving frequent failure to understand how the hours best functioned and for whom. As a daily counterpart of a weekly eucharist, the hours have much in their favor. But rarely since the fourth or fifth century has the church achieved such a balance for the worship life of large numbers of the laity. This is due not only to the difficulty of observing daily public worship for most people but also to the church's frequent confusion of the distinct functions of sacramental and nonsacramental worship. There can be little question as to the value that a basically biblical service, such as the liturgy of the hours, can provide; neither can the value of eucharistic worship be doubted. But the church has experienced continual difficulty in achieving an adequate balance. In the past hundred years, many Anglican parishes have moved to a more balanced diet, anticipated by John Wesley; and Roman Catholics have made tentative steps in recent years. But in most of Western Christendom the average worshiper is forced to choose between sacramental or nonsacramental public worship instead of having the possibility of constant encounter with God through both the spoken word of the hours and the acted sign of the eucharist.

II

We have already recognized in the synagogue service—with its combination of scripture, psalmody, preaching, and prayers—an ancestor of the **ministry of the Word.** Christian converts from Judaism would all be familiar with such a pattern of public worship, and probably many continued to worship in the synagogue while also celebrating the eucharist "in private houses" (Acts 2:46). But soon Christians were expelled from the synagogue; and, by the middle of the second century A.D., we find that a fusion of these two types of worship had taken place, tentative at first but soon to become permanent. The synagogue pattern was grafted on to the upper room pattern, and two media fused: the spoken word and the acted sign. From the sixth to the sixteenth century, the ministry of the Word and the eucharist became inseparable except on rare occasions such as Good Friday.

Though the union of Word and sacrament may have occurred earlier, our first evidence of it appears in **Justin Martyr's** *First Apology,* written in Rome around the middle of the second century. Justin gives us two examples of a eucharistic gathering. The first followed a baptism. The newly baptized (probably at Easter) were led to the eucharistic assembly, which offered prayer for the one just baptized, gave the kiss of peace, and immediately started the eucharist. It would appear that initiation, when celebrated, replaced the ministry of the Word but not the eucharist. The other service Justin describes seems to have been the normal Sunday service:

And on the day called Sunday there is a meeting in one place of those who live in cities or the country, and the memoirs of the apostles or writings of the prophets are read as long as time permits. When the reader has finished, the president in a discourse urges and invites [us] to the imitation of these noble things. Then we all stand up together and offer prayers. And, as said before, when we have finished the prayer, bread is brought, and wine and water.[22]

In modern terms, there were readings from the Old and New Testaments, a sermon, and general **intercessions** or **prayer of the faithful,** i.e., prayer for others. Apparently the amount of reading was flexible but included several lections.

Hippolytus indirectly corroborates these details two or three generations later. The two eucharists he describes are both special ones: baptismal and ordination. In neither is mention made of the ministry of the Word, which, apparently, is still separable when another celebration precedes the eucharist. Even today, on Good Friday the ministry of the Word is detachable and stands in its original simplicity apart from the eucharist (Sac., 211-22; BCP, 276-82; LBW—Ministers Desk Edition, 138-43). This illustrates Anton Baumstark's discovery: "Primitive conditions are maintained with greater tenacity in the more sacred seasons of the liturgical year."[23] Even today, the first part of the Good Friday service shows the same stark simplicity as we see in Justin: lessons, psalmody, sermon, and intercessions. Even the form of the Good Friday intercessions—bidding to prayer, silent prayer by all kneeling, and a summing-up prayer where all stand—is primitive (early). No nonessentials appear in the early ministry of the Word. Augustine tells us: "I came into the church, greeted the people with the customary greeting, and the lector started the lesson"[24]—about as sparse and abrupt a beginning as one could imagine.

But it was not long to remain that simple. If we think of a river laying down sediment, we can imagine successive layers of liturgical strata being deposited. This is a useful way to picture developments, except that liturgical items were also moved around or dropped entirely, something even an earthquake cannot quite duplicate! First to disappear were the **Old Testament lections** from the law and prophets, which started to vanish beginning with the fourth century. The **dismissal of the catechumens** (those who had not yet been baptized) disappeared in the West by the end of the sixth century. The words remain still in the East. Catechumens had been allowed to be hearers of the word but not to participate in the prayers of the faithful, the kiss of peace, or any of the eucharistic action. The **intercessions** or prayers of the faithful also disappeared from the ministry of the Word by the seventh century in the Roman rite.

The rest of the earliest stratum survived: the greeting, the Epistle, the responsorial psalm, the Gospel, and the sermon. The passage of time brought further accumulations, especially at the beginning of this stratum.

The second stratum represents basically introductory materials, including both song and prayer. Apparently these accretions began in the fifth century, after Christian worship had become public and more elaborate. Functionally, many of them tended to mask such vital actions as getting the clergy to the altar-table and everyone in place to begin worship. Actions performed in silence, no matter how essential, always seem to invite verbal or choral accompaniment, as if we never quite trusted bare action.

Obviously these developments occurred at different times in different parts of the Christian world. We can only suggest the outlines of development in the Roman rite of the West. We have seen how terse was the beginning of Augustine's service, but within a few decades after his death Rome had elaborated an **introductory rite** that still persists: introit, *Kyrie, Gloria,* and collect. This second stratum of liturgical development seems to have been the result of unrelated accretions. The **introit,** the first in order of the variable parts (proper) of the mass, was originally basically travel music, to accompany the procession of clergy to the altar-table by a psalm set to music. Late in the fifth century, the older prayer of the faithful was replaced in Rome by prayer in the form of a **litany** (a series of petitions, each followed by a recurring response) located before the lessons and sermon. The response was the *Kyrie Eleison* ("Lord have mercy"). By the beginning of the seventh century, the petitions themselves had disappeared in Rome though complete litanies still remain in the Byzantine rite. Only the *Kyrie* remained in Rome, a tiny Greek island in a sea of Latin words. The successive disappearances of the prayer of the faithful and the litany left the Roman ministry of the Word devoid of intercessions. A third item added was the *Gloria in excelsis* (Glory to God in the Highest), or greater doxology, usually sung. Of Eastern origin, its use as part of the ministry of the Word is confined to the West, the *Trisagion* ("thrice Holy") filling an equivalent function in the Byzantine rite. The **collect, oration,** or **opening prayer** brings the entrance rite to a close. A Western form, collects follow a formal literary pattern usually consisting of (1) an address to God, (2) a relative clause referring to some characteristic of God, (3) a petition, (4) a result clause, (5) a concluding doxology. At this point, the collect functions to conclude the introductory rite and to introduce the lessons for the day. Collects are another variable part of the eucharist. Collections of collects form an important part of the great sacramentaries.

Let us recapitulate. The fifth and sixth centuries had seen a great elaboration of the introductory rite. Gone was the terse move from the greeting directly into the lessons, and in its place had come a stately and musical progression of introit, *Kyrie, Gloria in excelsis,* and collect.

But there is yet a third stratum, deposited through gradual accumulation during the early Middle Ages. It is common even today for those leading public worship to spend a few moments of preparation in personal devotions in the sacristy before entering the church to begin the public service. Previously personal devotions of the same type crept out of the sacristy and into the sanctuary. They tended to have a specific character; they were basically **apologies** for unworthiness and petitions to be made more worthy to serve God in leading worship. Such devotions tend now, as they did then, to be individualistic, subjective, and introspective. None of these is a bad quality in itself, but when the function of these personal devotions was changed by their incorporation into public worship itself, a major shift occurred. It was a slow and subtle shift, not something debated and decided in public synods. But it signaled a shift in emphasis away from an assembly gathered to rejoice in what God had done to an assembly met to bemoan their sins before the Almighty. Eastern churches avoided much of this shift; Western churches unconsciously majored in it.

The result was a **preparatory rite** of opening devotions appended to the very beginning of the ministry of the Word. These began with Psalm 43 (42), of which verse 4 provided an apt antiphon. The fourteenth century prefaced the Psalm with a trinitarian blessing. The next of these prayers at the foot of the altar-table is the *confiteor,* or prayer of **confession** and an **absolution,** operating as a cleansing station before the priest is really prepared to begin. The *confiteor's* penitential language shaped much of medieval, Reformation, and modern eucharistic piety. Short prayers next accompanied the priest's going up to and kissing the altar-table before beginning the introit.

A further medieval accretion was musical elaboration of the responsorial psalm, the **gradual,** which originally followed the Old Testament lessons. When these disappeared, the gradual was placed after the Epistle and shortened to a single verse. There it joined the **alleluia** or **tract** (for penitential occasions). Nonbiblical elaborations of the alleluia, known as **sequences,** flourished in the Middle Ages but were virtually abolished in 1570.

The Middle Ages (in the West) also added the **Nicene Creed** immediately after the sermon. This appears to have occurred as a rearguard action against Arianism (which denied the divinity of Christ) and in forgetfulness of the proclamatory nature of the eucharistic prayer. This practice of saying the Creed probably originated in Spain, and was promoted by Charlemagne. It was not adopted in Rome until the early eleventh century. In the East, it was adopted in the sixth century as a part of the eucharist.

The result of all these developments is the ministry of the Word that the sixteenth century inherited, the Reformers changed slightly, and the Counter-Reformation even less. Let us chart the various strata, with parentheses marking items that disappeared:

First three centuries	Fourth to sixth centuries	Medieval
greeting		
		Psalm 43
		confiteor
	introit	
	(litany), *Kyrie* response	
	Gloria in excelsis	
	collect	
(Old Testament lections)		
psalmody		
Epistle		
psalmody	gradual, alleluia, tract	(sequence)
Gospel		
sermon		
		Nicene Creed
(dismissal of catechumens)		
(prayer of the faithful)		

For better or for worse, the Reformers themselves had been shaped by this service with its heavy dose of penitential elements and loss of the Old Testament and intercessory prayer. If they had known more of the history of the rite, they would have had more freedom to reform it; but not knowing sufficient history, they could not be set free by the truth. The Reformers did contribute greatly in advancing preaching, congregational song, and vernacular rites. In his *Formula Missae* of 1523,[25] Luther saw little to change in the ministry of the Word. He delighted in the musical elements, the introits, *Kyrie, Gloria in excelsis,* graduals, alleluia, and sung Creed. Luther eliminated the opening devotions and nonbiblical sequences, but encouraged congregational song in German, especially after the gradual. He suggested that the sermon might precede the entire service. In 1525 Luther produced his **German Mass**[26] and introduced more vernacular hymns and a paraphrase of the Lord's Prayer after the sermon.

Though Luther did not intend such, gradually the ministry of the Word, or Ante-Communion, by itself came to be the normal Sunday service among Lutherans, thus dividing the two so long wed, Word and sacrament. The process was slow in Sweden, where a more conservative rite and more pronounced eucharistic piety lasted longer than in Germanic lands. The new *Lutheran Book of Worship* returns to the sixth-century pattern. There is a Brief Order for Confession and Forgiveness, which may precede the service. Three musical settings are provided (LBW, 57-119). The sequence when the eucharist is not celebrated is: entrance hymn, greeting, *Kyrie, Gloria in excelsis,* collect, first lesson, psalm, second lesson, alleluia or tract, Gospel, sermon, hymn, Creed, offering, prayers (which may be intercessions), Lord's Prayer, and blessing. Most of it would have been familiar to a sixth-century Christian.

In the Reformed tradition, greater change occurred on the assumption that the early church was being followed. We shall look at **John Calvin** primarily, since his *Form of Church Prayers . . . According to the Custom of the Ancient Church*[27] of 1542 (Geneva, Strassburg 1545) was the fountainhead from which this tradition spread (though much of its originality is due to the Strassburg reformer, **Martin Bucer**). The service is heavily penitential and didactic. This tradition seemed to relish the medieval apologies. The rite begins with a vigorous prayer of confession noting that we are "incapable of any good, and that in our depravity we transgress thy holy commandments without end or ceasing." Absolution follows, then an item introduced by Bucer, the singing of the decalogue. Extempore prayer is offered, a metrical psalm is sung, and then is said a collect for illumination, an item that, it was believed, was common in early Christian worship but that has instead become a distinctive Reformed contribution.[28] The lesson and sermon follow. A long pastoral prayer of intercession, a petition, and paraphrase of the Lord's Prayer precede the concluding blessing.

Calvin preferred the eucharist to occur weekly but was thwarted by the conservatism of the Genevan magistrates. But it is important that the model for Sunday worship in the Reformed tradition is the ministry of the Word, not the liturgy of the hours. Singing of psalms came to be a hallmark of Reformed worship. They give considerable relief to the stern penitential and disciplinary character of the service.

The *Westminster Directory*[29] imposed a blend of Free Church and Reformed worship on the national churches of England, Scotland, and Ireland in **1645,** superseding the BCP for fifteen years and terminating the authority of the Scottish *Book of Common Order* (1564). The *Directory* is basically a book of rubrics. The order for the "Publique Worship of God" is as follows: the minister calls the congregation to worship and begins prayer reminding the people of "their own vilenesse and unworthinesse to approach so neare him [God]; with their utter inability of themselves, to so great a Work." Reading of the Word follows ("ordinarily one Chapter of each Testament" on a *lectio continua* basis), singing of a psalm, and intercession, a very long pastoral prayer of confession and intercession, preaching of the Word, a prayer of thanksgiving, the Lord's Prayer, a sung psalm, and a blessing. In the absence of a liturgy of the hours, this ministry of the Word has, for several centuries, provided the basic structure of worship for much of the English-speaking Reformed and Free Church traditions. Preaching is obviously the dominant act of worship. The medieval apologetic and penitential approach looms large, but there is clear gain in the recovery of Old Testament lections and high regard for congregational psalmody and preaching.

The new Presbyterian *Worshipbook* (1970) represents greater historical consciousness of early patterns and yet reflects Reformation tendencies. Its structure is: call to worship, hymn of praise, confession of sin, pardon, response, prayer for illumination, Old Testament lesson, psalm, New Testament lesson(s), sermon, Creed, concerns of the church, prayers of the people, peace, offering, prayer of thanksgiving, Lord's Prayer, hymn, charge, and benediction (Wb, 25-42). The *Worshipbook* strongly encourages the use of the eucharist each Lord's Day but this has not become common.

Different decisions were made by the **Anglican Reformers**. They benefited from gratuitous advice, based on two decades of experience with vernacular liturgies, of the continental Reformers. Basically a conservative revision of the Sarum ministry of the Word, Cranmer's 1549 rite began with an introit psalm, Lord's Prayer, the collect for purity, *Kyrie, Gloria in excelsis,* greeting, collect of the day, and collect for the king.[30] The Epistle and Gospel followed immediately, without psalmody, then came the Nicene Creed and sermon. The service then moved into exhortation and the eucharist. Two items were transplanted into the eucharist itself: intercessions appeared right after the *Sanctus,* and confession came before communion. In the 1552 version there was a move in the Reformed direction; the introit psalms had disappeared, while the decalogue was added immediately after the collect for purity.[31] The intercessions had been moved back to just after the sermon and offering, while the confession now followed the exhortations, just prior to the *Sursum Corda.* The *Kyrie* disappeared and the *Gloria in excelsis* was banished to just before the final blessing in the eucharist. A rubric provided for ending the service after the general prayer of intercession when communion was not celebrated, thus detaching the ministry of the Word from the eucharist after a thousand years of union. For centuries, this "ante-communion" or "second service" with sermon followed morning prayer and the litany on most Sundays in Anglican churches and the eucharist was not celebrated frequently.

The years since have seen a gradual unscrambling of this pattern. The most recent American BCP (pp. 316-409) represents major gains in the restoration of the Old Testament reading and psalmody and the down-playing of confession. The ministry of the Word is entitled "The Word of God" and includes a greeting, collect for purity, *Kyrie* (or *Trisagion*), *Gloria in excelsis,* collect of the day, two or three lessons (interspersed with psalms, hymns, or anthems), sermon, Nicene or Apostles' Creed, prayers of the people, optional confession of sin, and the peace. In short, this is the sixth-century pattern again.

Quaker worship does not necessarily involve the spoken word. It takes its center in a silent waiting upon God. After a period of centering down, people may rise to speak as the Spirit prompts them. There is a high sense of discipline, a strong reluctance to rush into words or to speak from oneself. Such worship does not fit into any of our patterns traced for other traditions.

Methodism inherited the Anglican pattern of morning prayer, litany, and ante-communion with sermon. The *Sunday Service of the Methodists in North America* (1784)[32] made minor changes in the ministry of the Word aside from omission of the Creed. The major change was the expectation of hymn singing, which brought a distinctive warmth to Methodist worship. While some British Methodists tended to cling to Anglican morning prayer, Wesley proved to be a poor judge of the American situation. By 1792, the year after Wesley's death, the printed text of the ministry of the Word was set aside and none was published until 1932. For the forty years after 1932 the tendency was to reappropriate the 1549 BCP rite (BoW, 15-22).

What happened in the nineteenth century? The *Disciplines* of the century carry only a scant outline: "Let the morning service consist of singing, prayer, the reading of a chapter out of the Old Testament, and another out of the New, and preaching." On balance, that sounds slightly more like morning prayer than the ministry of the Word, though the monthly eucharist was also appended to it. Nineteenth-century Methodism moved close to the **Free Church** tradition, itself heavily influenced by the Reformed tradition. Most of the Anabaptists had settled for an informal style of worship with rich hymnody. The English Independents triumphed in the *Westminster Directory* by imposing a structure rather than a liturgy. Whether the average Free Church morning service belongs more to the tradition of the hours or to the ministry of the Word is hard to say. The Reformed model had been the ministry of the Word, but this was largely abdicated in favor of the *Westminster Directory.* Anglican and Methodist influences favored the pattern of the hours somewhat. The Free Church pattern that prevails in most of American Protestantism today combines elements of both structures. Methodism, in turn, influenced the Free Church tradition by its hymnody and strong involvement in **revivalism.** The upshot for much of American Methodism, the Free Churches, and the Reformed tradition was worship heavily oriented to evangelistic purposes, defined as bringing souls to Christ through a conscious conversion experience. A frontier development was the Disciples of Christ, who insisted on rejoining the eucharist to the weekly service.

Revivalism having paled, Methodism, the Free Churches, and Reformed churches in America turned increasingly toward **aestheticism** in the early twentieth century and to **historicism** by the middle of the century. Now all three traditions have moved into an era of **pluralism,** with a common concern to recover the early roots of Christian worship. For United Methodists, this has taken the form of the 1972 Alternate Text, *The Sacrament of the Lord's Supper* (SWR #1) and *Word and Table* (SWR #3), which interprets it. The basic pattern "when the Lord's Supper is not celebrated" (*Word and Table,* p. 10) includes: gathering, greeting, hymn or song, opening prayer(s), act of praise, prayer for illumination, lection, psalm or anthem, lection, hymn or song, lection, sermon, responses to the Word (e.g., Creed or confession), concerns and prayers, the peace, offering, prayer of thanksgiving, Lord's Prayer, hymn or song, and dismissal with blessing.

The Free Church tradition, represented in the United Church of Christ, has produced two services of Word and Sacrament (HUCC, 12-29). The first pattern contains sentences, confession, *Kyrie,* pardon, *Gloria in excelsis* or psalm or *Gloria Patri* or hymn of praise, an Old Testament lesson and one or two from the New, sermon, Creed, and intercessions. The second pattern is basically the same, somewhat simplified.

Pentecostal worship, beginning at the onset of the twentieth century, has preferred spontaneity to clear structures. Its most dramatic form involves the use of the gift of speaking in tongues and interpretation. But more important is the insistence on freedom from set forms and the unexpected possibilities in spontaneous singing, testimonies, and biblical readings.

If one thing can be clear in all these traditions, Roman Catholic and Protestant (except Quakers and Pentecostals), it is the return to the priorities of the first six centuries. We now see how captive the Reformers were to medieval assumptions in making the ministry of the Word heavily penitential, didactic, and disciplinary. Even recent elimination of those portions of services does not remove lingering feelings among many people that they still go to worship primarily to be scolded, to feel sorry, and to make amends.

Much of the impetus for the newer (and older) approach came from Vatican II. It mandated simplicity and clarity in the mass, and stressed that "the treasures of the Bible are to be opened up more lavishly" (CSL, 51), that preaching should be normative on Sundays (CSL, 52), and that "there is to be restored, after the Gospel and the homily, 'the common prayer' or 'the prayer of the faithful' " (CSL, 53). The results can be seen clearly in the *Roman Missal* of 1970. The Order of Mass is: entrance song, greeting, blessing rite or penitential rite or neither, *Kyrie, Gloria in excelsis,* opening prayer, first reading, responsorial psalm, second reading, alleluia or Gospel acclamation, Gospel, homily, profession of faith, and general intercessions (Sac, 403-13). Not only could it be used almost interchangeably with the newest rites of the Protestant traditions mentioned here, but it could also almost pass for what Roman Christians did each Sunday fifteen hundred years ago. Muted is much of the penitential preparatory material and recovered are emphases on Old Testament lections, responsorial psalmody (in preference to graduals), preaching, and prayer of the faithful. Recovery of our roots has given us wings!

III

The liturgy of the hours and ministry of the Word have a common ancestry and a parallel history. Both moved toward a systematic and orderly way of reading scripture and praising

God. Both serve as vehicles for expressing the common prayer of God's people, however much they differ in the ways it is structured. Both function primarily through the medium of the spoken word. Because of these similarities, it is possible to discuss the theological priorities of the hours and the ministry of the Word together. We shall not attempt a detailed theology of proclamation here, since that is frequently studied in connection with preaching itself and readily available in a variety of books.[33]

Fundamental to both types of worship is hearing and responding to God's Word, mediated and expressed through human speech. What God does here is done primarily through the spoken word. We must recognize the medium and its powers and limits. Speech acts in worship as a means of giving oneself. Through words we are present to others, God is present to us. Words express our thoughts, our emotions, our very being, that others may share in them. In worship, God gives Godself to us through human speech; and we, through God's power, give ourselves to God through our speech.

Structurally, this means that these types of worship evolve around God's Word as read in the lessons and expounded in the sermon (if any). This was certainly the intent of the Reformers and has become much more obvious in the new *Liturgy of the Hours.* A Reformation collect declared that God "hast caused all holy Scriptures to be written for our learning" (cf. Rom. 15:4). That "all," it is recognized today, means both covenants must form a part of worship, old as well as new. To communicate the corporate memories of the community of faith, its written records—the scriptures—need to be read again and again. The corporate memories contained in scripture give the church its self-identity. Without the continual reiteration of these memories, the church would simply be an amorphous conglomeration of people of good will but without any real identity. Through the reading and exposition of scripture, the Christian recovers and appropriates for his or her life the experiences of Israel and the early church: escape from slavery, conquest, captivity, hope for a Messiah, incarnation, crucifixion, resurrection, and mission. The church's survival depends on reinforcing these memories and hopes just as did

Israel's. Worship is indeed an "epiphany of the Church," through the recapitulation of salvation history.

Of course it is not just the recollection of past events that occurs in the readings and their interpretation. In the events narrated in scriptures the Christian community discerns meaning that illumines all history. The black and white of all history is transformed into a color presentation as the scriptural events give history meaning. The meaning-events chronicled in the Bible give the Christian community clues for interpreting present and future as well as past events. It is as if the playwright steps into the play to tell us what it is about.

An excellent way to describe both types of worship would be to call them Bible services. The reading of scripture—whether used selectively or consecutively—is basic to both. Quite possibly what oral reading now does can someday be presented by media other than the human voice, though the spoken word doubtless will continue to be central just as it is now and will be the primary mode of communication for the rest of human life. The transmitting of the corporate memories narrated in scripture is crucial to Chrstian worship.

The importance of **preaching** is closely linked to the centrality of scripture. Preaching is a form of communication based on the conviction that God is central in the process. The preacher speaks *for* God, *from* the scriptures, *by* the authority of the church, *to* the people. Four items are vital in conceiving of preaching: power of God, source in scripture, authority from the church, and relationship to people. It would be presumptuous to believe that we preach on our own power. God uses our voices to speak God's Word; what we have to say has little power by itself. But through the power of God our voices have the power to heal and reconcile. The substance of preaching is grounded in scripture. Otherwise we get solemn lectures, not preaching. It is simply not true that the only difference between a sermon and a lecture is thirty minutes. Preaching is grounded in God's Word, though all other forms of learning may help interpret the scriptures. The value of preaching from a lectionary is that it gives us a catholic canon, even though imperfect, rather than a private canon of favorite passages. We preach not an individual faith but rather the faith of the church, which examines and licenses us, thereby authorizing us to speak for it in preaching the faith of the universal community of believers. Preaching cannot occur without hearing. A congregation of faithful people who can hear and respond to preaching is a necessary part of preaching. Through the presence of hearers of the Word, God acts to give Godself through preaching.

Not only does God speak to us through lessons and sermon, but we also speak to God. This takes place through prayer, psalms, and canticles. Of help here is the definition of worship as revelation and response that we see articulated by Hoon and Underhill. God takes the initiative, and we respond with our words to God's Word. God's Word does not return empty; it evokes ours. But we can respond only on the basis of what God has done.

Prayer takes many forms: invocation, praise, thanksgiving, confessions, supplication, intercession, oblation, and others. Each of these forms functions in a somewhat different way; yet all have in common that they are the creature's voice to the Creator. We may beg forgiveness, offer praise, plead for someone else; but whatever the function, the method is similar: the articulating of deeply felt human needs as we confess, rejoice, or beg. Prayer gives us the opportunity to speak the right words, to say to God whatever concerns us most deeply. It is an essential part of all worship. Recovery of the importance of the intercessions in the ministry of the Word is a major advance for both Protestants and Roman Catholics.

Psalmody has probably reached the lowest ebb in all its history in much Protestant worship today. This is despite the central role that the reading or singing of psalms had in the Reformed ministry of the Word and the Anglican hours. Part of this feebleness is due to a lack of understanding of how psalms have functioned traditionally in Jewish and Christian worship. They are not substitutes for lessons; they are responses to lessons. In many services, psalms or canticles are interwoven between the lessons and function as responses. They provide a jubilant form of congregational or choral response to what has been read. The psalms articulate our wonder and marvel (and occasionally our despair) at what God has done. Sometimes they are deeply and intimately personal; at other times they are a recapitulation of salvation history. Psalms may be also used as invitatories to worship or as opening acts of praise, but their usual use is as responses to the lessons. **Canticles,** poetic fragments from other books of scripture plus a few early Christian hymns, function in the same way as psalms. Most familiar are the *Magnificat, Benedictus,* and *Nunc dimittis* all from Luke 1 and 2 and the *Te Deum,* a late–fourth-century hymn.

In the fourth century, Christians began to supplement biblical poetry with **hymns.** Hymns, like prayer, function in a rich variety of ways. They serve to express praise, thanksgiving, proclamation, contrition, invocation, oblation, and a long list of other purposes. Like prayer and psalms, hymns are usually addressed to God and frequently are recitals of God's acts. But hymns add another dimension, the ability to shade our meaning by adding melody, harmony, and rhythm. Hymns provide a more intense form of address to God than speech by adding another layer of participation: music that involves our whole body. Frequently hymns provide a rather subtle bridge between different portions of a service, sometimes eliminating the need for a spoken rubric.

Finally, there are times in worship in which we speak to one another, especially the greeting, announcements, various spoken rubrics ("let us . . ."), dialogues, the Creed, and the blessing and dismissal. These are not just necessary stage business; these reflect the communal nature of our approach to God. We come to meet our God and meet our neighbor. It is as a community that Christians worship, and members of any community talk to one another. We use greetings and dialogues to encourage and cue one another, while the Creed helps us to build one another up as we profess together allegiance to the church's faith as symbolized in spoken words.

God speaks to us, we address God, and we speak to one another. All these are vital parts of worship in both the pattern of the liturgy of the hours and the ministry of the Word.

IV

Only on the basis of historical and theological priorities can we make the necessary practical and pastoral decisions that worship leadership entails. The practical decisions will vary from tradition to tradition. For Roman Catholics, Lutherans, and Episcopalians the decisions will chiefly involve choosing the most apt materials provided in service books and, of course, preaching the most suitable possible sermon. Even these traditions have become increasingly open to prayer composed for the occasion (*ex tempore*). Considerable time must go into planning and preparing for worship in these traditions. Decisions of a pastoral nature must take place in terms of where one is in the liturgical year, where worship will be located, and, above all, the actual people who will be worshiping.

For people in the Reformed, Free Church, and Methodist traditions, more decisions are necessary. Although denominational publications are available in most instances, many pastors prefer to devise their own order of worship. Many, though not all, of the decisions to be made revolve around the **order of worship,** both published ones and newly concocted ones. Sometimes the published orders are defective; frequently the original ones also miss important historical and theological issues and, consequently, fail pastorally as well. Sometimes the order is a legacy from the previous pastor. (The hardest tradition to overcome is usually the most recent one.) And sometimes the order of worship seems to be designed after a system that passes all understanding.

Quite clearly there is no one right order of worship. But it may be of help to specify some criteria to keep in mind while planning an order of worship. First of all, we must realize the centrality of scripture—all of scripture—in these types of worship. Every major church in Christendom is rediscovering the importance of a richer diet of God's Word in worship. Gone are the days when we could be content with a few verses read as a sermon text. God's Word speaks for itself and should be read whether there is a sermon or not.

Second, there ought to be an obvious sense of progression in worship as one goes from greeting to benediction. This can be overdone. There is no clear indication where the Lord's Prayer, for instance, belongs. But one can trace development from introductory types of acts to proclamation and on to commitment.

Third is the need for **clarity of function.** Generally, acts of worship that have the same function ought to come together. It is astonishing to see how far the location of preaching strays from the reading of scriptures. Yet reading and preaching of God's Word are about as similar in function as any two acts can be. Offerings of money, service, and prayers for others have a similar affinity of purpose. Functional questions need to be asked about each act: What does it do? What is its purpose? Usually this will help clarify the obvious sense linkages. To be pastorally responsible, orders of worship must be designed so that clarity of function enables the congregation to follow the order with ease.

In addition to the basic problem of ordering the service, there are several other problems. The first of these is that we have usually not been sensitive to the process of gathering and going forth and to the interaction of people during these preliminary and final acts of worship. But these are important parts of worship and need to be pondered and planned more carefully rather than simply masked by music. Spatially this means areas outside the worship location must be inviting and stimulate a desire to linger and socialize rather than to rush inside or outside.

The problem of penitential portions of the service has been mentioned. These portions may make some sense as personal devotions for minister or priest in the sacristy before leading public worship, but that does not mean that penitential acts are the best way to begin public worship. They need not appear at all in most services. Contemporary thought seems inclined to suggest that penitential rites be occasional acts, particularly appropriate in Advent and Lent. But when they do occur, they often make more sense after God's Word is read and interpreted and the congregation knows for what omissions and commissions confession is needed.

Psalmody may vie with the pastoral prayer for the distinction of being the deadest part of Protestant worship. But neither need be in this unenviable position. At best, the psalms ought to be sung. There is a variety of ways of doing this, ranging from metrical paraphrases (hymns) to the Gelineau settings where a soloist or choir sings the verses of varying lengths and the congregation joins in the refrains. Most of these methods can easily be taught to congregations, especially with choir help. When the psalms cannot be sung (if there ever are such circumstances), they ought to be shouted back and forth across the central aisle between halves of the congregation at a fairly rapid pace. The psalms make more sense when tied closely to the lections read, most easily done by following the psalms listed in some versions of the new ecumenical lectionary (other than Wb or HUCC).

The chief problem with the **pastoral prayer** is that often it tries to do everything and ends by doing nothing. At its best, it can be a magnificent articulation of the congregation's deepest feelings and needs. Some pastors have this gift; others of us do not. Too often the pastoral prayer simply is overloaded and tries to cover confession, thanksgiving, intercession, and all points between, as if one try were better than several. If we think through the differing functions of these (and other) types of prayer, it may make better sense to have separate prayers for each main function. Some lend themselves well to congregational participation, such as confession (unison), supplication (litany or bidding), or intercession (spontaneity). Then the pastoral prayer can fill a single function and do it well. The Reformed tradition, which gave us this type of prayer, too often yielded to the temptation to use it for instruction. This we would now consider a dubious function for prayer, no matter how badly Christians in the sixteenth or twentieth century need instruction. But the pastoral prayer can enlarge our vision while leading us in intercession or in thanksgiving, for example. One thing done well may be better than many done poorly.

The function of choral music, especially anthems, is problematic (cf. chapter 3). Frequently the anthem can be used as a part of the proclamation of the Word, provided it is carefully selected to join with the lections read. When simply dropped in as a musical interlude to cover some action or, worse still, as a bit of entertainment, it is highly questionable. One might almost say that the lectionary is as useful for good choral work as it is for comprehensive preaching. Thus when the anthem functions as a musical commentary on God's Word it can be a major asset to worship. Even then it ought not to deprive the congregation of opportunity for singing hymns and songs.

The Creed is a rather late addition to worship in the West and far from necessary. But it can function as an appropriate response to the Word, especially after a doctrinal sermon, by giving an opportunity to affirm together the faith that makes the church one. It is hard to see how a modern affirmation of faith can function in this way. The Apostles' and Nicene Creeds can be joined in by all Christians, and maybe the Athanasian on some occasions, such as Trinity Sunday. All other affirmations of faith are denominational or local and more or less divisive. They simply fail to function as symbols of the faith of the universal church.

Acts of offering seem to come best as a result of what has been said and heard, whether they be offerings of money, service for others, or prayer. "Concerns of the church" may be statements asking for help for those in need. Prayer of intercession reaches out to all humanity: the church, those in positions of power, those in need or distress, the local community, the world community, and (in some traditions) the dead. This is the most obviously worldly part of worship. It is far too easy to thank God that we are not like other people. Intercessory prayer opens us to their needs and is an important act of growth and love on our part.

The liturgy of the hours and the ministry of the Word will continue to evolve in form and yet remain much the same in function as they enable the church to remember and to hope. The survival of the church depends upon them, just as the survival of Israel depended on the synagogue service.

V
The Acted Sign

We encounter God through the use of the spoken word in worship. But there is another medium of equal importance in Christian worship, the use of certain meaningful actions known as sacraments. For most Christians, the sacraments are the most common experience of worship. In the worship life of almost all other Christians, sacraments play a significant, if not such a dominant, role. Accordingly, the second half of this book will examine the sacraments.

Sacramental worship is distinguished by its use of **sign-acts,** i.e., actions that convey meaning. **Sacraments** are signs that involve actions, words, and (usually) objects. Calvin repeats Augustine's dictum: "Add the word to the element, and there results a sacrament, as if itself also a kind of visible word."[1] More specifically, we might say that in sacraments words become part of an action using an object such as bread, wine, oil, and water.

In Christian worship, both the spoken word (as found in the hours or ministry of the Word) and the acted sign (as found in the sacraments) reinforce each other. A handshake and a spoken greeting do not compete with each other; each strengthens the warmth and meaning of the other. The washing of baptism underscores words spoken about God's action in cleansing. Like eating and drinking, speaking and acting belong together in Christian worship. The same God who gave us ears to hear also gave us eyes to see and hands to touch.

Worship is true to the way humans communicate with one another. The kiss does what words cannot; words make the kiss have meaning. Much of the beauty and color of life would be lost if we had to choose between one medium or the other. Instead, we say much through a nod of the head, a wave of the hand, or an embrace. Each of these sign-acts, though small in itself, is nevertheless part of the whole galaxy of actions that add to what we express in words. These revelatory actions are a means of giving ourselves to others as we convey to them what we mean or even who we are. Words do no more or less; only what they do, they do differently.

Ever since the New Testament, the church has found certain sign-acts essential for expressing the encounter between God and humans. These sign-acts signified sacred things and became ways of expressing to the senses what no physical sense could perceive, God's self-giving. The sacraments call us to "taste, then, and see" (Ps. 34:8), to touch, to hear, even to smell "that the Lord is good." In them, the physical becomes a vehicle of the spiritual as the sign-act causes us to experience what it represents. Obviously, only certain sign-acts out of the myriads we use in daily life function as sacraments. The process of reaching consensus as to which sign-acts to designate as sacraments has been complex, as we shall shortly see.

The number of sign-acts that can be used universally in worship is limited, and there seems to be a built-in bias to conservatism in retaining those that communicate well. Those in common use today would have been familiar at any time in Christian history. Sign-acts do not change rapidly the way spoken words do. Perhaps this is one reason they seem so faithful at the solemn crises of life: birth, marriage, sickness, and death.

There is a tendency in Christianity, when the original function of something becomes obscure, to overlay it with symbolic meaning and then at a later date to lay it aside as irrelevant. Purtians and Roman Catholics alike have tended to trivialize actions and to bury them under a haystack of words. A meal became a snack; the act of washing got underplayed while we interpreted in words what was happening instead of doing it. Only in recent years have we become fully aware of the sign value that actions have in and of themselves and have at last become willing to let them "speak" for themselves.

In this chapter, we shall trace the gradual development of Christian reflection on what the church experiences in sacraments. Part of this discussion will involve familiarizing ourselves with terms Christians have selected over the centuries as the most nearly adequate to explain what they experienced in the sacraments. Then I shall attempt a contemporary statement of the meaning of sacraments. Practical exposition will accompany the individual sacraments in following chapters.

I

The practice of the sacraments has seen but few dramatic changes over the centuries. Development in practice, for the most part, has been like the slow unfolding of a bud. Nor have new ways of understanding what was experienced in the sacraments been articulated rapidly except in a few times of controversy. Many a term we now regard as essential was unknown in the first thousand years of church history. Even the number of sacraments remained indeterminate throughout most of the time Christians have been receiving sacraments.

Once again we must begin with the Jewish mentality and practices that made sacraments a possibility for Christians. It is hard to imagine a sacramental life evolving from any other religion than Judaism. The Jews held in tension the transcendence of God with God's concrete involvement in the actual events of human history. God was made known through events and objects that disclosed the divine will, yet were never confused with the deity. Humans, in turn, could respond to God by appropriate actions.

Christianity's deepest debt to Judaism in this area, then, is the mentality that conceived of the use of certain actions and physical objects as means that God and humans can use to communicate with each other. And yet God remains transcendent, never to be confused with the created. In this way, even inanimate objects can gain a power to speak and yet never become identified with God themselves. A pillar of fire, a cloud, a volcano, daily bread, all can become ways through which God is revealed, though God is none of these. Thus a false split between the material and the spiritual is avoided. Even ordinary objects such as water can be used to convey God's love to us. From time to time, Christians need to remember that they are not called to out-spiritualize God; the path to the spiritual leads through many material realities.

Throughout the Old Testament, we encounter a variety of forms of prophetic symbolism in which dramatic actions signify to humans God's will and purpose. Frequently the actions not only reveal but help initiate events. Jeremiah makes a yoke of iron, or Elijah smashes a pot of clay. Such actions give impetus to the ensuing denouement of what God intends. They are part of the very events they anticipate and thus have potency to fulfill God's will.

From Judaism also comes a profound understanding of each meal as a sacred event. This most common of human social activities became for Judaism an opportunity for praising and thanking God as well as for forming a bond of unity between partakers. Far from being simply physical necessity, the meal becomes a means of encountering God as provider, host, and companion.

Judaism discovered that humans can also use actions to reach God. Practices of sacrifice of food and drink became ways of establishing and maintaining relationship with God. Though the forms and interpretations of sacrifice are complex, the central concept seems to be the use of objects of value to convey one's meaning, one's very being, in surrender of self for communion with God.

Without this Jewish mentality and these practices, the sacramental life of Christianity would never have been born. But, since the earliest Christians were also Jews, these ways of thinking and doing things came naturally to them. Though surrounded by a wide variety of idolatrous religions, early Christians were able to use the material as a channel of the spiritual without confusing the two. Their sense of the transcendent set them free to use the material in spiritual ways without risk of idolatry. It was a freedom tempered by responsibility to the weaker brethren (I Cor. 8) who had not shaken off the shackles of idolatry.

The Gospels show Jesus and his disciples using the sacramental patterns of Judaism. The disciples began baptizing early in Jesus' ministry (John 4:2), following a custom that had gradually developed of baptizing converts to Judaism. Jesus himself had submitted to baptism at the hands of John the Baptist, a fact the Evangelists explain (with some difficulty) as conforming "with all that God requires" (Matt. 3:15). It was obvious to Jesus, as to any other Jew, that the annual Passover commemoration brought to life the crucial moment in Jewish history. The Passover meal itself was a series of sign-acts that recalled what God had done to make the Jews a distinctive people. These customs were part of the very air that Jesus and his disciples breathed. Nothing could be more natural than to transform these familiar practices in establishing a new covenant, or rather, a means of commemorating a new covenant.

It is not nearly so clear just what Jesus intended for his followers to do. It is open to debate whether we have in scripture express commands in the actual words of Jesus to baptize (Matt. 28:19), to remit sins (John 20:23), or to eat and drink as a memorial of him (I Cor. 11:24-25). On the other hand, there can be little doubt that the early church considered itself to be fulfilling the Master's will in continuing these practices in his name. There is no room for doubt that Jesus received baptism, that he forgave sin, or that he kept the feast. In this sense, Jesus' own actions are a firmer basis for the sacraments than reports of his words. At an even deeper level, Jesus himself, as the visible manifestation of God, is the primordial sacrament itself; and the church, in doing what he did, simply carried on his sacramental reality.[2]

The church continued to repeat Jesus' actions from the time of his death on, i.e., long before the scriptures were put into written form. What we find recorded in the scriptures, then, represents sacramental practices that the church had already long observed. The various **institution narratives** of the Lord's Supper (Mark 14:22-25; Matt. 26:26-29; I Cor. 11:23-26; Luke 22:15-20) may tell us as much about the fulfillment by churches in various locations of the Lord's will as they do of the Lord's directives themselves.[3] In short, the sacraments are older than the written scriptures, which refer to current liturgical practice as well as to a remembered past.

The church's acts of obedience to the Master, then, rather than words of institution, are our chief evidence for the foundation of the sacraments. There is no reason to believe that the church's practice did not faithfully obey what it understood to be Jesus' own intentions. The apostolic practices of Jesus' followers who baptized (Acts 2:41), laid on hands (Acts 6:6), prayed (Acts 2:42), healed (James 5:14), and broke bread together (Acts 2:46) are acts of obedience. These actions of the apostles reveal Jesus' intentions just as much as any red-letter formulas. This also means that we are not limited to a handful of passages in interpreting Jesus' intentions with regard to acted signs but can draw on Acts and the Epistles, which supply far more detail.

The New Testament is full of references to what later generations would call sacraments. Most numerous of all, as might be expected in a church afire with missionary zeal, are references to baptism. Second are allusions to the Lord's Supper. Widely scattered references appear to other signifying actions, such as laying on of hands, healing, sealing, and forgiving. In none of these instances do we get much more than a glimpse at apostolic practice. Even less do we find an exposition of what these practices meant to the participants. But, taken as a whole, these references give us innumerable rich and varied sights of the sacramental faith and practice of the apostolic church. The manifold views of apostolic practice are like the different facets of a jewel, which, to be fully appreciated must be turned around so the sparkle from all its facets can shine. Unfortunately, throughout its history the church has tended to look at only a single facet or two and to ignore the rest. We shall try in subsequent chapters to examine the rich variety of these biblical facets so as to get a balanced view.

Thus we can be thankful there is not a single New Testament chapter devoted exclusively to portraying sacramental life and doctrine. In the diverse and scattered fragments, we have a broader and deeper reality depicted. In our urge to systematize, we must beware the temptation to settle for a narrowly coherent view instead of accepting the richly varied assortment that scripture presents. The Bible does not give us liturgies or sacramental theologies, but it lays the foundations on which these can be built. The church uses the New Testament, then, not as a book of laws and statutes but as the fundamental constitution for its ministry of sacraments.

We must beware of asking the early church our questions about the sacraments. The very terms and categories in which we think, are products of later ages. Our terms would seem hopelessly legalistic and mechanically precise to an age that was more inclined to experience the sacraments than to consider them objects of theological study. Yet we, in turn, may learn much from the church's use of the sacraments in the first six centuries.

A basic insight is revealed in the Greek word normally used for a sacrament, *mystérion*. The usual translation, "mystery," is misleading. As the New Testament uses the term, it refers to the secret thoughts of God, which transcend human reason and therefore must be revealed to those whom God wishes those secrets to reach. In Mark 4:11 Jesus tells the disciples that "to you the *mystérion* of the kingdom of God has been given" while others must depend (rather obscurely) on parables. Paul uses the term to refer to Christ himself, to the apostolic preaching, to that which is spoken in the spirit, and to the hidden wisdom of God. The basic insight in the use of this same term for those sign-acts which we call sacraments is that *mystérion* implies acts in which God discloses Godself to us. These heavenly mysteries are completely dependent upon God's acting to give Godself to us.

Unfortunately the Latin word chosen by Tertullian to replace *mystérion* has none of that rich depth. *Sacramentum* is a term that referred to an oath of allegiance taken by a soldier or a vow to keep a promise. It is much more legalistic and lacks the cosmic dimension of divine personal self-giving that *mystérion* implies. It is, though, the word the Western church chose from the third century onward.

Whatever the term used, the sacraments were more experienced by the early church than debated. Heresies abounded in other topics, but relative tranquility reigned in this aspect of the church's life. The precise definitions with which we are familiar were unknown because no one pushed the church to define what it meant. Concepts such as an exact number of sacraments or the moment the Holy Spirit was given in initiation or the moment the eucharistic elements were consecrated would have been puzzling in the church's heroic age. For well over a thousand years there was no consensus as to just how many sacraments there were. For Augustine, the list included such things as the baptismal font, the giving of salt at baptism, the ashes of penance, the Creed, the Lord's Prayer, and Easter Day. One thing mattered: that in these acted signs God was presented to humans.

Consequently, what we know of early practice and reflection on the sacraments comes indirectly. Tertullian wrote a short treatise, *On Baptism,* early in the third century, but it tells us more of baptismal discipline than of theology. In *On Penance* he gives us a bit more theology but mostly practical advice. We get glimpses of actual rites in Hippolytus but practically no interpretation. Ambrose and Cyril of Jerusalem are more detailed in their lectures given to newly baptized Christians. These date from the fourth century but are as dangerous as they are tantalizing. For us it is tempting to read back subsequent developments in the West and East into their terse statements about what occurs in the eucharist. But these are our concerns, not theirs. Augustine baffles us with apparent contradictions in presenting side by side realistic and symbolic interpretations of Christ's presence in the eucharist. But what to us is inconsistency never troubles this great thinker. Clearly our categories are not his, and our exclusivistic language seems a bit trite by comparison.

Augustine did nudge the church forward in several irreversible directions in understanding what it experienced in the sacraments. He began the attempt to define a sacrament, finding it a sacred sign that represents what it signifies, as bread and wine do body and blood. Most important are his phrases "visible form" and "invisible grace," which shaped the standard late medieval definition (in Gratian and Lombard) that "a sacrament is the visible form of an invisible grace." Furthermore, Augustine distinguished between the visible sacrament itself and the power of a sacrament. Apart from the invisible grace the sacrament has no power of itself; only this invisible power or force can give it effect.

Through his involvement in the Donatist Controversy, Augustine had to clarify who had actually been baptized. In refuting a group of North African schismatics known as the **Donatists** (and the Catholic bishop Cyprian), who believed only good men could perform good sacraments, Augustine imparted some concepts that have lodged themselves permanently in the church's thinking about the sacraments. First of all, Augustine had to argue that the schismatic Donatists nevertheless possessed genuine baptism though they had it unrightfully. This is true because the sacraments depend not on the human who administers them but on God. Their power is not a human one, contingent upon the moral character or doctrine of the celebrant; it depends, instead, on God, who uses sacraments to bring about God's own purposes. This is at once the most important and most controversial theological statement ever made about the sacraments. Others elaborated it as the *ex opere operato* doctrine, i.e., God operates simply through the work being done independently of the human agent. Augustine's great contribution is to make it clear that the source of sacraments is divine agency, not human.

If the Donatists had genuine baptism, they nevertheless had it contrary to the Catholic Church's laws and without baptism's benefits. Remaining obstinate in schism, they could not profit from the love and charity of the community into which baptism initiates one. Augustine does not draw these conclusions to their precise definition, but implicit here are the germs of much later distinctions: sacraments as **valid** or **invalid, regular** (legal) or **irregular,** and **efficacious** or **without efficacy.** But once Augustine bent the twig in this direction, it was bound to grow into a major branch of sacramental theology and canon law.

Let us sum up what can be learned from the early church about the sacraments. The number of sacraments was indeterminate, and how they operated was undefined. More concern was expressed about who could receive the sacraments and who could perform them, though even here there seemed to be considerable imprecision. What was to become a juridical encrustation of the sacraments in theology and canon law had hardly developed. But what was apparent and characteristic was that Christians experienced in the sacraments God's self-giving and rejoiced in these sign-acts. Much later Calvin was to say of the eucharist: "I shall not be ashamed to confess that it is a secret too lofty for either my mind to comprehend or my words to declare. And, to speak more plainly, I rather experience than understand it."[4] That seems a good summary of the early Christian witness to the sacraments.

The medieval period shows a slow move to more definitions and new terminology, a process speeded up greatly in the twelfth and thirteenth centuries. Most of our approaches to the sacraments today are so heavily colored by these late medieval developments that it is hard for us to go behind them. How late these developments came about is extraordinary. A debate over the nature of the eucharist flared up in the mid ninth century between two monks of Corbie, **Paschasius Radbertus** and **Ratramnus**. In the eleventh century, **Berengarius** found out, to his consternation, that there were limits as to what was acceptable eucharistic doctrine. He was forced to retract his unpopular views. But even then considerable latitude was still possible. As late as the twelfth century, the number of sacraments was a subject of varying opinions. **Hugh of St. Victor** listed such diverse things as the blessing of palms, the receiving of ashes, bending the knee, or reciting the creeds as sacraments as late as 1140; and the Third Lateran Council in 1179 speaks of instituting priests and the burial of the dead as sacraments. In short, from Augustine to the twelfth century not much had been settled as far as sacramental doctrines were concerned.

Meanwhile popular practice and piety had continued to change. The practice of penance underwent a drastic shift from the seventh century onward, changing from a public office for gross offenders only to a private office for everyone. Slowly but surely the rites of initiation were pulled apart in the West. Even more slowly the church tightened its grip on the marriage ceremony. Healing became associated almost exclusively with death and was known as extreme unction. Eucharistic practice moved ever more to celebrating the mass as an awesome spectacle with rare lay communion and little participation by the laity. Even ordination underwent changes as accessory ceremonies came to dominate the rite.

The twelfth century marked a time of synthesizing of scripture and the fathers, summarizing of what had been learned thus far, and the division of such knowledge into manageable segments. Sacramental theology showed a meteoric development. Most influential was the work of **Peter Lombard,** professor and (briefly) bishop at Paris, whose *Four Books of the Sentences* was completed about A.D. 1150 and became the basic textbook for Christian doctrine for almost five hundred years. It is the funnel through which all preceding developments of any significance passed on to future elaboration. In a key passage, Lombard tells us:

Let us now come to the sacraments of the new covenant; which are baptism, confirmation, the blessing of bread, that is the eucharist, penance, extreme unction, ordination, marriage. Of these some offer a remedy for sin, and confer helping grace, as baptism; others are merely a remedy, as marriage; others strengthen us with grace and virtue, as the eucharist and ordination.[5]

Within a half century, this became the standard list of sacraments and was made dogma by subsequent councils.

Lombard summarizes previous teaching on each of these seven sacraments. Following Augustine, he distinguishes between sacraments of the old covenant (such as circumcision), "which only promised and signified salvation" and those of the new covenant, which "give it."[6] Using language developed by Augustine, Lombard defines a sacrament as "the sign of a sacred thing (*res*)." But Augustine's distinction between the *sacramentum* (that which is apparent to our senses) and the *res* (thing) or fruit of the sacrament, is refined further by Lombard to a threefold distinction between the sacrament itself (the outward and visible), the *res* (the inward fruits), and the **sacrament and** *res* (the two combined, i.e., both sign and reality). An indication of future developments occurs in his statement that "a sacrament is properly so called, because it is a sign of the grace of God and the expression of invisible grace, so that it bears its image and is its cause."[7] Thus a sacrament sanctifies as well as signifies, and this the following century was to pursue in detail.

At another point, Lombard looks backward rather than forward. With the coming of the thirteenth century, it was taken for granted that a sacrament could only be instituted by Christ, an addition to the definition as a "visible form of an inward grace" that caused an explosion at the Reformation. But Lombard, while clear that Christ instituted baptism and the eucharist, apparently follows earlier belief that the apostles instituted the rest and relates that unction of the sick was "instituted by the apostles."[8] Unfortunately Lombard and the past were not followed at this point.

Other problems were tackled by thirteenth-century theologians, especially the questions of proper ministrants, recipients, and the effects and operation of grace in the sacraments. In a period of brilliant theological activity, the church's experience of the sacraments was reduced to words. The clarity of language so formulated has endured, and until recently all subsequent discussions were tied to the terminology developed in this period. The councils of Florence and Trent in the fifteenth and sixteenth centuries did little more than place an official cachet on the theological work done during the thirteenth century.

The most convenient summation of all this work occurs in the *Decree for the Armenians* published by the Council of Florence in 1439. It begins by listing the by then conventional list of seven sacraments, which "both contain grace and confer it upon all who receive them worthily."[9] Three things are necessary for each of these sacraments: the proper **matter** (objects such as water), the correct words or the **form** (such as the baptismal formula "I baptize you . . ."), and the person of the designated **ministrant,** who must have "the **intention** of carrying out what the Church effects through him," i.e., doing what the church does in the sacraments (such as baptizing). That means even a priest cannot perform a sacrament while acting in a play or by using the proper matter and form for some purpose other than that the church designates. "Three of these sacraments—baptism, confirmation, and ordination—impress indelibly upon the soul a **character,** a certain spiritual sign, distinct from all others, so they are not repeated for the same person."[10] The Council then goes on to specify for each sacrament the proper matter, form, minister, and the benefits conferred upon the recipient.

It is all very neat and coherent, a far cry from Augustine's imprecision about even the number of the sacraments. What happened is that the sacraments had become a system, a carefully worked out way of life in which every major human passage is ministered to by an appropriate sacrament. Birth, growth, marriage, ordination, and sickness—each is marked by a sacrament. One is nourished in the eucharist and recovered from falling through penance. The effects of each sacrament are carefully worked out so that those who receive it with proper **disposition,** i.e., without imposing an **obstacle** to its operation, receive the designated grace.

What are the results of these late medieval developments? The church, at last, made up its mind about what it experienced in the sacraments. For better or for worse, it had the tools of Aristotelian philosophy and could give a rational accounting of what it experienced. But this is also its weakness. What we perceive in the **scholastics** is a rationalism of the right, fully orthodox but more a matter of rational categories than experiential ones. The definition of the miracle of the eucharist in terms of localized substance is an example of this, although the term "substance" in the thirteenth century was a far more experiential term than it is today.[11] One cannot help feeling, in these neat distinctions about the operation of grace, a danger of knowing too much, a forgetfulness that one is dealing with heavenly mysteries, not that which is susceptible to philosophical solution.

The sacramental system embracing all of life was a brilliant product of human ingenuity. That was its problem. There are limits to human ingenuity when reality breaks out in unexplained ways not comprehended in our philosophy. Too neat a system led Roman Catholicism, especially after the Reformation, to treating the sacraments in excessively juridical ways and to overemphasis on the question of validity, an obsession reaching its peak in the eighteenth century. The necessary concern with affirming the sacraments' dependence on God alone, *ex opere operato,* could sometimes be diverted from its proper affirmations to a mechanical, almost *quid pro quo,* concept of grace. Far more free were the **sacramentals,** an indeterminate number of pious practices such as table blessings, use of holy water, and almsgiving, whose benefits were contingent upon the disposition of the performer (*ex opere operantis*). Furthermore, the whole sacramental system was tied very heavily to the ministry of the ordained clergy. Only baptism and matrimony could be administered by the laity, while in the West usually only bishops could confer confirmation and ordination.

Still, even those who question the sacramental system cannot but admire its comprehensiveness and thoroughness in caring for human needs, though they may question the wisdom of knowing too much about how God acts. Questionable, too, may be the late medieval restriction of the number of sacraments to seven, the belief that all seven were instituted by Christ, and the whole structure of such a tightly interlocking system. When one is dealing with so sublime a subject as how God gives Godself to humans, neat scholastic divisions and distinctions may not be an adequate substitute for awe and wonder.

Rebellion against such a finely conceived system finally exploded in the person of Martin Luther. Luther's most vehement blow at the sacramental system was struck in the **Babylonian Captivity of the Church (1520),** in which he successively breached the walls the Romanists had erected to protect the mass. Written in white hot anger, it was no logical exposition but a forceful blast at the whole sacramental system. It is hard to overestimate its force; it changed all subsequent Protestant thought on the sacraments. Except for small groups such as the Quakers and Salvation Army (which dispute the need for outward sacraments at all), all major Protestant groups have accepted Luther's final conclusion that there are only two sacraments instituted by Christ and therefore there are only two sacraments. Luther drew the restrictions even closer than his late medieval predecessors had by declaring that the only sacraments are those for which explicit words of Christ are recorded in the New Testament. In being so restrictive as to insist on these **dominical injunctions** in which Christ clearly commands sacraments, Luther builds his case on a biblical literalism that today seems questionable. Even Luther had trouble with penance, for which John 20:23 seems to indicate something close to a dominical injunction. If Luther had had the freedom that prevailed as late as the twelfth century to accept other institution than by Christ alone, the Reformation would have taken another course; but he is captive himself to the thirteenth-century qualification, "instituted by Christ."

The force of Luther's attack led the **Council of Trent** to assert in defiance: "If any one saith, that the sacraments of the New Law were not all instituted by Jesus Christ, our Lord; or that they are more, or less, than seven . . . let him be anathema."[12] Trent (wisely) did not go into details as to how all seven were instituted or the contrasting opinions of the church fathers. Protestants, just as stubbornly, maintained that only two sacraments had divine authority. Unfortunately it was no longer possible to agree that the number of sacraments was unknown or that some could have been instituted by the apostles following Christ's own practices. Late medieval definitions had closed those doors for Protestants as well as for Catholics.

The shattering of the sacramental system may not have been what Luther wanted, though he certainly deplored its clericalism, its Aristotelian philosophy, and its works righteousness. But shatter it he did, and the pieces have never gone back together again within Protestantism. Unfortunately Luther and his contemporaries knew less about the early church than they thought they did and far less than we think we do. And in their zeal to reform the system they sometimes overlooked its humane side, its ability to minister to the deepest human needs from birth to deathbed. Granted that it was not all biblical, but it ministered in a comprehensive way to deeply felt human needs that are permanent.

Pressure on one portion of the **sacramental system** was sure to produce distortion on other parts. When the sacrament of penance was abolished, how could the contrite sinner find the same concrete assurance of absolution that this sacrament had guaranteed? The result was to push the eucharist into being a penitential sacrament too, a process already strongly developed in late medieval piety. Ever since the Reformation, the Protestant eucharist has had to do double duty as both a sacrament of penance and of thanksgiving. After all, the deep human need to be forgiven did not disappear simply because the sacrament of penance had been abolished; it simply overloaded the eucharist. It is perhaps more accurate to say that Protestantism has two and a half sacraments: a penitential eucharist and baptism.

The dethroning of confirmation as a sacrament was almost equally destructive. Instead of being reunited to baptism, the Reformation changed it into a didactic experience expressed as a graduation exercise, and much of Christian education has been built on such a disaster. Medieval rationalizations of confirmation's effects were not much better, but at least Roman Catholicism considered confirmation an act of God rather than an educational process.

It is more speculative to guess what would have happened had matrimony been retained as a sacrament. Would Protestantism have been less supine when faced by the pressures of secular culture in yielding to easy divorce? Perhaps not; Roman Catholicism is slowly conceding to the same pressures. But as long as the community of faith is involved in a sacramental union, there can be more communal help in maintaining this relationship of love than when marriage is viewed as a merely private arrangement.

It can be debated whether ordination ever ceased being a sacrament. Most Protestants treat it as imparting an indelible character and do not reordain clergy who return to the ordained ministry after secular work. Ironically, Protestantism never developed a similar rite of passage for entrance into secular vocations.

Protestants have paid a penalty for the loss of healing as a sacrament, partly by the outcropping of bizarre and spectacular efforts to minister to a basic human need: the desire for God's help in restoring health. And it can seriously be asked what ministers better in conditions of extremity: saying the right words or performing significant actions.

What did the Reformation accomplish with regard to the sacraments? Many of its results were not intended, especially pushing sacramental worship from the center to the periphery of the Christian life despite recoveries in early Methodism, the Oxford Movement, and the Disciples of Christ. Luther suggested some profound insights on baptism as life-style that have never been done justice by his successors. Calvin succeeded better than his contemporaries in fusing reason, biblicism, and a sense of awe before holy mysteries. In this he came closest to the early church's understanding and left a legacy to which John Wesley resonated. The attempt of several Reformers to restore frequent communion to the laity could have been a tremendous gain had it not been too radical a change from the late medieval practice of yearly reception of the sacrament. Unfortunately, the Reformers were children of the late Middle Ages too. But they did achieve clear gains in sacramental worship through simplified vernacular rites, more congregational participation, congregation song, a well catechized laity, and new emphasis on preaching of the Word.

Perhaps the Reformation was overly dramatic, for, despite the outbursts, much more of the Augustinian and medieval apparatus of thinking about the sacraments was retained than discarded. Even in railing against transubstantiation, Luther was committed to thinking of the eucharist in spatial terms. And many of the Reformers preserved the essence of *ex opere operato* in thinking of the sacraments as acts of God. For most of the Reformers God is the chief actor in the sacraments and humans the recipients of what God chooses to do for our benefit through sacraments. Calvin saw the sacraments as "visible signs best adapted to our small capacity" in which Christ acts "giving guarantees and tokens."[13] This approach is frankly supernatural in insisting that God uses the physical objects and actions of this world to accomplish God's will for us. The efficacy of the sacraments does not depend on us, but is a gift of grace. God makes the sacraments happen, though humans are free to receive or to refuse God's gift in them.

The closing years of the seventeenth century and the eighteenth century saw a more subtle change but one just as drastic as that of the Reformation in sacramental theology. It came about in the desacralizing tendencies of the **Enlightenment,** which found repugnant the very notion that God would intervene

161

in present time or use physical objects and actions to accomplish the divine will. Slowly, for some Protestants, these views eroded the traditional Roman Catholic and Reformation view that God acts to accomplish God's purposes through sacraments. The desacralizing tendencies preferred to play down God's role in the sacraments and to magnify humanity's. Biblicism was still firm enough that Christians accepted two sacraments as required by Jesus' teaching.

For a vast segment of Protestantism, the two sacraments became simply pious memory exercises. The sacraments were occasions for humans to remember what God had done in times past. They were credited with immense practical value in stirring humans up to greater moral endeavor. Remembrance of God's past actions was looked upon as one of the strongest possible incentives for leading a better life. But the emphasis in desacralized Protestantism was not on God's acting now but in remembering what God had done in times past. The agency is human; we remember, we act. The same humanizing tendency characterizes the way many Protestants have treated time (chapter 2).

There are premonitions of these developments in **Ulrich Zwingli's** treatise *Of Baptism* in 1525, though they are less apparent in his understanding of the Lord's Supper. But the real split developed, as the eighteenth century progressed, between those who followed the traditional Roman Catholic and Reformation concept of *ex opere operato* and those for whom the sacraments had become basically pious memory exercises. The latter included a wide variety of Protestants ranging from Anglican bishops to frontier Baptists. Even Ben Franklin indulged in some prayer-book revision, making show of the practical benefits of remembering Jesus for amending one's character. This is the rationalism of the left. If the rationalism of the right encrusted medieval piety in a shell of Aristotelian philosophy, that of the eighteenth century created a rigidly desacralized universe in which nothing was more than its outward appearance.

God no longer made sacraments happen; that depended on humans. It was far more constricting because all depended upon human fervor in generating the ability to remember.

Frequently that ability failed to produce an enduring fervor for remembering God and adjusting behavior. This was a Gethsemane type of piety ("If Christ did, . . . can't you at least?"), and its fervor was often fragile. The result was a great drop in sacramental worship in several Protestant traditions.

The value of the *ex opere operato* doctrine is clear; if the sacraments are only pious memory exercises, then they have little chance of being the center of a vital worship but only remain legalistic survivors because Jesus once said "do this." Traditionally the purpose of the sacraments was not to induce good ethical behavior but to give humans access to God (which, of course, does change behavior drastically).

Today there is a real split in Protestantism between those who follow Luther, Calvin, and Wesley in the traditional view that God acts in the sacraments, using them as a means of grace for divine self-giving, and those who follow the desacralizing tendencies of the Enlightenment, which saw the sacraments as something humans do in order to stimulate our memory of what God has already done. This split is at least as great as that between the Reformers and their Roman Catholic contemporaries. Fortunately neither approach is frozen in ice, and there are signs that both are beginning to change. Today we see more clearly the divine self-giving that occurs in the sacraments, and we also are discovering more about their anthropological nature.

II

In recent years there have been major changes across Western Christianity in the ways sacraments are understood. These changes have swept across denominational boundaries and changed both faith and practice in vast segments of the Christian world.

The most obvious changes in practice have been in Roman Catholicism since Vatican II. But change has been underway since the beginning of this century, when receiving communion weekly began to be common for Roman Catholics for the first time in over a millennium. The liturgical movement brought further changes in the direction of increased biblical study, more congregational participation, and a firm grasp of the church as community. Vatican II accelerated this process with important advances in the presentation of doctrine (especially with regard to the church and sacraments) and in major changes in worship. The post–Vatican II revision of the liturgical books has brought major changes in the outward form of each of the sacraments, though most conspicuously in penance and healing. Less obvious has been a move away from treating the sacraments in legalistic, juridical terms (especially of validity and regularity) to more concern about the fruits (efficacy) in people's lives.

Within Protestantism, changes of equal significance may be detected in the widespread growth of a deeper sacramental piety. Recent years have seen more frequent communion services, progressing from quarterly to monthly or even weekly in many congregations. The emerging recovery of the eucharist as the norm for Sunday worship has also been accompanied by more concern with baptism as a congregational act. Less detectable, but even more significant is the gradual shift away from regarding worship as an intellectual experience of instruction or as an emotional outlet to the realization that worship encompasses our total being—body, emotions, and intellect. A greater sensitivity has developed to the crucial role sign-acts play in relations between humans and in the encounter between God and humans. Many have discovered that such a heavily emotional sign-act as the imposition of ashes on Ash Wednesday is as much a part of worship as the doctrinal sermon. Probably the impact of these changes reflects something broader than worship alone: we are discovering more about what it means to be fully human. Revived interest in the sacraments simply shows how deeply anthropological the sacraments are, i.e., how closely they reflect what it is to be human.

Changes in sacramental practice have often reflected new ways of understanding what is experienced in the sacraments. The most significant breakthrough in this century began with the German theologian Odo Casel, Benedictine monk of Maria Laach in Germany. Casel's mystery theology stressed that Christian worship is basically a time mystery in which the reality of past events is again offered to us through our reenactment of them in worship. He avoided many of the Scholastic terms from the thirteenth century and concentrated on showing how, through the church's corporate recalling of salvation history, each Christian can appropriate these events and live "our own sacred history."[14]

Postwar theological developments in the Netherlands and Belgium associated with the names of Piet Schoonenberg and **Edward Schillebeeckx** led to further significant breakthroughs. Schillebeeckx's *Christ the Sacrament of the Encounter with God* was the most influential work on sacramental theology of the Vatican II years. In it, Schillebeeckx presents Christ as the primordial sacrament through whom we encounter God. The visible sacraments are means through which we can experience gracious personal relationship with God. The categories Schillebeeckx uses are personal human relationships, not static and juridical terms. At points, some of the insights of Calvin seem to appear; at others, modern phenomenological philosophy comes to the forefront.[15]

A variety of factors has shaped the new approaches to the sacraments. Biblical studies have greatly illuminated our understanding of the richness and complexity of the biblical witness to the sacraments, while historical studies have traced the slow development of Christian experience of and reflection on sacraments. Ecumenism has made each branch of Christianity willing to share its particular experiences and to appropriate those of others. Old controversies have been bypassed, frequently on the basis of better understanding of the common heritage of the New Testament and the early church. Modern communications theory, anthropological studies, and sociological research have clarified the human content of the sacraments and led to more profound understanding of how humans relate to one another and to God.

Given all these factors, how can we best express the role of sacraments in the life of a Christian today? Practice and theory, experience and understanding, must all come together. It is not easy to concoct a clear teaching in short space any more than it is to weave a coherent pattern of too many disparately colored and textured threads. But the remainder of this chapter will attempt, in briefest possible terms, a contemporary statement of what the sacraments can mean for the Christian of today. I can only treat the sacraments in general here. Not all comments apply equally to each sacrament. Besides having much in common, the sacraments obviously differ. Only a few Christians receive ordination; almost all receive baptism. The generalizations of this chapter must be tempered by the specifics of following chapters.

It should be obvious by now that I regard the number of sacraments as indeterminate, just as did Christians for most of church history. The number seven is just as arbitrary as two, and the possibilities entertained in the first twelve Christian centuries seem richer than those selected during the last eight.

First of all, it would seem that any satisfactory understanding of the sacraments must start from the belief that *God acts in the sacraments.* That is to say, the sacraments depend upon what God makes of them, not on human moral character, ability, or personality. The outward, visible form is shaped by humans and may vary in detail from generation to generation, but the inward grace depends upon God. The *res,* the thing or fruit of the sacrament, depends upon God, although humans can impose an obstacle to what God offers. In this sense, we can speak of the objectivity of divine grace in the sacraments.

These, of course, are the concepts Augustine used so forcefully in his debate with the Donatists. The sacraments are not contingent upon the moral character of the celebrant but depend on God alone. Humans are freed from the need to make the sacrament happen; only God can do that. Thus the desacralizing position is profoundly unsatisfactory, for it makes the sacraments depend upon human agency and forces their fruitfulness to rest on the degree of fervor with which the sacraments are approached. That is to confuse the roles of God, the giver, and humans, the recipients. Some form of the *ex opere operato* doctrine seems essential to safeguard the crucial sense of divine activity, though this must not be pushed so far as to make grace irresistible or to leave humans completely passive.

Sacraments, as Calvin saw so clearly, are God's idea, designed by God to lead us to God. "Our merciful Lord,"

Calvin says, "so tempers himself to our capacity that . . . he condescends to lead us to himself even by these earthly elements, and to set before us in the flesh a mirror of spiritual blessings."[16] God knows us best and knows the need to strengthen our faith. And the Creator knows best how to address us creatures. Sacraments, then, are God's way of acting. The sacraments are far more than pious memory exercises, for in them, Calvin continues, God "imparts spiritual things under visible ones."

Second, *God acts in the sacraments to give Godself to us.* God takes the initiative in the sacraments. What is given is not some abstract idea or mechanical infusion of energy but a gracious personal relationship, God's life entering ours. We receive God's gift of self. Christianity proclaims that God is love, and it is the very nature of love to be self-giving. In various ways in different sacraments, God acts to give Godself to us in forms appropriate to the time and occasion—as forgiveness and reconciliation in one sacrament, as acceptance in another. Gifts are the human way of giving ourselves to others. God does no less in the sacraments. Indeed, because God is given to us in the sacraments, we are able to give ourselves to others in broader and deeper ways. When God gives Godself to us, say in the eucharist, we are made one with our fellow worshipers and enabled to serve all the world. Thus the sacraments have the power to change all that we do through power based on God's initial self-giving.

God's self-giving is by no means confined to sacraments. The whole Old Testament and New Testament are chronicles of ways God has been given to humans in times past. Frequently it was in unexpected ways of giving, not to the proud and mighty but to the meek and lowly. God is given to us in creation, in law and prophecy, and in the life together of a chosen people. God is given to us in the human Jesus, who "made himself nothing, assuming the nature of a slave" (Phil. 2:7). The scriptures are a record of God's self-giving in the past.

The sacraments are a third testament of God's self-giving. Through them, God gives Godself to us as present reality in our own here and now. The reality of past events is made present to us in reading and expounding the scriptures. Likewise, both

167

past and contemporary actions are imparted to us in the sacraments. They form yet another testament to the self-giving nature of God. All three testaments—old, new, and sacraments—make known to us God's will to give of self for our benefit.

In the third place, *through the sacraments, God gives Godself to us as love made visible.* For Christians, God's self-giving is perceived as the giving of God's love. "God is love; he who dwells in love is dwelling in God, and God in him" (I John 4:16). There is no love that does not make itself manifest in some way. Any human emotion as powerful as love is reflected in actions in the way we relate to the loved one. Love is constantly seeking sign-acts by which to reveal itself to the object of our love. It may take such affectionate forms as hugs and kisses, it may crop out in the giving of a gift, or it may manifest itself by one's doing the dishes for someone. One writes letters or visits the hospital or telephones as visible manifestations of love. These visible sign-acts are identified with love. We know another one loves us because of how she or he acts toward us.

This is not an abstract principle; this is simply how people are. We need to be shown. In Jesus Christ, God showed us the fullness of divine love embodied in the Incarnate One. But we need to be shown this love again and again. In the sacraments God continues in present visibility what God has already done in self-giving in the historical visiblity of Jesus Christ. Love manifests itself in various ways according to our varying stages and circumstances of life. God as love is given to us to uphold us in making a lifelong pledge to love another. The diverse self-giving is witnessed to as the community prays for our return to health. Love is made visible as the community rejoices in the gifts that someone has received for ministerial leadership.

In these and other ways the love of God is made visible to us through actions. Just as we depend upon the handshake, the kiss, or the embrace to express our love so others can recognize it, so we depend upon sacraments to know the love of God. We make human love visible by acting it out; it is no different with divine love. Distinctions between the act and love itself soon disappear. The kiss becomes love itself; the act is part of the emotion. The loving deed is love made visible. The sacraments are God's love made visible.

Fourth, *God's self-giving as love is made visible through relationships of love in community.* Though the sacraments involve a vertical—i.e., God-to-human—relationship, they also always involve horizontal—i.e., human-to-human—relationships. The sacraments are social through and through. They grow out of life in community. Throughout the biblical narrative, God chooses to act in and through a community of faithful people. The sacraments function within the community, enabling Christians to build one another up in love, faith, and hope.

The sacraments function as visible vehicles of love within community in two ways. They establish new relationships of love. And they maintain and nourish existing relationships of love. When two people give themselves to each other in marriage, God acts through the community to strengthen the couple's relationship of love by support and blessing. An ordination without a community of faith would come close to travesty. In baptism and confirmation we move into a new relationship of love within the community as God incorporates us into Christ's body. Death marks yet another transition in which, by God's grace, we pass into the Church Triumphant from the Church Militant. God enables the community to surround us in sickness by its witness of caring love. Throughout life's journey, God is offered to us. The eucharist nourishes us, and reconciliation raises us when we stumble. In all these sign-acts we are built up in love, faith, and hope through the establishment of new relationships of love or the maintenance of existing relationships of love within the church.

In either case, it is God who acts within the actions of the community to make these relationships of love fruitful. The community of faith acts to perform the outward and visible forms of the sacraments. But it knows that the *sacramentum* is meaningless without the *res,* that inward giving of God's love. The sacrament and the reality are experienced together as the community gathers to receive God's gift of self expressed as love in visible form. This we experience within the community, which is itself visible manifestation of God's love. By its sign-acts, the church nurtures our love through new or renewed relationships of love. Of course such love spills over in mission to God's entire world. Just as God uses the words of a preacher to make God's word audible, so God uses the sacraments to make God's love visible. In the sacraments, God acts to give Godself as love made visible by upholding relationships of love in community.

Much of this will be made clearer as we explore the sacraments one by one in subsequent chapters. Though we shall explore in some detail the outward form of each sacrament, the essential concern is not what we do but how the reality of God's love is made manifest in each case. We shall need to remember, when we become preoccupied with the intricacies of matter, form, and ministrant, that what ultimately matters is not what we do with the sacraments but what God does with them.

VI
Initiation
and Reconciliation

No one is born a Christian. One becomes a Christian through becoming part of a community with a distinctive way of life involving definite ethical and creedal commitments. This change in our being is marked by sacraments that proclaim what God is doing to bring us to faith.

In this chapter, we shall survey how Christians experience and understand the ways God acts to initiate us into the community of the faithful and to reconcile us when we injure that relationship of trust and love. The Christian way of life is an intensely social life-style, involving the community of faith intimately in both initiation and reconciliation. The community recognizes that the power given in these sign-acts transcends the church itself. God's love made visible in the sacraments of initiation and reconciliation establishes us and maintains us within the Christian community.

When we speak of **Christian initiation,** we refer to a variety of sign-acts: those relating to the **catechumenate** (a period of instruction, catechesis, and examination) that surround the actual washing of baptism; various subsequent acts frequently known as "confirmation" or "reception into the church" (a term used by some Protestants as the equivalent of confirmation); and first communion. The entire ritual process of the making of a Christian will be referred to as initiation, and individual portions will be named as encountered. **Reconciliation** may be an unfamiliar term to many, though recognizable under older terms such as penance or confession. Reconciliation is the preferred contemporary term and certainly is more descriptive of the purpose served.

Initiation and reconciliation have a number of points of contact, though they do not always dovetail conveniently. Their relationship is more a matter of life than logic. Reconciliation has ties to healing almost as strong as to initiation, a relationship evident in James 5:16 and elaborated by Tertullian. On the other hand, since most people are spared serious illness in any frequency but no one is exempt from sin, reconciliation has parallels with the eucharist in maintaining us in a continuing relationship of love. One advantage in relating initiation and reconciliation is that one establishes and the other maintains the relationship to the Christian community thus begun. Tertullian calls them planks after the shipwreck of sin. Initiation has been compared to a wedding, which makes visible the establishment of a permanent relationship of love. But even in such a relationship there are times of conflict and the need to "make up" or to be reconciled. We can profit from considering initiation and reconciliation together as they mark the start and travel on the Christian's journey through life.

It is not always easy to draw a line between practice and the understanding of it, between rite and reason, between liturgiology and sacramental theology. But that is the course we shall attempt in this chapter. First we shall survey what Christians have done and do now in these sacraments. Then we shall examine their understanding of these acts. Finally some conclusions for pastoral use will be drawn.

I

Current changes in the practices of initiation and reconciliation are only the latest chapters in a long history of development. Once again we must look for roots in Judaism. The sources lie deep in prophetic symbolism and the use of acts and objects for encountering God. The Jewish belief that the material can affect the spiritual is central to these sacraments.

The most conspicuous Jewish antecedent of initiation was **circumcision,** a sign-act that placed males within the covenant relationship between Israel and God. This sacrament of the old law (as Christians saw it) brought the eight-day-old Jewish male into lifelong relationship with a people with whom God had covenanted to be God and king. Even when Christian writers denied that circumcision could do any more than promise and signify salvation, the concept—of being engrafted into God's people through a sign-act—persisted.

More questionable is whether first-century Judaism practiced **proselyte baptism,** i.e., of male and female gentile converts. We know that Judaism eventually did baptize converts, and it seems unlikely that such a practice would have been copied from Christianity. The first-century Qumran community practiced daily ritual washing as a sign of spiritual cleansing. Washing with water is, after all, the obvious natural sign of cleansing, as I Peter 3:21 recognizes: "Baptism is not the washing away of bodily pollution, but the appeal made to God by a good conscience." Acts 22:16 echoes this: "Be baptized at once, with invocation of his name, and wash away your sins."

There is no question, though, of the influence of **John the Baptist,** who baptized Jesus and many others. Paul interprets: "The baptism that John gave was a baptism in token of repentance, and he told the people to put their trust in one who was to come after him, that is, in Jesus" (Acts 19:4). That sums it up fairly well: John's baptism was a baptism of repentance and a baptism of eschatological expectation. It was ethical and anticipatory. The church could never forget that Jesus himself submitted to John's baptism as a part of conforming "in this way with all that God requires" (Matt. 3:15). Thus the weight of Jesus' own action in receiving baptism and in allowing his disciples to baptize (John 4:2) gave paramount authority to baptism. Furthermore, Jesus identified his baptism with his passion and death (Mark 10:38 and Luke 12:50). Thus baptism became an image of Christ's sacrificial death.

Other acts the church appropriated were the **laying on of hands** and **sealing** or **anointing with oil.** Both acts signified the transmission of power and blessing (Isaac blessing Jacob, Gen. 27; or Jacob blessing his grandsons, Gen. 48), or the certification of power (Samuel anointing David, I Sam. 16:13). Priestly and royal power seem associated with the use of oil, both symbols applying to the gifts of the Holy Spirit for those initiated into the "royal priesthood" (I Pet. 2:9; Rev. 5:10). The association of "anoint" and the words "Christ" and "Messiah" could not be missed in Greek or Hebrew.

Much more dubious is the influence of the initiatory rites of the various pagan mystery religions popular in the Roman empire during the days of the New Testament. Certainly there were obvious parallels to Christian initiations in the initiatory rites of these secret sects, but that was probably more a cause of embarrassment to the church than a source of ideas. Justin Martyr dismissed the pagan rites as imitations by "wicked demons" of authentic Christian rites.

The New Testament itself gives us only tantalizingly brief glimpses of actual initiatory practices and even fewer of reconciliation. But what we see there has become determinative for all subsequent developments. Easily the most detailed account of a baptism is Philip's baptism of the Ethiopian eunuch in Acts 8:35-38. Verse 37 is absent in some texts but present in others. The whole is worth repeating.

Starting from this passage, he told him the good news of Jesus. As they were going along the road, they came to some water. "Look," said the eunuch, "here is water: what is there to prevent my being baptized?" [Philip said, "If you whole-heartedly believe, it is permitted." He replied, "I believe that Jesus Christ is the Son of God."]; and he ordered the carriage to stop. Then they both went down into the water, Philip and the eunuch; and he baptized him. (Bracketed portion is a footnote in the NEB.)

We begin with a form of catechesis, Philip instructing the eunuch. Then comes a profession of the eunuch's faith, in which he gives the correct creedal statement. Whereupon they go down "into" (eis) the water, and Philip baptizes the eunuch. It is essentially the core of baptism as practiced today.

The creedal statement focuses on the second member of the Trinity, not the whole Trinity. There are other texts that indicate that the earliest Christian baptisms were "in the name of Jesus" (Acts 2:38; 8:12, 16; 10:48; 19:5; 22:16). Paul makes a short creedal statement in Romans 10:9: "If on your lips is the confession 'Jesus is Lord' "; and repeats it in Philippians 2:11: "and every tongue confess, 'Jesus Christ is Lord.' " Consequently, it is all the more problematic that Matthew 28:19 gives a baptismal formula that is clearly trinitarian and that says literally: "Baptizing them into the name of the Father and of the Son and of the Holy Spirit." Very likely this represents a second stage of development in actual liturgical practice and was read back into the words of the Lord by the Evangelist. This is corroborated by the early *Didache*, which uses exactly the same baptismal formula as have virtually all baptismal rites since.

The witness to the **laying on of hands** is far more perplexing. The Ethiopian eunuch story makes no mention of it, but this act occurs repeatedly in ambiguous and conflicting passages in Acts. For moderns this raises questions about the relation of reception of the Holy Spirit to baptism. Acts 2:38 links repentance, baptism, the forgiveness of sins, and the gift of the Holy Spirit. But at Caesarea the Holy Spirit got there first, obviously being poured out before baptism (Acts 10:47), whereas in Samaria the newly baptized did not receive the Holy Spirit until they received laying on of hands (Acts 8:17). At Ephesus after baptism "when Paul had laid his hands on them, the Holy Spirit came upon them" (Acts 19:6). Two things seem likely from these accounts: the Holy Spirit and baptism are directly and intimately related, and the laying on of hands, or **sealing (anointing)** (II Cor. 1:22; Eph. 1:13 and 4:30), seems to testify to this relation by emphasizing the presence of the Spirit in those baptized.

There has been speculation as to whether I Peter is a baptismal sermon. It addresses its audience as "new-born infants" (2:2) who "are now the people of God, who once were not his people" (2:10). The waters of Noah's flood are seen as prefiguring "the water of baptism" (3:21), an allusion echoed in baptismal rites down to the present. And baptism is compared to a clean conscience (3:21).

Practical problems began to emerge as the church started to age. Hebrews raises the question of apostasy by those who have been baptized: "when they have had a taste of the heavenly gift and a share in the Holy Spirit, . . . and after all this have fallen away, it is impossible to bring them again to repentance"

(6:4-6). This problem has vexed the church ever since: how to deal with the backslider. The *Shepherd of Hermas,* from the second century, is a bit more lenient. Acknowledging that some deny any repentance beyond baptism, the author concedes that "after that great and holy calling [baptism], if a man be tempted by the devil and sin, he has one repentance, but if he sin and repent repeatedly it is unprofitable."[1]

It is surprising that the New Testament tells us little about baptized sinners. Paul threatens to show them "no leniency" in Corinth (II Cor. 13:3), and a notorious sinner is to be consigned to Satan (I Cor. 5:5). Ample precedent was available in the Old Testament for penitential practices of supplication, fasting, mourning, and wearing sackcloth. In light of the major role it played in subsequent ages, it is amazing the early church placed little emphasis on John 20:23, the most obvious text giving it authority to forgive or retain sins. Clearly the return of sinners is sought in the Gospels, and Paul equates bondage to sin with death. Evidence for the practice of reconciliation beyond the cleansing of baptism is not clear in the New Testament.

In modern times, the most vexing problem has been whether the New Testament accounts are compatible with the **baptism of infants (pedobaptism).** All agree there is no explicit evidence either for or against the baptism of infants in the New Testament. Those who practice infant baptism are likely to be convinced that the *oïkos* (household) passages, which speak of the baptism of whole households (Acts 16:15 and 33; 18:8; I Cor. 1:16), are likely to have included children of the family and resident slaves. Since the fathers usually determined the religion of the whole family, it is likely, they argue, that baptism was applied to all within the household as a matter of course. Those who do not practice infant baptism are likely to argue against it on the basis that the demands for repentance and faith on the part of those to be baptized (Mark 16:16; Acts 2:38) preclude baptism of infants.

On historical evidence alone, we must agree with Kurt Aland that "infant baptism is certainly provable only from the third century,"[2] though there are some theological grounds for asserting it was practiced in the New Testament times.[3] The irrefutable historical evidence is in early–third-century passages of Tertullian, who deplores the baptism of "little children" who may later embarrass their sponsors, and in a contemporary passage of Hippolytus, who speaks of baptizing the "little children" (*parvulos*) first, some of whom apparently cannot yet "speak for themselves." By the fifth century, infant baptism had become widespread. Ever since, most Christians have practiced the baptism of infants.

The second-century church fills out more details of initiation practices beyond the hints the New Testament accounts give us. The *Didache* forbids those unbaptized "in the Lord's name" from eating and drinking the eucharist. Those about to be baptized are to fast. Baptism is preferably in cold running water; but, lacking this, water is poured "thrice upon the candidate's head in the name of the Father, Son, and Holy Spirit."[4] Justin gives slightly more detail. The catechumenate involves instruction, the promise to "live accordingly," prayer, and fasting. Baptism is at a place "where there is water," and candidates are washed in the name of the Trinity. Those baptized are then led to where the church is assembled and share, for the first time, in common prayer, the kiss of peace, and the eucharist.[5]

Much more information appears in the next century in Tertullian's treatise *On Baptism* and scattered throughout his other writings. Tertullian indicates a rigorous discipline for those about to be baptized involving "prayers, fasts, and bendings of the knee, and vigils all the night through."[6] The most solemn occasion for baptism, he tells us, is the Pascha. Pentecost comes second, though any moment is possible. The normal administrant is the bishop, if present, then authorized presbyters and deacons; but "even laymen have the right, for what is equally received can be equally given."[7] Just before baptism comes **renunciation** of "the devil, and his pomp and his angels." Candidates are "thrice immersed" after "interrogations rather more extensive than our Lord has prescribed"[8] and then "thoroughly anointed with a blessed unction" such as Moses used to anoint Aaron into the priesthood. Next, "the hand is laid on in blessing, invoking and inviting the Holy Spirit as Jacob blessed his grandsons."[9] Yet another Old Testament image appears in the act of giving the newly baptized "a mixture of milk and honey," a symbol of the promised land (Exod. 3:8).

Hippolytus corroborates all of this, giving us extensive detail, particularly on a long and rigorous catechumenate that could last as long as three years. During this strenuous period, catechumens are hearers of the word but cannot pray with the faithful, give the kiss of peace, or remain for the eucharist. Advanced and suitable candidates are set apart each year and their conduct examined (eventually ritualized as the **scrutinies**). They undergo a period of intense preparation with daily exorcism. The candidates fast on what we would now call Good Friday and Holy Saturday.

The climax of the initiation process occurs on Easter Eve after an all-night vigil of scripture reading and instruction. At cockcrow, prayer is made over the water, the candidates undress, and the bishop prepares oils of exorcism and thanksgiving. Then, after the renunciation of Satan, each candidate is anointed thoroughly with oil of exorcism, goes down into the water, and is asked three questions that are virtually the words of the **Apostles' Creed** (which to this day the West uses as the baptismal creed). Each time after affirming belief in a different member of the Trinity, the candidate is baptized. After the third washing, he or she comes up out of the water and is anointed with the oil of thanksgiving. Then, after dressing, the newly baptized meet the assembled church where the bishop lays hands on each, asking God to "make them worthy to be filled with Thy Holy Spirit."[10] The bishop then pours holy oil and lays his hands on the heads of each. Finally, the bishop seals each on the forehead, presumably with the sign of the cross (**consignation**), and gives each the kiss of peace. The new Christians now join the congregation for the first time in prayer, the kiss of peace, and the eucharist. On this Paschal occasion there are three cups: water ("a token of the laver"), milk and honey, and wine. As can be seen, the whole rite has a variety of actions, all involving a strong sense of touch: anointings, washing, laying on of hands and signing, embracing (kiss of peace), and eating and drinking.

Other pre-Nicene materials add a few details. The third-century *Didascalia Apostolorum* stresses the need for a "woman deacon" to "anoint the women . . . for the ministry of a woman deacon is especially needful and important."[11] Egeria tells us that in late–fourth-century Jerusalem at the beginning of Lent the names of those to be baptized that Easter (the *competentes*) are given in.[12] After inquiry into their life-styles, three hours of daily catechizing and exorcism takes place. After five weeks, they are given the creed to learn which they must recite back, one by one, to the bishop, who examines their understanding. Egeria noted nothing much unfamiliar in the Paschal vigil but mentions the eight days of Easter week when the newly initiated have interpreted to them all the mysteries that they have just experienced for the first time.

Fortunately, several examples of this method of **mystagogical catechesis** have survived in the forms of lectures given by Ambrose in Milan, Cyril (or his successor) in Jerusalem, and John Chrysostom and Theodore of Mopsuestia in Antioch. **Ambrose** tells the new Christians the meaning of the *ephphetha,* the ceremonial opening of the ears and nostrils (Mark 7:34). Then: "Thou wast anointed as Christ's athlete; as about to wrestle in the fight of this world."[13] After baptism, there is a footwashing, though Ambrose is aware that Rome does not do this.

Cyril gives us much more detail and elaborates on symbolic meanings: "Ye were stripped, ye were anointed with exorcized oil, from the very hairs of your head to your feet, and were made partakers of the good olive tree, Jesus Christ."[14] Theodore adds other details, such as the role of the sponsor and the clothing of the newly baptized in a radiant garment. John Chrysostom gives us the **adhesion,** or pledge after the renunciation, "And I enter into thy service, O Christ." He also uses the typical Eastern baptismal formula: "So-and-so is baptized in the name of the Father, and of the Son, and of the Holy Spirit," in contrast to the active form the West adopted subsequently: "I baptize you. . . ." Chrysostom also tells us the candidate's head is thrice lowered into the water and raised.[15]

The most perplexing part of these rites is the variety of anointings and signings. **Anointing** tended to be originally a covering of the body with oil, much as soap is used in bathing today, thus suggesting a preliminary to the bath of baptism or preparation for an athletic contest. **Signing,** or marking with the sign of the cross (sometimes with oil), is a form of sealing or giving definite identity to the newly baptized. It is all the more puzzling since apparently most Syrian rites lacked post-baptismal anointing. As early as the fourth century, in some places, these post-baptismal acts had become associated with the gift of the Holy Spirit. Ambrose speaks of the "spiritual seal, . . . when, at the invocation of the priest, the Holy Spirit is bestowed," and lists the sevenfold gifts (Isa. 11:2).[16] Cyril calls anointing "the emblem of the Holy Ghost."

Tertullian tells us much about the early practice of reconciliation in his treatise *On Penance*. Sin is not only an offense against God but a wound of the church, for it endangers all Christians (especially in time of persecution). It is far better to acknowledge one's sin and suffer embarrassment before the community than to enter hell after this life. God cannot be deceived. Penance involved a rigorous public discipline of daily deprivation for those guilty of gross sins such as apostasy. Penitents were excluded from the eucharist until reconciled to the church on Easter just as the newly baptized were being admitted to their first communion. Reconciliation was indeed the plank after shipwreck for those who have sinned grievously and destroyed the cleansing effects of their baptism. Often involving a period of fasting, wearing penitential clothing, and continence, reconciliation was usually practiced once in a lifetime. Tertullian considered it medicinal, as a way of healing a wound in the community just as astringent medicine heals. Thus Easter morning publicly celebrated the reconciliation of lost sheep both to God and to the offended Christian community.

In summation, the early church's rites of initiation and reconciliation were public, involving the whole community. The full rites of initiation came at Easter at the end of a long catechumenate and consisted of a variety of acts at the Easter vigil: anointings, renunciation, creedal profession, washing, laying on of hands, sealing, and eucharist. Post-baptismal catechesis followed. It was a formalized way of ritualizing the whole process of conversion from first inquiry to final and total commitment, all tied directly to the celebration of the resurrection.

Much of this was to change with the advance of the Middle

Ages. In the East, the whole of initiation was kept together by the priest's performing the whole rite, using chrism (olive oil and balm) consecrated by the bishop for the final anointing. This portion of the Eastern rite is known as **chrismation.** It corresponded to the laying on of hands for confirmation, which the West insisted must be done by a bishop. But the West saw a slow movement toward fragmentation and privatization of the whole. The disintegration of the unity of the rite was a long and unconscious process, not really complete until the end of the Middle Ages. (As late as 1533 the future English Queen Elizabeth I was baptized and confirmed three days after birth, a practice soon forbidden by the 1549 BCP.) Unfortunately most of these changes came about for nontheological reasons. In Italy there was a bishop in every sizable town, and it was possible to have initiation with all its parts at one time (Easter) and place (a baptistry such as those in Pisa, Parma, Florence). But as Christianity spread into the geographically vast tribal dioceses of northern Europe, it became impossible to bring everyone to the bishop for his part in the rite. What worked in Italy did not work elsewhere, and the bishop's portion of initiation was simply postponed though there was experimentation in allowing priests to do the complete rite in Gaul, Spain, and Ireland.

The origins of the word **confirmation** are problematic, though Ambrose used a verb form of it in the context of sealing in *Of the Mysteries.* In the fifth century "to confirm" applied to the post-baptismal anointing and hand-laying by the bishop, but not until the ninth century does it "become the normal term to use of this part of the initiatory rite."[17] Slowly its meaning changed from that of "to complete" to that of "to strengthen."

Other factors brought about changes too. A lengthy catechumenate made no sense for infants. The pressure of Augustine's theology and fear of infants dying unbaptized and thus being excluded from the kingdom (John 3:5) brought about the custom of having infants baptized within a few days of birth. Even so, in some places, people waited until the Paschal season for baptisms as late as the thirteenth century. Other factors sheared off parts of initiation. First communion followed baptism for infants well into the Middle Ages, but growing scrupulosity about the consecrated elements led to termination of this practice. As late as the twelfth century, infants were communicated by placing in their mouths the priest's finger dipped in the wine. Such a practice fell into abeyance, and children were denied communion until reaching the age of reason; but "infant communion . . . was not finally abolished in the West until the Council of Trent."[18] Confirmation was gradually postponed until years of discretion, which came to mean at least seven years of age. For vast numbers of medieval people, and even after the Reformation, this meant that the practical difficulties of meeting a bishop rendered confirmation an unlikely experience. Confirmation was desirable but, unlike baptism, not a necessity for salvation.

The result by the late Middle Ages was that infants were baptized within eight days after birth by being dipped into the font in their parish church in a private ceremony. Then they might be confirmed after reaching the age of seven (usually in a private ceremony, too) if they chanced on a bishop. And at this age they could receive communion, whether confirmed or not. The whole corporate and Paschal character of initiation had been shattered.

Changes in reconciliation were no less drastic. Indeed no sacrament has reversed its original form so much and then been restored. Originally administered by bishops, it became performed by presbyters; from being openly public it became private and secret; from being once or twice per lifetime, it became yearly at least and weekly in modern times; from being the rare exception, it became required of all. Much of the impetus for these changes came about through the dissemination throughout Europe of Celtic **penitentials,** handbooks prescribing penalities for wrongdoings.[19] From the seventh century onward, the influence of these books spread, popularizing a type of penance wholly separated from that of the public assembly of the church. Indeed, some of the early Irish confessors were lay men and lay women, but eventually only priests could be confessors. Late medieval councils decreed that confession was necessary before receiving communion, both of which must be received at least yearly, a fateful linkage for both sacraments.

The Reformation era was largely one of missed opportunities with regard to initiation and reconciliation. For the first time in centuries, the churches began to engage in vast missionary efforts, which should have brought drastic changes in initiation but failed to do so. The Church of England did not even have a rite for administering "Baptism to such as Are of Riper Years" (adults) until 1662. Rubrics in previous prayer books spoke merely of the "children." Rome was content simply to codify the late medieval developments.

The Protestant Reformers made two significant advances with baptism. They insisted that it be made a public office in the vernacular. The 1549 and 1552 BCP insisted that it be administered on "Sondayes and other holy dayes, when the most numbre of people maye come together." The Reformers also simplified the ceremonies. Unlike his first (1523) rite, Luther's 1526 *Order of Baptism Newly Revised*[20] omitted breathing on the child, the giving of salt, the first exorcism, the *ephphetha,* the two anointings, and the lighted candle, though he retained the white robe. It was a drastic pruning of accessory ceremonies, but Calvin went even further, "abolishing them, so that there might be no more impediment to prevent the people from going directly to Jesus Christ."[21] He did not exercise similar restraint with regard to didactic exhortations.

The Church of England at first was less stingy with the medieval ceremonies. Retained were an exorcism and procession into the church to the font (both abolished in 1552), dipping the child thrice in the font so as to cover the entire body, the chrisom robe and anointing (both abolished in 1552), and the sign of the cross (which became a stumbling block to the Puritans). John Wesley followed the same rite with considerable modifications. In his early years, he insisted on dipping the infant, but late in life gave sprinkling as an alternative mode. Central theological statements of Wesley's service were lost in 1858 and 1916 among American Methodists.

The most drastic changes came about among the **Anabaptists,** who insisted that the only proper candidates for baptism were adult believers. They maintained that baptism should only be given to those of known purity of life and doctrine. They preferred the pure church, consisting of believers, to the state church consisting of everyone. Anabaptists were no less adamant on reconciliation; the ban was imposed on baptized backsliders who could only be reconciled after a period of public ignominy.

The earliest Anabaptists seemed to have practiced baptism chiefly by pouring. Eventually other groups such as the English Baptists came to demand immersion, although some Anabaptists still practice pouring. Roman Catholics and Protestants alike continued to baptize infants by dipping until well past the Reformation. Not until the eighteenth century did this form of immersion become unfashionable among Anglicans and pouring was substituted.

An early Anabaptist baptismal order by **Balthasar Hubmaier,** "A Form for Baptism," indicates that candidates must first be examined as to faith by the bishop, then presented to the congregation. The rite involves prayer for the Holy Spirit to fill the candidates' hearts, creedal questions based on an amended Apostles' Creed, renunciation, questions as to willing obedience and desire to be baptized, baptism, prayers, laying on of hands and welcome into "the fellowship of Christians."[22] Though rejecting infant baptism, some Anabaptists such as Hubmaier and Pilgram Marpeck advocated a public service of infant dedication.

At first, English Baptists practiced the laying on of hands at baptism.[23] Since only believers were baptized, Anabaptists and Baptists alike had no need for a separate rite of confirmation. Christian initiation was complete at one event, as it had been in the early church.

Quakers took an even more radical step. They eliminated any outward act, insisting that the Bible commanded none; they commended instead an inward "baptism in the Spirit." Twentieth-century Pentecostalists distinguish between the two. Water baptism they practice (usually) for adult believers by triune immersion, but baptism of the Spirit is a separate manifestation of charismatic gifts.

Confirmation was a problem for the Reformers. Luther did not draw up a rite but did not object "if every pastor examines the faith of the children . . . lays hands on them, and confirms them."[24] Martin Bucer cast the die for subsequent Reformed and Anglican developments by tying confirmation to an examination of the child on his or her knowledge of the catechism. Partly as an antidote to Anabaptists, Bucer probably introduced in Strassburg a confirmation service that was more an examination and graduation ceremony than anything else, though the pastor does conclude by stretching his hands out over the children with a blessing.[25] Calvin followed suit after a diatribe about confirmation "doing injustice to baptism." He preferred "a catechizing, in which children or those near adolescence would give an account of their faith before the church."[26] The Church of England agreed in restricting confirmation to "suche as can say in theyr mother tong, tharticles of the faith the lordes prayer, and the tenne commanundementes" (1549 BCP). The bishop was the minister, crossing the candidates on the forehead (1549) and laying his hand upon their heads (1549 and 1552). Confirmation was made requisite for admission to communion, thus ratifying the late medieval end of centuries of infant communion.

The unfortunate consequence of these developments was that confirmation came to be contingent upon human knowledge—the learning of the catechism. The sacramental sense of the laying on of hands as a gracious act of God became dissipated in favor of a graduation exercise. The Reformers' misreading of church history led them to salvage confirmation in a way that caused new problems. It was left to portions of the Free Church tradition to improvise an act of profession of faith as a substitute with no sacramental overtones.

Reconciliation also was a lost opportunity. Luther drew up "A Short Order of Confession before the Priest for the Common Man" in 1529 and wrote "How One Should Teach Common Folk to Shrive Themselves" two years later.[27] These seek to avoid the artificiality of cataloging one's sins by number and species and to give one the peace that reconciliation can offer. Both forms are for private confession to a priest or father confessor. The other Reformers were content to append penitential prayers to their public Sunday service.

All in all, the Reformation saw more subtraction than addition in the rites of initiation and reconciliation. Recent years have seen reversal of this retrenchment, with Roman

Catholics and the major Protestant traditions often moving in similar directions.

The most common move has been toward recovering the **unity of the initiatory rites.** The most striking instance of this occurs in the new Roman Catholic "Rite of Christian Initiation of Adults." This represents a recovery of the extended catechumenate, which ritualizes the whole process of conversion so the congregation shares in the individual's growth in faith. The catechumenate is spread out over months or even years in three stages or gateways. It begins with the inquirer's reaching the stage of acceptance as a catechumen, continues when the catechumenate nears completion with election or enrollment of names at the beginning of Lent, and concludes with reception of the three initiatory sacraments at Easter (Rites, 40-106). Lent is used as a period of enlightenment or illumination, marked on three Sundays by scrutinies, exorcisms, and the presentation and recitation of the Apostles' Creed and Lord's Prayer. The whole is a recovery of primitive practice refined to fit the life of a missionary church in the world today. The new "Rite of Baptism for Several Children" (Rites, 197-213) and "Rite of Confirmation within Mass" (Rites, 306-13) have been simplified, congregational participation has been increased, and a greater emphasis placed on the use of scripture. The baptism of children testifies to greater responsibility on the part of parents.

A different course has been taken by Lutherans, Episcopalians, and United Methodists, though they also stress the unity of the initiatory rites. These downplay confirmation as a separate and distinct rite and introduce the **reaffirmation** or **renewal** of baptismal promises by all Christians. The new Episcopal service advocates that the bishop be the normal celebrant as far as possible. There is a laying on of hands on all baptized, chrism may be used in making the sign of the cross, and the service may continue with confirmation, reception ("into the fellowship of this Communion"), and reaffirmation. The whole is to be set normally in the context of the eucharist (BCP, 299-311). The new Lutheran rite contains the laying on of hands and consignation immediately after baptism (LBW, 121-25). A separate service, "Affirmation of Baptism,"

provides possibilities of confirmation, reception into membership, and restoration to membership (LBW, 198-201). The 1976
alternative United Methodist *Service of Baptism, Confirmation, and Renewal* (SWR #2 and #10) combines water baptism
and laying on of hands and provides for confirmation and other
renewals of the baptismal covenant in addition to profession or
renewal of full membership in The United Methodist Church.
The whole congregation is encouraged to participate periodi-
cally in the act of renewal. The central prayer, the thanksgiving
over the font, is recovered after a sixty-year lapse. The
Presbyterian *Worshipbook* (48-52) and the *Hymnal of the
United Church of Christ* (31-34) have adopted separate services
of confirmation just at the time other churches are seeking to
avoid such.

Mention should also be made of the new emphasis on the
"Renewal of Baptismal Promises" as part of the Easter Vigil
among Roman Catholics (Sac, 256-58) or "Renewal of
Baptismal Vows" on the same occasion (BCP, 292-94) among
Episcopalians, Lutherans (LBW, Ministers Desk Edition,
152), and United Methodists (*From Ashes to Fire, SWR #8*).
The addition of the Baptism of the Lord as an important
occasion in new Western calendars is likewise significant.

A common note in most of the new initiatory rites has been
concentration on the essential actions: the ethical change
expressed by the renunciation; the creedal change expressed by
the trinitarian affirmation; the blessing of the water; the
washing of baptism; the laying on of hands, or sealing; and the
first eucharist. Other accessory actions, such as multiple
anointings, the *ephphetha,* the giving of salt, the white garment,
and the lighted candle tend to be made optional or eliminated.

Recent changes in initiation have been substantial, but those
in reconciliation have been even more dramatic. We have seen
how the Middle Ages brought drastic changes to this
sacrament. Vatican II mandated revision of the "rite and
formulas" of penance but gave no hint of such major changes as
three distinct rites such as appeared in 1973: those for
"Reconciliation of Individual Penitents," for "Several Penitents with Individual Confession and Absolution," and for
"Several Penitents with General Confession and Absolution"

(Rites, 311-79). Easily the most controversial has been the last, but it has stimulated some important experiments. In all three rites there is provision for the reading of scripture. The last two rites dramatize the "relation of the sacrament to the community." All participants share in general confession and praise for God's mercy. The whole represents both recovery and advance beyond early practice in emphasizing the communal nature of sin and our need to be reconciled to one another by God's mercy.

During the Vietnam war years, many Protestant congregations experimented with various types of corporate services of reconciliation. Unfortunately these tended to disappear once that trauma was over. Now there are signs that the deep human needs to which reconciliation ministers are being met more directly. Lutherans now provide services for both "Corporate Confession and Forgiveness" and "Individual Confession and Forgiveness" (LBW, 193-97). Episcopalians, following practices recovered in the Oxford Movement of the nineteenth century, now make provision for private "Reconciliation of a Penitent" (BCP, 447-52). United Methodists are at work on services of reconciliation.

Most of these churches include penitential elements in the liturgy of the hours and in the eucharist. The Lutherans now provide an optional preliminary "Brief Order for Confession and Forgiveness" before the eucharist (LBW, 56). Episcopalians provide a rather free-floating "Penitential Order" (BCP, 319-21; 351-53) for use at the eucharist and rather strongly hint that, in its absence, a general confession should follow the intercessions. For Roman Catholics, United Methodists, Presbyterians, and the United Church of Christ, the introductory rites of the normal Sunday services can begin with acts of confession and pardon, a legacy of the Middle Ages.

Increased concern has been shown in recent years for penitential seasons such as Advent and Lent and occasions such as Ash Wednesday. The Free Church tradition long had special days of humiliation as well as days of thanksgiving. There is also an old Methodist tradition of watch-night services and covenant services. The first BCP had a service for Ash Wednesday with fierce curses from Deuteronomy 27, a service renamed in 1662 as "A Commination, or Denouncing of God's Anger and Judgements Against Sinners." Somewhat more mellow observations of Ash Wednesday have become common in many churches, and a service with optional imposition of ashes appears in the BCP (264-69); the LBW, Ministers Desk Edition (129-31); and the United Methodist *From Ashes to Fire* (SWR #8). Much of the value of corporate reconciliation is of an occasional matter and could work best when tied to special times in the church year or civil life.

Rites of initiation and reconciliation are obviously still developing and changing. Recent shifts involve recovery of many early Christian practices and a critical attitude about much medieval practice.

II

As the rites themselves changed over the centuries, there have been equally important changes in the ways Christians understood what they experienced in initiation and reconciliation. We cannot understand the rites themselves without understanding what concepts they were expressions of and how the rites were instrumental in shaping ideas about themselves in turn.

The New Testament witness to initiation is fascinating and complex. A vast array of hints and metaphors is thrown out as to what initiation meant to the first Christians, but no systematic exposition of these ideas appears in scripture. Nevertheless, these biblical metaphors are the foundation of all subsequent attempts at understanding what God is doing through the rites of initiation.

For the sake of convenience, we can identify the chief of these as **five New Testament metaphors of initiation.** This should not blind us to the fact that there are other minor themes in the New Testament relating to initiation: naming the name of Jesus, sealing, and entering the royal priesthood are some of them. But the five chief metaphors or themes seem to be used most frequently and to have had the most influence on both faith and practice. They are: union with Jesus Christ, incorporation into the church, new birth, forgiveness of sin, and reception of the Holy Spirit.[28]

We shall begin with the theme of initiation as bringing one into **union with Jesus Christ.** Paul expresses it thus:

Have you forgotten that when we were baptized into union with Christ Jesus we were baptized into his death? By baptism we were buried with him, and lay dead, in order that, as Christ was raised from the dead in the splendour of the Father, so also we might set our feet upon the new path of life. For if we have become incorporate with him in a death like his, we shall also be one with him in a resurrection like his. (Rom. 6:3-5)

The same idea recurs in Colossians 2:12. Baptism conveys to each one baptized both the death of Jesus and the possibility of resurrection through him. What Christ has done is done for the individual named in baptism. It is a personalizing and internalizing of the climax of history as holy events are given to individuals through union with Christ. The ancient practice of designing baptisteries so as to suggest a going down into and rising from a grave is a literalizing of this sharing in Christ's death and resurrection.

Very closely related to this theme is that of **incorporation into the church,** Christ's body. "For indeed," Paul says, "we were all brought into one body by baptism in the one Spirit" (I Cor. 12:13). Probably the most egalitarian statement in all scripture is Paul's assertion that for those "baptized into union with [Christ] . . . there is no such thing as Jew and Greek, slave and freeman, male and female; for you are all one person in Christ Jesus" (Gal. 3:27-28). Baptism is the sign-act of entrance into the church no matter at what age it is practiced. Hence fonts are often placed near the entrance to church buildings, and some rites involve an entrance procession into the midst of the building and people.

Initiation is also the **new birth.** Closely tied to union with Christ in death and resurrection and to joining a new body, the church, the image of new birth appears in Jesus' discussion with Nicodemus: "No one can enter the kingdom of God without being born from water and spirit" (John 3:5). Implicit in this image is being a new creature in Christ Jesus, having put one's past, the Old Adam, behind one. More controversial has been the history of Titus 3:5: "He saved us through the water of rebirth and the renewing power of the Holy Spirit." The key word, *paliggenesía,* or regeneration, has been a focus of controversy. Various liturgical representations of new birth occur; it is the most feminine of images. In the most explicitly sexual act in Christian liturgy, the Paschal candle is plunged into the baptismal font at the Easter vigil in anticipation of those who will be born from this womb (font) into a new body (church) during the ensuing year.

The most obvious thing about baptism (so obvious it is often overlooked) is the cleansing action of water representing the **forgiveness of sin.** In Acts 22:16, Ananias commands: "Be baptized at once, with invocation of his name, and wash away [*apólousai*] your sins" (cf. also I Cor. 6:11). Both I Peter (3:21) and Hebrews (10:22) compare baptism to an outward washing and the inward cleansing of "a good conscience." The relation of baptism and forgiveness is clear in Acts 2:38—"repent and be baptized, every one of you, in the name of Jesus the Messiah for the forgiveness of your sins"—and became dogma in the Nicene Creed—"One Baptism for the remission of sins." Reconciliation for post-baptismal sin comes to mind, though the most obvious text to us in this connection is John 20:23: "If you forgive any [person's] sins, they stand forgiven." The act of washing in baptism and the pre-baptismal anointing with oil (the predecessor of soap) are the most obvious enactments of forgiveness. The giving of a new white garment after baptism reinforces the idea of a newly clean conscience and the putting on of Christ (Gal. 3:27).

Reception of the Holy Spirit is a complex metaphor partly because the eventual splintering of the rites of initiation in the West has raised questions as to the role and timing of this reception. When this metaphor is seen in conjunction with incorporation into the church, some of these problems disappear. The church is the environment of the Holy Spirit's activity. One cannot be a part of the spirit-filled community and not receive the Holy Spirit. Hippolytus repeats the refrain, "in the Holy Spirit and the holy Church," suggesting where the Holy Spirit is known and experienced. The Acts 2:38 passage, quoted above, continues "and you will receive the gift of the Holy Spirit." Jesus' own baptism has a theophany of the Holy

Spirit visible as a dove (Matt. 3:16). Sometimes, as we have seen, the coming of the Spirit seems manifested most clearly by one portion of initiation, the laying on of hands (Acts 19:1-7). Other images seem to refer to the activity in initiation of the Holy Spirit: "illumination," or "enlightenment" (Heb. 6:4), or "sanctification" (I Cor. 6:11). The giving of salt (wisdom) or a lighted candle (preparedness) to those just baptized, and the visual symbol of the dove, underscore the Spirit's work in initiation.

The most important witness in the New Testament accounts is that initiation is far deeper than any single interpretation of it. Our problem is to obtain a balanced understanding that does justice to all five chief metaphors. All subsequent developments are to be held accountable to this standard of balanced understanding. Initiation is a jewel with many facets. We do not sense its full brilliance until we see all facets reflecting the light.

Probably as concise as possible a statement of these five metaphors occurs in Justin Martyr's two short accounts of initiation in his *First Apology*. He speaks of being "made new through Christ," being led into and greeted by the Christian assembly, the "rebirth by which we ourselves were reborn," the repentance of sins and being "washed in the water" and the "washing is called illumination."[29] Irenaeus beautifully combines several of these themes by speaking of baptism as the water without which "dry flour cannot be united into a lump of dough, or a loaf . . . so we who are many cannot be made one in Christ Jesus without the water which comes from heaven."[30] Clement of Alexandria favors the theme of "enlightenment"; others of the fathers have their favorites, but taken together there seems to be a fair degree of balance. What one does not find in one is likely to appear in another.

Unfortunately this balance was always a fortuitous matter and always subject to extraneous pressure. In this case, it came about in a most unintentional fashion. Augustine, who made a fairly balanced use of these metaphors himself, as a result of the controversy with Pelagius pushed the church very strongly in the direction of looking at baptism as the remedy for two kinds of sin: original, i.e., the guilt we all inherit from Adam's sin; and actual, that which we get to commit ourselves.[31] It is a bit ironic that Augustine himself was not baptized until fairly late in life since the consequence of his systematic development of existing concepts of original sin was to hasten the baptism of infants for fear that children dying unbaptized would be brought by the guilt of original sin to the gates of hell.

The whole medieval development tilted emphasis in the direction of the forgiveness of sin, especially that of original sin in the case of infants. As we have seen, the Paschaltide portrayal of union to Christ was underplayed, while incorporation in the church, when that was equivalent to civil society itself, was of little account. The sense of new birth lost much of its drama when only infants were baptized. The teaching of the work of the Holy Spirit was undernourished in the West, and baptism was a good example of such malnutrition. Peter Lombard has much to say about baptism, but it all boils down to one word: "remission."[32] The forgiveness of sin is an important part of the biblical witness to initiation, but when it became so dominant that it crowded out the other themes we cannot but feel that a one-sided understanding of what God does in initiation had occurred.

One of the saddest of the medieval developments was in the understanding of confirmation. We have seen how this portion of initiation was split off in the West because of conservatism about limiting it to a bishop. Throughout its whole subsequent history, confirmation has been a practice looking for a theology. Peter Lombard could find very little to say about confirmation (two pages), but he said all the early medieval church had provided: "The virtue moreover of the sacrament is the gift of the holy Spirit for strength, who is given in baptism for remission." Lombard goes on to attribute to Rabanus the statement that one is strengthened through the laying on of hands "to proclaim to others that which he has attained in baptism."[33] Lombard also suggests that persons need confirmation "to be complete Christians." A sermon of the fifth-century Faustus of Riez had apparently first suggested the terminology that "after baptism we are confirmed for combat," leading "to confirm" to be identified with "to strengthen." These are the raw materials, and practically the only raw materials, the Scholastics had with which to build their systems.

The 1439 *Decree for the Armenians* sums up the late medieval development (or lack of it) by telling us: "In this sacrament the Holy Spirit is given to strengthen us, . . . that the Christian may confess boldly the name of Christ,"[34] The matter "is the chrism made from oil . . . and from balsam . . . blessed by the bishop. The form is: 'I sign thee with the sign of the cross and confirm thee with the chrism of salvation, in the name. . . .' " The normal ministrant is the bishop, though occasionally a priest can administer confirmation with chrism blessed by a bishop. Shorn of connection to baptism, confirmation became a dangling participle.

By contrast, Lombard has much to say about reconciliation (seventy pages), indicating great development in the frequent use of this sacrament by all. Most important, he tells us "that by penance not only once, but often, we rise from our sins. . . . True penance may be done repeatedly."[35] The process of reconciliation, which Lombard discusses in detail, is summed up by the Council of Florence as involving as the matter three acts of penitence: "contrition of the heart . . . confession with the mouth . . . [and] satisfaction for sins . . . chiefly by prayer, fasting, and almsgiving." The form was the words of the priest (the minister of this sacrament): "I absolve you."[36]

By the time of the Reformation, baptism, confirmation, and first communion had become completely detached entities. The Council of Trent simply solidified late medieval practices and beliefs. Baptism was not a major point of controversy between Protestants and Roman Catholics, though a lively debate developed within Protestantism over it. The Reformers do not sift out conveniently on our five New Testament metaphors of initiation, though we can point out certain centers of gravity among them. The fear that infants dying unbaptized could not be saved troubled them less, so that forgiveness of sins tended to recede from dominance. But new considerations, such as the doctrine of election, brought new pressures.

Luther shows some of the most profound insights, insights that still have not yet been fully appropriated. Luther's special stress is on baptism as a "promise" in which, as he says, "Christ is given us." What ensues is a lifelong covenant relationship of faith whereby our baptism is victorious over doubt and sin, for "baptism is in force all through life." Indeed, in moments of deepest despair Luther could assert that "I am baptized, and through my baptism God, who cannot lie, has bound himself in a covenant with me."[37] And, in a famous line, he exclaims: "There is no greater comfort on earth than baptism."[38] Luther suggests the possibility of looking at the Christian life as a baptismal spirituality, i.e., as a lifelong living out of one's baptism. Luther probably comes closer to stressing union with Jesus Christ than any of the other biblical themes.

Zwingli introduced a new concept altogether: that baptism is merely a dedicatory sign. He based his argument on the Romans 6:3-5 passage, which he interprets figuratively. Baptism, for Zwingli too, is union with Christ; but he is leery of physical signs, for "it is clear and indisputable that no external element or action can purify the soul." "Hence," he concludes, "water-baptism is nothing but an external ceremony, that is, an outward sign that we are incorprorated and engrafted into the Lord Jesus Christ and pledged to live to him and to follow him."[39] Zwingli's concept of baptism as dedication, as pledge, or as covenant sign, tends to make of it an external matter of record rather than the source of a warm inward relationship, as in Luther.

Calvin deplores Zwingli's view of baptism as a "token or mark" of profession. Calvin stresses baptism's power to save through forgiveness or cleansing and union to Christ. But the predominant metaphor for him seems to be that of being "received into the society of the church, in order that, engrafted in Christ, we may be reckoned among God's children."[40] He is concerned to refute the Anabaptist critique of infant baptism. Infants too, Calvin insists, are within the covenant and members of the church.

The Anabaptists, of course, insisted that since "young children are without understanding and unteachable; therefore baptism cannot be administered to them without perverting the ordinance of the Lord, misusing His exalted name, and doing violence to His holy Word."[41] Clearly, for them, baptism was to be contingent upon human faith and repentance. Only those already reborn could join the baptismal covenant. Though their concept of the church is quite different from Calvin's, incorporation into the company of regenerate believers is probably their dominant theme. For many of them, baptism involved not only water and Spirit but their own blood of suffering and martyrdom (I John 5:6-8). They taught and lived as if all of life were a baptism.

The Anglican prayers in the 1549 and 1552 baptismal services achieved a remarkably good balance of the biblical metaphors partly because they tend to collect biblical images. The Articles of Religion called baptism "a sign of Regeneration or new Birth," a phrase that caused controversy in the nineteenth century as to whether baptism caused or signified regeneration. Anglicans retained confirmation, but by 1552 it had become more a rite of praying for strengthening than an objective conferring of grace.

The Free Church tradition was split between Anabaptist and Reformed understandings of baptism. None confused baptism with election; but the degree to which the elect were visible as a small select company of baptized saints, or as those known only to God within a baptized civil community, was a subject of much dispute.

John Wesley added further complications by placing an emphasis on **conversion** as a necessary part of the Christian life even after baptism. For reasons not clear, he omitted confirmation while retaining most of the Anglican rites of baptism. Nineteenth-century Methodists instituted a service of reception into the church for those already baptized.

Reconciliation as a sacrament disappeared in all the Reformation churches, though penitential elements became a conspicuous part of Sunday worship. With all its shortcomings, the medieval practice of penance did enable men and women to live life with the concrete assurance that God had truly acted to forgive them when they had been truly contrite, confessed to a priest, and performed works of satisfaction. The Reformation brought the sense that all Christians could exercise a priestly role to one another in confessing and pardoning one another. But often where power is available to all, it is exercised by none. All Protestant traditions found standards of discipline and judgment necessary, though means of enforcement varied. Calvin tied the disciplinary action of **fencing the tables** (i.e., excluding notorious sinners, I Cor. 11:27) to the eucharist, and Wesley demanded communion tickets from his class members. Both practices placed an undue disciplinary burden on the eucharist.

The recent past has seen some important developments in efforts to understand Christian initiation as it became the center of much controversy and, hopefully, some enlightenment. Two areas have stood out as storm centers: Who is a proper candidate for baptism? and, What is the relation of baptism to confirmation?

The first of these storms was stirred up by a lecture given by **Karl Barth** to Swiss theological students in 1943 and first published in English five years later as *The Teaching of the Church Regarding Baptism.* In it, Barth contended that infant baptism "is necessarily clouded baptism" and that only adults capable of understanding the event should receive baptism. Essentially Barth's approach was a cognitive one; baptism is a "representation" or "message" to the one baptized.[42] By contrast, Barth's leading opponent, **Oscar Cullmann,** replied that baptism is causative in that it places a person within the community where faith becomes a possibility rather than simply informing that person of something. Cullmann insisted that potentially Christ has died for all and that this possibility is actualized when one is incorporated into the church and receives the possibility of growing up in a faith environment.[43]

The fray was also joined on strictly historical grounds by two New Testament scholars, Joachim Jeremias and Kurt Aland.[44] The debate goes on, with everyone from Baptists to Roman Catholics expressing doubts over their own practices and teachings. Baptists have misgivings about treating children as outside the church; Roman Catholics fear that all too often many baptized children never become part of the church's life.

Much of the debate over baptism of infants vs. believer's alone seems to be a superficial shortcut around more basic questions as to the nature of a sacrament. If a sacrament is a self-giving act of God, then surely infants or anyone else can receive its benefits. If, on the other hand, we are speaking of an ordinance that is only a high-level bit of religious education, a pious memory exercise or representation, then it could be appropriate only to a person who has reached the age of reason. Thus most pedobaptists and those who practice only believer's baptism can never agree because they are discussing from two entirely different concepts of the sacraments, whether it be with regard to infant baptism, infant confirmation, or infant communion.

The other debate was sparked by a lecture **Gregory Dix** gave in Oxford in 1946 and published as *The Theology of Confirmation in Relation to Baptism.* Dix deplored the attribution to baptism of the giving of the Holy Spirit, which, he claimed, downgraded what applied in the earliest church to the act of sealing with the Spirit "for which 'Baptism in water' is only a preliminary."[45] To this extreme view, G. W. H. Lampe replied with an equally one-sided emphasis on water baptism in *The Seal of the Spirit.* Lampe argued that Dix had split the Holy Spirit in a way unbiblical and untrue to the practice of the early church.[46] The upshot of this debate has been a gradual swing to affirming the unity of initiation. The practical question rises when confirmation is postponed from baptism as to what is confirmation's proper age: seven, twelve, eighteen, or even later?

Practical questions cannot be settled apart from study of the whole issue: What is initiation itself? Here the chief way forward seems to be by recovering the richness of all the biblical images with a clear sense of balance. Initiation is forgiveness of sin, but it is also incorporation into the church and other themes as well. The new initiatory rites are hopeful signs that this biblical balance is being recovered.

Thought about reconciliation is much less sophisticated in Protestantism, but recent excitement in Roman Catholicism has begun to spill over. Much reflection remains yet to be done. In the future, some forms of public reconciliation may have widespread appeal in Protestantism. Then the eucharist can be liberated from the burden of also having to be a penitential office.

III

Numerous pastoral possibilities arise out of the current ferment in initiation rites and theology. We shall mention three prime practical concerns. First and foremost is that initiation is **evangelism.** This was obvious to the early church, which grew by initiation. It is a lesson the modern church has been slow to learn despite the great missionary expansion of the last few centuries. But now the experiences of the church outside Western civilization has reached lands once considered thoroughly Christian. Initiation is how the church grows.

There are several practical implications from this. Initiation must cease to be "promiscuous," i.e., unrestricted and indiscriminate. Strangers who call to have the baby "done," or unfamiliar people who troop down the aisle for "walk-in" baptisms must be politely told that the pastor will be glad to call on them to begin the process of initiation. At least, pastoral visitation with parents or prospective candidates must always precede baptism, and such often could accomplish much afterward, too. For the unbelieving parents, it means that the church has to say no; but in the process of calling and explaining the demands of initiation the pastor has perhaps the only opportunity for witnessing to what Christians believe. For the adult inquirer, it means enrollment in some kind of catechumenate. Hippolytus' three-year catechumenate was a bit rigorous, but those who had been through it were willing to die (and frequently did) for their faith. The new (and very old) Roman Catholic "Rite of Christian Initiation of Adults" is worth serious study by all Christians. Not only does it give the inquirer the full support of the community during his or her growth toward full incorporation, but it also causes the congregation to reexamine the basis of its own faith.

Baptizing and teaching belong together (Matt. 28:19-20). The church year gives opportunities to preach on the meaning of initiation, especially at the Baptism of the Lord, Easter, and Pentecost. It is no wonder that most Christians are confused about initiation; they have never had any kind of mystagogical catechesis to explain it to them. But they deserve to know more, so that, whenever they serve as witnesses to initiation, they can be put in mind of what God has already done for them. Baptism builds up the church from within as well as from without. For mature initiates, the catechumenate would seem to be a crucial form of evangelism.

The second point is the importance of the **sign-value** of what is done in initiation. Initiation is basically actions; something happens for which words alone cannot suffice. The actions must be allowed to speak and not be muffled by indifference or lack of sensitivity to their sign value.

Initiation is a communal act; and the community must be present, for the whole congregation is a sponsor. How can one marry by proxy without losing much that is meaningful? How can one be engrafted into the body when the community is absent? Methodists and the Free Church tradition have usually been careful to make initiation a part of Sunday worship with the whole congregation present. Other traditions are now moving in this direction. The community itself is the foremost sign of incorporation, not a vacant church building.

Baptism is washing. It is a highly tactile act that demands that water be seen, heard, and (in effect) felt by the whole congregation. Under present practices, in many Roman Catholic and Protestant congregations, that would be to expect a miracle. Both the facilities and practices in most churches that do not immerse are defective. Baptism often looks more like a dry run than a vigorous cleansing, and it has been lampooned as "dry cleaning." If one's only concern is validity, then a teaspoonful of water is enough. But if one's concern is to communicate the life-giving flood in which God acts, then a tubful communicates better. Obviously this means that baptismal bowls are insufficient and that most modern fonts will not do. Medieval and post-Reformation fonts were large enough for dipping a baby. That was the mode Luther clearly preferred, that the Church of England's rubric has always specified (though ignored for two hundred years), and that the new Roman Catholic and Episcopal rites suggest first. But it does imply facilities and practice different from those that most pedobaptist churches now have.

If our concern is to show forth by actions what God does, then sprinkling with a few drops of water is most insufficient (unless we have a very anemic doctrine of God). Pouring is somewhat better if the water can be seen and heard. Dipping (infants) or immersing (children and adults) is clearly best. If we are willing to let the act speak for itself, we will not bury it under verbiage but will actually wash people. Above all, we will avoid making it an act of Christian cuteness; the center is God, not the baby.

The laying on of hands or anointing are dramatic actions that must be allowed to make their own witness. They should be made as personal as possible with the use of the Christian names of all those involved. Each candidate should be touched individually. When the entire congregation participates in baptismal renewal, sprinkling of the whole congregation is greatly to be desired. In no way a repetition of baptism, renewal is a vivid recalling of what God has already done for us in baptism. Once a year is frequent enough, but services of renewal or reaffirmation have been widely appreciated in recent years.

The third point is the need to make visible the **unity of the whole process of initiation.** Ideally all portions of the rites ought to be performed at the same time on Sundays or at Easter in the midst of the congregation as the new Episcopal and United Methodist rites suggest. In churches with bishops, when possible, the bishop can be the minister of the whole integrated rite, thus clearly manifesting the universal church.

Baptism, the laying on of hands, and first communion ought to come together. Anything that implies halfway membership or preparatory membership is a contradiction in terms. When God acts, it is not halfway or preparatory. God's acts are unqualified self-giving. We may reject them eventually, but God remains faithful to God's promise of acceptance offered to us in initiation. The unity of the initiatory rites should witness to this. Certainly baptism and the eucharist belong together. The early church was right in understanding the eucharist as the only part of initiation that is repeated. Those who have received baptism and the laying on of hands or anointing ought immediately to be welcomed to the Lord's table, no matter at what age they have come. If anyone is old enough to become a part of the Lord's body, he or she is old enough to be welcome at the Lord's table.

As practices of corporate reconciliation develop, creative imaginations will be needed to help in examination of conscience (both individual and social), to proclaim God's mercy, and to praise God accordingly. The reforms underway in Roman Catholicism can be suggestive of possibilities, but this is an area demanding creativity, such as a visual litany (slides and response), to help us recall what we have or have not done and to proclaim what God promises.

VII
The Eucharist

The eucharist is the most characteristic structure of Christian worship. It is also the most widely used form of worship among Christians, being celebrated daily and weekly in millions of congregations and communities all over the world. In chapter 4, we examined the ministry of the Word, which, since early times, has formed the first half of the eucharist. We now turn to the second half, the acted sign.

Various groups use a variety of names for both halves combined: "eucharist" (i.e., thanksgiving), or "Lord's Supper" (I Cor. 11:20), "breaking of bread" (Acts 2:46; 20:7), "divine liturgy," "mass," "holy communion," and "Lord's memorial." The second half by itself is also sometimes called the "eucharist," or "mass of the faithful," "offering of sacrifice" (Tertullian), "service of the table," "sacrifice," "the holy," "the Lord's," "offering," or "anaphora" (in a broad sense). Ever since the end of the first century, the term "eucharist" has been used. It is the most descriptive term available and the one we shall use most frequently.

Whatever the name, the content throughout Christianity is the same: a sacred meal based on Jesus' actions at the Last Supper. Despite all the diversity in practice throughout the Christian world, there is also remarkable constancy in the form that the rite takes. All churches profess loyalty to following what the writers of the New Testament interpreted to be Jesus' words, actions, and intentions.

The widespread similarity in eucharistic practice throughout Christianity witnesses to the imprint Jesus left on this type of worship. No wonder, then, that despite strong Jewish roots, the eucharist is the most characteristic form of Christian worship. The eucharist bears the authority of direct connection with the Savior himself.

In this chapter, we shall examine very quickly the eucharistic practices of Christians across time, their understanding of what they experience in their eucharistic celebrations, and the consequences for pastoral action of this information. There is much to cover, so we may not linger long over any topic, however important, but can only sketch the bare outlines of historical, theological, and practical matters.

I

Nowhere else are the Jewish roots of Christian worship so important—or so complicated—as in regard to the eucharist. Every type of Jewish public worship made a contribution to the Christian eucharist almost as if Jesus and his followers had deliberately sought to build on the foundations the Jewish people had laid. We now realize that whenever these Jewish foundations have been forgotten, the eucharist has been distorted in practice and misunderstood in experience. An understanding of the Jewish contribution can hold Christians true to their own eucharist. Three locations for Jewish worship are particularly important in this regard: the temple cult, synagogue worship, and family meals.

From the seventh century B.C. on, Jewish **sacrificial worship** had been nationalized in the **Jerusalem temple.** The whole sacrificial cultus had developed as a means of relating to God as a nation and achieving communion with God as individuals. Sacrifice was a way of life, and the daily morning and evening sacrifices of the temple (Exod. 29:38-39) were remembered in the prayers of devout Jews everywhere. Sacrificial imagery is picked up in the narratives of the institution of the Lord's

Supper ("blood of the covenant, shed for many") and recurs throughout the New Testament, especially in Hebrews.

Psalms sung daily in temple worship became part of the eucharist. Conspicuous examples are the entrance song, "I shall come to the altar of God, the God of my joy, . . . thou God of my delight" (Ps. 43:4) and the *Benedictus qui venit,* "Blessed is he who comes in the name of the Lord" (derived from Ps. 118:26). And responsorial psalmody forms an important part of the Christian ministry of the Word.

We have already seen how the **synagogue** service evolved into the liturgy of the hours and ministry of the Word, but its contribution does not end even with all that. Synagogue worship involved prayer, prayer that came to have a specific form and content. The form was that of blessing God for what God had done, especially as narrated in the readings. Blessing God and thanking God are equivalent terms. The Christian term *eucharistía* simply translates the Jewish term *berakah,* or thanksgiving, in the synagogue prayers for what God has done. This means that the contents of such prayers are largely a recital of the *mirabilia Dei,* God's mighty acts for God's people. The *berakah* is basically a thankful response to what is narrated in the word of God. Such prayers have a creedal function. God is blessed by reciting those acts one wishes to recall, thus making prayer also a form of proclamation.

It is only a natural evolution to turn from those works of God already accomplished to beseeching God to bring about those yet hoped for in the future: "restore thy Shekinah into Zion thy city, and the order of worship into Jerusalem" (after A.D. 70). Supplication for further mighty works is the sequel to proclamation of what God already has done. Much of the form and content of synagogue prayers was simply adopted as the pattern for Christian eucharistic prayer, especially the sense of blessing (thanking) God through creedal prayer.

The same understanding of prayer as thanksgiving also appeared during **family meals,** but there actions were equally important. The Last Supper was obviously a sacred meal, but so were all those many other meals which Jesus shared with his disciples. Each Jewish meal is a holy event shared only with family or close friends. If the Last Supper was the Passover meal, as the Synoptic Gospels insist, Jesus was transforming the most solemn occasion of the Jewish year (the festival when the Jews hoped and prayed the Messiah would appear). Jesus used the specified words and actions of a familiar pattern to state that the Messiah had come indeed. Jews, who do not agree the Messiah had come, continue to perform the Passover **Seder** (sacred meal) to this day; Christians, who agree that Jesus was the Messiah, celebrate the eucharist instead.

Jesus deliberately used the climactic occasion of the Jewish year to establish the new covenant, but he did it in terms of the old worship. According to the Synoptics, at the Last Supper Jesus followed the conventional reenactment of the original Passover meal as commemoration of deliverance from captivity in Egypt. It is a liberation saga, mandated in Exodus 12:25-27. Normally, children ask: "What is the meaning of this rite?" (vs. 26). Replies of interpretation (*haggadah*) are given. This is the model for the words with which Jesus instituted the eucharist. But just as important are the actions: special food is eaten, bread is broken, and cups of wine are shared at the Passover. Words and significant acts help recover the saving power of God's acts culminating in the great event of liberation and help people look forward to God's future works of deliverance. Throughout, God is blessed for past events, once again made present in their ability to save, and implored to confer future benefits. Eating and drinking, thankful remembering and anticipating, all go together.

The New Testament gives several accounts of the institution of the eucharist plus fleeting glimpses of it as celebrated in Jerusalem, Troas, and Corinth. There are also stories of meals of Jesus, his disciples, and multitudes before the resurrection and of Jesus with his disciples after the resurrection.

Two parallel sets of institution narratives appear in the New Testament: Mark 14:22-25 and Matthew 26:26-29, which are quite similar, and I Corinthians 11:23-26 and Luke 22:15-20, with strong similarities. The Lucan account is unique (in some texts) in mentioning two cups. The slight differences between the accounts may be explained by the theory that what we have in these texts is a description of what was being said and done by several churches in different places when celebrating the eucharist. They all would have understood themselves as following the intentions, words, and actions of the Lord himself at the Last Supper. The churches, after all, had been celebrating the supper from Pentecost onward, long before any written accounts had been made. Thus our links from the Last Supper itself to the narratives of its institution are actual eucharistic celebrations. Even so, Joachim Jeremias is of the opinion that one can come close to discerning the eucharistic words of Jesus himself. Jeremias considers the Marcan account the closest with the most likely wording resembling:

> This is my body / my flesh
> my blood of the covenant
> the covenant in my blood
> which . . . for many[1]

The **words of institution** have important dimensions. In their context, they are sacrificial in speaking of a covenant made in blood. All accounts, especially the Lucan, are oriented in an eschatological direction (as was the Passover itself) in looking forward to the coming kingdom of God. In giving interpretations, albeit new and shocking interpretations, to the food and actions of the meal, Jesus simply was following convention. Jeremias believes that Jesus' word about not eating (Luke 22:16) is in the form of a vow (such as Paul's attackers take in Acts 23:12) and indicates that Jesus did not partake himself. A key word in the Pauline and Lucan accounts is *anámnesis*. No single English word conveys its full meaning; remembrance, recalling, re-presentation, experiencing anew are all weak approximations. The sense in which *anámnesis* is used expresses that in doing these actions, one experiences once again the reality of Jesus himself.

The actions of institution are no less important than the words. **Gregory Dix** made much of **four actions** that form the basic "shape of the liturgy."[2] Mark 14:22 reads: "He *took* bread, and having *said the blessing* he *broke* it and *gave* it to them." The same actions are used over the cup, except there is no breaking. The same actions occur elsewhere, as in the miracle of the five loaves and two fish (Mark 6:41), the Emmaus road account (Luke 24:30), and even among a shipload of pagans (Acts 27:35). The foods used at the Passover meal involved symbolic actions as well as utilitarian ones (dipping in bitter herbs, eating unleavened bread). Dix's most lasting contribution has been to remind us that the eucharist is basically action. He considered four actions central: taking, giving thanks (blessing), breaking, and giving. Of these four, the giving of thanks and the giving of bread and wine are now seen as the more significant.

John's Gospel does not give details of the actual meal at the Last Supper except for words exchanged with Judas. It does give, however, a unique description of another sign-activity, the **foot washing** (John 13:3-17). Apparently the early church understood this not as an imperative but as an acted parable. The action of foot washing became part of the initiation rite in Milan and eventually part of the Maundy Thursday observance elsewhere. But we have no evidence for it as apostolic practice. In the eighteenth century, "feetwashing" became an important observance for the Church of the Brethren.[3]

The dating of the Last Supper is an unresolved controversy. The Synoptic Gospels present the Last Supper as the Passover meal, whereas John says "it was before the Passover festival" (13:1), or on the day (beginning with nightfall) on which the lambs were slaughtered (cf. also 18:28). In John's chronology, the sacrifice of the lambs coincides with the crucifixion. Probably the majority of New Testament scholars follow the Johannine dating of the Last Supper on the evening before the Passover, though many others present the Last Supper as the Passover meal. For this author, given John's propensity for symbolism, it does not seem unlikely that he could have combined the sacrifice of the lambs and the crucifixion for symbolic effect.[4] Accordingly, we have followed the Synoptics and presented the Last Supper as the Passover meal. In any event, climactic events of Christ's passion and death occur in the context of the Passover festival and are heavily colored by its significance of past deliverance from captivity through blood and anticipation of future liberation by divine action.

The insights the New Testament gives us of first-century eucharists are brief. Acts 2:46 speaks of the Jerusalem Church as "breaking bread in private houses, [they] shared their meals with unaffected joy [literally, with glad and generous hearts]." A phrase in Paul's stern warning to First Church, Corinth, against unworthy partaking of the "Lord's Supper" links the eucharist to proclaiming "the death of the Lord, until he comes" (I Cor. 11:26). Paul threatens those guilty of eating and drinking unworthily, i.e., without discerning the Lord's body in the community, with sickness and death. Some scholars have tried to discover two kinds of eucharist in the New Testament and early Christian literature, a joyful and a somber type.[5] These theories now seem highly unlikely, for the death of the Lord is both a sobering thought and yet a source of joy.

We catch a fleeting view of another eucharist as Paul prepared to leave Troas (Acts 20:7-12), where Eutychus slept through even Paul's preaching; but we learn little else about the eucharist itself. A unique reference occurs in the Epistle of Jude, where there appear to be problems similar to those in Corinth. "These men are a blot on your love-feasts [*agápais*], where they eat and drink without reverence" (verse 12). The *agape,* or love **feast,** apparently was a full meal. Hippolytus goes to pains to distinguish it from the Lord's Supper. At what time the Lord's Supper stopped being a full meal is unknown; apparently one could still be a glutton and a drunkard when Paul wrote. There is slight evidence in an early (*c.* A.D. 112) letter from Pliny in Bithynia to the Emperor Trajan that can be interpreted to mean that Christians in Bithynia were accustomed to an early Sunday morning eucharist and an *agape* in the evening but gave up the *agape* under persecution. For Hippolytus, the *agape* was an occasional church supper put on by private benefactors with clergy present. Leftovers were sent to the poor. Too easily the *agape* degenerated into abuse and was proscribed by councils from the fourth century on. Possibly the distribution of blessed (but not eucharistic) bread, the **antidoron,** distributed after the liturgy in Eastern Orthodox churches, may be a survival. The love feast was revived among eighteenth-century Brethren, Mennonites, and Moravians and still flourishes.[6] John Wesley borrowed the practice and introduced it into Methodism in 1738. The *agape* has been used ecumenically in recent years when a eucharist is not feasible.

It is tempting to read back into the New Testament period the information we have on eucharistic practices in following centuries. Yet this is risky, and we must admit that our knowledge of the first-century eucharist is very limited. Much more evidence appears in the second and third centuries. The *Didache* may contain prayers from either a eucharist or an *agape*. It includes a strict warning about not giving communion to the unbaptized, instructions to be reconciled to one's neighbor before the sacrifice (Matt. 5:23-24), and a famous line: "As this piece [of bread] was scattered over the hills and then was brought together and made one, so let your Church be brought together from the ends of the earth into your Kingdom."[7] This and a subsequent phrase have a strong eschatological flavor. Prophets, we are told, may give thanks in their own way. The *Didache* (14) and Justin's *Dialogue with Trypho* (41) quote Malachi 1:11 on a "pure sacrifice" and specifically refer to the eucharist in sacrificial language.

In Justin's *First Apology* we find our first outline of the eucharist. In one case it follows a baptism but ordinarily would come after the ministry of the Word:

On finishing the prayers [petition and intercession] we greet each other with a kiss. Then bread and a cup of water and mixed wine are brought to the president of the brethren and he, taking them, sends up praise and glory to the Father of the universe through the name of the Son and of the Holy Spirit, and offers thanksgiving at some length that we have been deemed worthy to receive these things from him. . . . When the president has given thanks and the whole congregation has assented [with an "amen"], those whom we call deacons give to each of those present a portion of the consecrated [literally, "eucharistized"] bread and wine and water, and they take it to the absent.[8]

The **kiss of peace** (Rom. 16:16; I Pet. 5:14) is a warm sign of love and unity that concludes the intercessions and bridges to the offertory (as in chapter 14 of the *Didache*), a position it retains in the East but lost in the West until recently. Apparently the wording of the prayer by the president (bishop or presiding presbyter) is still fluid at this stage. Justin, in his second account (chapter 67), tells us the president "sends up prayers and thanksgivings to the best of his ability." The mixture of water and wine Cyprian explains (in Epistle 62) is a symbol of the unity of people (water) and the blood of Christ (wine). It probably was originally utilitarian. The deacons carry bread and wine to those sick and in prison, setting an early precedent for extended communion and eventually **reservation** of the consecrated elements in churches between eucharistic celebrations. A collection is also taken up for the benefit of the needy.

Our most important source of information about the early eucharist is, once again, our old friend, Hippolytus. This staunch reactionary, trying to stem liturgical experimentation in the third century, has sparked much innovation in the twentieth. His wording (chapter 4) of the eucharistic prayer after the ordination of a bishop has been widely copied by Protestants and Roman Catholics alike. It is the basic source for Roman Catholic Eucharistic Prayer II (Sac, 510-13). Readers are advised to study Hippolytus' text to accompany the following discussion.[9]

As soon as a new bishop is ordained, Hippolytus tells us, all offer him the kiss of peace. Then deacons bring the offering (bread and wine); and the bishop, "laying his hands on it, with all the presbytery,"[10] begins the thanksgiving. Deacons bring the offering, but the presbyters share (here silently) in the prayer, a practice known as **concelebration.** The **great thanksgiving (eucharistic prayer, canon, anaphora, prayer of consecration)** begins with a dialogue between chief celebrant and the congregation. The dialogue includes the *Sursum Corda*—"Lift up your hearts"—and invites the congregation to join in the thanksgiving, which the bishop speaks. This is the way almost every eucharistic prayer still begins. All share in it, though one expresses the words.

Most subsequent liturgies turn next to the *Sanctus* ("Holy, holy, holy") based on Isaiah 6:3 and Revelation 4:8. Hippolytus does not mention the *Sanctus* either because it was not in use, occurred elsewhere, or he did not consider it necessary to mention. The **post-***Sanctus* continues thanksgiving for what God has done in Jesus Christ, recites Christ's works, and concludes this section with the words of institution. Then a section known as the *anámnesis*-**oblation** summarizes what is being recalled and offers the bread and cup to God. Hippolytus' final portion is an invocation of the Holy Spirit, or *epiclesis*, in which the Holy Spirit is invoked to make fruitful the communion of those who partake. Other rites often have either a consecratory *epiclesis* (usually before the words of institution), or a communion *epiclesis* after the *anámnesis*-oblation (like Hippolytus), or both. Hippolytus cites benefits desired from the Holy Spirit. It is a short step from this to **intercessions** for others, both living and dead, just as synagogue prayers had easily moved from thanksgiving by recital to supplication for further divine action. Hippolytus had not moved in that direction but it was a natural development that soon followed. The whole prayer then concludes with a trinitarian **doxology** and **amen.**

Now why is all this so important? What Hippolytus gives us is the prototype of the central prayer of the central act of Christian worship. The eucharistic prayer was in his time and for several centuries afterward the most common theological statement of the Christian faith. In thanking God, the church followed the Jewish custom of summing up its faith in what God had done. The prayer is largely a recital of the *mirabilia Dei,* God's saving acts. It is proclamation and creed rolled into one. The structure is basically trinitarian: thanking God the Father, commemorating before God the Father the works of God the Son, and invoking God the Father to send God the Holy Spirit. The whole is then concluded with a doxology praising all three members of the Trinity. The form is thoroughly Jewish: praising God by recital of God's past acts and invoking their continuation. The contents are thoroughly Christian: the recalling of what God has done in Jesus Christ and continues to do through the Holy Spirit.

The ability to lead in this central prayer demanded a person who could faithfully represent the beliefs of the Christian community. Hippolytus even says that "it is not at all necessary to recite the same words we have proscribed . . . in giving thanks to God, but let each one pray according to his ability, . . . only let him pray what is sound doctrine (*orthodoxia*)."[11] One of the most important functions of the ordained ministry is the ability of presbyters and bishops to sum up the faith of the church and proclaim it in prayer. No wonder Ignatius limited the celebration of the eucharist to being "by the bishop or by someone he authorizes."[12] Each such pastor is a theologian for the congregation. To such pastors is entrusted the statement of the community's faith through its supreme expression, eucharistic prayer.

Slight changes occurred after Hippolytus in the eucharistic prayer, chiefly in an expansion of the words calling to give thanks after the *Sursum Corda*. This is called the **preface** and is a beginning of the recital of thanks. In the West, it could vary according to the season or occasion and formed a **variable preface.** In Eastern rites and some Protestant rites it is fixed and unchanging. The *Sanctus* comes next and often the *Benedictus qui venit*—"Blessed is he who comes in the name of the Lord" (Ps. 118:26; Matt. 21:9). In some rites, a **preliminary epiclesis** occurs in the early part of the post-*Sanctus*. The final *epiclesis* can give way to quite extended intercession. Like Hippolytus, Protestant rites, in general, have avoided the preliminary *epiclesis* and the intercessions. Once one has mastered the basic form of eucharistic prayers, it is possible to improvise them in as many different ways as one can write sonnets in the specified form. The usual form of eucharistic prayers includes:

> dialogue
> preface
> *Sanctus*
> post-*Sanctus* (and preliminary *epiclesis*)
> words of institution
> *anámnesis*-oblation
> *epiclesis* (and intercessions)
> doxology
> Amen

But, as Hippolytus hints, not all "have the ability of praying at length in solemn form." Shortly we begin to find more or less fixed texts coming into use. One of the earliest comes from the hand of **Sarapion,** bishop of Thmuis, Egypt, about the middle of the fourth century. The most distinctive element is an *epiclesis* directed to the second member of the Trinity.[13] A generation later came a very lengthy text in book 8 of the *Apostolic Constitutions.* Though probably never actually used, it represents the victory of prescribed forms over the freedom expressed by the *Didache* and Justin.

Hippolytus' ordination eucharist contains rather obscure references to the offering and to giving thanks over oil, cheese, and olives. In his Paschal eucharist (chapters 23 and 21), milk and honey, water (symbols of baptism) and wine are given after the bishop has broken the bread (the **fraction**) and distributed the fragments with the words: "The bread of heaven in Christ Jesus." The three chalices are given with a trinitarian form to which each recipient responds, "Amen." The service ends abruptly as all leave and "each one hastens to do good."

In the post-Nicene era a variety of **liturgical families** came to light scattered around the perimeter of the Mediterranean. All have common characteristics. By the sixth century the ministry of the Word and the eucharist had been wed for the next millennium. The fourfold actions, foreshadowed in the New Testament accounts, in Dix's famous words, "constituted the absolutely invariable nucleus of every eucharistic rite known to us throughout antiquity."[14] However much the actual words vary, the basic contents of the second of these acts—the giving of thanks or eucharistic prayer—likewise evince remarkably similar functions. But in the fourth, fifth, and sixth centuries, important divergences in style and wording appear, witnessing to the diversity of peoples yet retaining constancy of purpose. The comparative study of these is a vast science; we can only suggest here a little of the richness of diversity present by following these liturgical families around the Mediterranean in a counterclockwise direction.

The characteristic **Alexandrian** or Egyptian eucharistic prayer is typified by that named after **St. Mark,** who, tradition has it, ministered in Alexandria. In these rites, the preface often has a long recital of God's works of creation and redemption from the Old Testament (noticeably absent in much of the Western tradition of eucharistic prayer). This moves into intercession (including prayer for the rising of the Nile) and the diptychs (a list of those for whom offering is made, dead and living). Then follows the *Sanctus*. Characteristically the post-*Sanctus* picks up with: "Full in truth are heaven and earth." A consecratory *epiclesis* leads to the institution narrative. After the *anámnesis*-oblation comes another *epiclesis* dealing with both consecration and communion and then a concluding doxology.

Further East we encounter the Antiochene, or **West Syrian,** family with important documents centered in Antioch and Jerusalem and probably combined under the name of the liturgy of **St. James.** This is familiar to many as the source of the hymn text "Let all mortal flesh keep silence." Characteristic of this family is the preface with its celestial roll call. The post-*Sanctus* picks up on the word "holy" in a recital of old and new covenant works. Acclamations and amens by the people have recently been copied in the West. A long series of intercessions for the living and dead follows the *epiclesis*. Each petition begins "Remember, Lord." The language is florid, poetic, and never brief.

Easily the most puzzling family is the **East Syrian,** originating in Edessa as the liturgy of **Sts. Addai and Mari.** Isolated by heresy and Islam, it has continued in use relatively untouched by other influences. As such it has early roots, perhaps reflecting third-century practice in that region. The most controversial aspect is an apparent lack of words of institution, which would make it unique among Christian liturgies. The *epiclesis* comes last after the intercessions.

To the family of **St. Basil of Caesarea** in Asia Minor we owe an early version known as the Alexandrian Basil since it may have been brought to Egypt by Basil himself around A.D. 357. This has been widely admired in recent years and forms the basis for the ecumenical text, "The Common Eucharistic Prayer." A later version, probably revised by St. Basil himself, is filled out with more scriptural references. It is used by the Orthodox churches of the world on ten days of the year, chiefly in Lent. Structurally both versions are of the Antiochene type, but the latter St. Basil has developed a detailed post-*Sanctus* recital of creation, fall, and redemption.

Somewhat dependent upon it is the liturgy of **St. John Chrysostom,** or the **Byzantine** liturgy, the second most widely and frequently used eucharistic rite in the world today. It, too, reflects Antiochene structure. St. John Chrysostom had been bishop in Antioch at the end of the fourth century. The post-*Sanctus* and intercessions are relatively short, and the whole prayer appears concise in comparison with most of those already mentioned.

Turning westward, we momentarily pass over the Roman family to note an assortment of Non-Roman Western rites known collectively as **Gallic** and subdivided into **Ambrosian** (or Milanese), **Mozarabic** (from Spain), **Celtic** (originating in Ireland but scattered where Celtic missionaries traveled), and **Gallican** in the narrow sense of Frankish-German. There are connections between these rites and those of the East, though the exact derivation is uncertain. The Ambrosian rite is still in use in the Archdiocese of Milan, and the Mozarabic in one chapel in the Toledo Cathedral. A common characteristic is florid language and eucharistic prayers, which, except for the *Sanctus* and words of institution, change entirely according to the day or season.

For two centuries following Hippolytus, there is a blackout of material regarding the **Roman rite,** though Ambrose foreshadows much that emerges in Rome and the few surviving North African fragments show some similarities. The mists lift in Rome when we discover several early **sacramentaries,** collections of the priest's prayers for the various masses of the year including initiation and ordinations, and various **ordines,** collections of rubrics. Of the oldest sacramentaries, the **Leonian** has preserved proper prayers from more than three hundred masses, many of which may actually go back to Pope Leo I (440–461). The older version of the **Gelasian** may contain opening prayers and prefaces shaped by Pope Gelasius I (492–496), who seems to have polished the canon itself. The **Gregorian** was named for Pope Gregory I (590–604), who presided over various reforms in the Roman rite and anchored the **Lord's Prayer** at the end of the canon.

Various sacramentaries were in circulation in the early

medieval West. Charlemagne sought standardization for purposes of imperial unity and requested a copy of an authentic Roman sacramentary. Pope Hadrian I transmitted one to imperial headquarters at Aachen. But it turned out to be drastically incomplete for parochial purposes. One of Charlemagne's ecclesiastical advisers, probably Benedict of Aniane, added a "Supplement" of materials drawn from the various Gallican rites then in use throughout the Empire. Any distinction between the mandatory official rites and the optional "Supplement" soon eroded, and the two were conflated. Two centuries later, the combined sacramentary was brought to Rome and imposed on Rome itself by Germanic emperors. Consequently, the Roman rite assimilated a variety of Gallican propers including additional **prayers over the gifts,** prefaces, and **prayers after communion.** These complemented those developed in Rome previously. In the West, by the fifth century the kiss of peace had been relocated after the eucharistic prayer.

Throughout the Middle Ages, the eucharistic prayer remained stable. But increasingly it and the other central action, the giving of bread and wine, were surrounded by subjective **apologies** for the unworthiness of clergy and people. These tended to be penitential and introspective in tone. Accessory actions, such as censing the altar-table and washing the hands of the priest, joined private prayers of the celebrant at the offertory. The *Agnus Dei* was introduced in the late seventh century at the fraction and **commingling** (mixing a particle of bread in the wine, a remnant of a symbol of unity of the pope and churches of his diocese). Individualistic prayers surrounded the giving of bread and wine. The **ablutions** (ceremony of cleaning the vessels and hands of celebrant) developed as a reflection of late medieval scrupulosity about each drop and crumb of the consecrated elements. The late Middle Ages also added a last gospel (John 1:1-18), and modern popes attached a few concluding prayers. Both of these anticlimactic elements have disappeared since Vatican II.

The resulting Western development may be charted in simplified form, with those elements moved or removed in parentheses:

Hippolytus	Fourth to sixth centuries	Medieval
(kiss of peace) offertory		
		offertory prayers and ceremonies
	prayer over the gifts	
eucharistic prayer	preface, *Sanctus,* intercessions Lord's Prayer kiss of peace	
fraction		*Agnus Dei* commingling priest's prayers "Lord, I am not worthy"
giving bread and wine	communion song	
		silent prayer ablutions
	prayer after communion blessing with dismissal	
		(last gospel) (concluding prayers)

This is the structure the Reformers inherited. Long lost had been any grasp of the original function of the eucharistic prayer as the great thankful summation and proclamation of the church's faith. Inasmuch as this occurred at all, it had been relegated to the Creed as part of the ministry of the Word (in the West) or as a prelude to the *anaphora* (in the East). The medieval subjective devotions (which had crept in before and after the eucharistic prayer and the giving of bread and wine) became the minor that the Reformation majored in. The Anglican Prayer of Humble Access ("We do not presume to come to this thy Table") is a good example.

The **Reformers** did, however, take some very important positive steps, although none of them caught the ancient significance of the eucharistic prayer. They put the mass into the vernacular, simplified it, and tried valiantly to restore frequent communion (except Zwingli and the Anabaptists).

But for a laity accustomed to receive communion once a year, frequent communion proved too radical a departure to win widespread success.

Luther gave the strongest, if not the earliest, impetus to reforming the mass with his Latin rite, *Formula Missae* **of 1523** and his vernacular *Deutsche Messe* **of 1525.**[15] Luther is conservative until he comes to the canon—"that mangled and abominable thing gathered from much filth and scum"[16]— which he simply slashes down to the words of institution and *Sanctus.* In one stroke he out-medievalizes the Roman Catholic Church, which had located the moment of consecration at these words. Luther advocated the addition of vernacular hymnody. His German mass still retained much ceremony, including the elevation of bread and wine and instructions that the "German *Sanctus*" or other hymns be sung during the distribution of the bread and hymns or the *Agnus Dei* during the giving of the cup.

Zwingli's 1523 *Attack on the Canon of the Mass* substituted four of Zwingli's Latin prayers for the canon. In 1525 Zurich adopted his *Action or Use of the Lord's Supper,* which made Luther's reforms look tame. Gone were virtually all ceremonial and music as well. What remained was an austere commemoration and fellowship meal, practiced four times a year.

Martin Bucer's work in Strassburg underlies much of Calvin's liturgical efforts and with Zwingli's rite helped mold the Reformed eucharistic tradition. Bucer was anticipated in Strassburg by Diobald Schwarz, and Calvin in Geneva by Guillaume Farel. Calvin's *Form of Church Prayers,* **Geneva, 1542,** represents the work of his predecessors brought to a definitive shape for the Reformed tradition and transmitted through John Knox's *Forme of Prayers,* Geneva, 1556, to the English-speaking world. Characteristic of the Reformed tradition, the eucharist is excessively didactic and includes a reading of the words of institution outside the eucharistic prayer as a warrant for the eucharist's observance. The fencing of tables (reflecting I Cor. 11:27-32) forbade evil livers from communicating.

Practices varied greatly among the Anabaptists, some of whom had serious doubts about any sacrament. Extreme simplicity characterized their celebrations, elaborated only by a highly developed hymnody. Among the English Free Churches, fixed liturgies were by no means eschewed in the late sixteenth and early seventeenth centuries. But the *Westminster Directory* eventually substituted ordines for sacramentaries or rubrics for rites, though it outlined a model eucharistic prayer. The Quakers, of course, insisted on silent and inward feeding on Christ while avoiding outward ceremonial.

The 1549 Anglican BCP carried a vernacular communion rite that was very recognizably a conservative blending of the *Sarum* rite with Reformation theology. Much of the 1549 BCP's eucharistic theology was deliberately ambiguous, permitting both a Catholic and Protestant interpretation. Three years later this rite was replaced with one that removed most ambiguity and involved drastic restructuring. The canon was cut in two. The oblation was placed after communion so as to eliminate any traditional sense of sacrifice. Despite minor changes in 1559, 1604, and 1662, basically the 1552 rite is still in use in England, though an alternative is now near completion. The American prayer books (1789, 1892, 1928) have utilized a much richer Scottish eucharistic prayer.

John Wesley followed the 1662 BCP eucharistic rite in his *Sunday Service,* **1784,** abbreviating it only slightly. Wesley's two great contributions were a eucharistic revival with weekly celebrations and (with Charles Wesley) a magnificent collection of 166 eucharistic hymns. These contain a rich variety of sacrificial, eschatological, and pneumatological emphases, absent from Protestant eucharistic piety for many centuries. But neither Wesley's strong eucharistic discipline nor eucharistic hymns were cherished by his followers. An abbreviated form of his rite continued in use in America.

Pentecostalists vary greatly in the use or nonuse of set forms. They do concur that the Holy Spirit must be free to break into any pattern through spontaneous elements.

Recent tendencies are restoration of the practices of the ancient church. It is generally agreed that most of the medieval developments were distortions, although contemporaries may be as prone to romanticize the early church as Victorians were the medieval. Many of the changes have been the result of historical studies of comparative liturgiology. The results of such studies are made more appealing in the realization that the church in a post-Christian era has much in common with a pre-Constantinian church. The results of liturgical revision are so similar that in many cases it is often hard to tell which tradition has produced a eucharistic rite if the title page is lost.

Basic to most rites, ever since the Church of South India rite first appeared in 1950, is structuring around the fourfold actions of which Dix wrote. Rediscovery of the centrality of the eucharistic prayer as the church's supreme faith statement has spurred revision of existing ones and composition of new examples. American Lutherans recovered it in 1958. The eucharist itself is being observed more frequently in most Protestant churches advancing from quarterly celebrations to monthly, and then to weekly. The same process occurred among Anglicans in the past century.

A common development has been the move to a variety of eucharistic prayers. This reflects the most significant of new developments, a forthright acceptance of **pluralism** as a positive good and consequent efforts for flexibility and adaptation. As a result, the Roman Catholic Church, after being restricted to a single canon for a millennium and a half, now has four eucharistic prayers for any occasion (Sac, 503-21) and (in the U.S.A.) others for masses with children and reconciliation. A rich assortment of prayers over the gifts, prefaces, and prayers after communion is provided. United Methodists have twenty-two eucharistic prayers (*At the Lord's Table*, SWR #9).

Pluralism is reflected in the 1979 Episcopal BCP by the inclusion of two entire rites: one with Elizabethan language and two possible eucharistic prayers, and another in contemporary language with four choices. A third outline rite also contains two eucharistic prayers (BCP, 316-409).

The 1978 *Lutheran Book of Worship* provides three complete musical settings that can be used with any one of the three eucharistic prayers: a traditional scheme, the institution narrative alone, and a brief form concluding with the institution narrative (LBW, 57-120).

The 1974 *Hymnal of the United Church of Christ* provides two services of Word and Sacrament (pp. 12-29). In one, the words of institution are part of the eucharistic prayer; in the other (in

Reformed tradition) they are not. In the "Service for the Lord's Day" of the 1970 Presbyterian *Worshipbook* (pp. 25-42), the words of institution also appear outside the prayer. It is clear that the eucharist is intended to be part of the usual Sunday service.

Methodists have a curious bifurcation; the 1964 *Book of Worship* eucharist (pp. 15-23) is the last of the Reformation rites, basically an updating of Cranmer's 1552 rite with some of its faults rectified (e.g., the *Gloria in excelsis* returned to the ministry of the Word). The 1972 Alternate (SWR #1) and the 1980 rite (SWR #10) are more comparable to the new Roman Catholic, Episcopal, and Lutheran rites and their ancient antecedents from Hippolytus through the sixth century. Much coalescence has occurred in recent years as Christians have learned from one another and studied the eucharistic practices of others in every time and place.

II

Just as with initiation, Christians have understood the eucharist in a variety of ways. Indeed, to reduce what Christians experience in the eucharist to a single interpretation would be to miss much of the eucharist's power, though such reductionism has often been a temptation. The method we shall follow here is to trace five key themes plus two sub-themes that Christians have used to explain what they experienced in the eucharist.

We shall use the terms of Yngve Brilioth, formerly Lutheran Archbishop of Uppsala, Sweden, though applying them somewhat differently and supplementing the terms. In his *Eucharistic Faith and Practice,* Brilioth defined **five New Testament eucharistic themes.** They are: eucharist or thanksgiving, communion and fellowship, commemoration or the historical, sacrifice, and mystery and presence. To these, following recent research, we would add two sub-themes: the eucharist as the work of the Holy Spirit and as an eschatological event.[17]

These themes, and possibly others, appear in fragmentary form in the New Testament, which is even more elusive in revealing the meaning of the eucharist for first-century Christians than in disclosing its form. But clearly one of the central acts in the Lord's Supper, as in its Jewish antecedents, is **thanksgiving.** All four institution accounts speak of Jesus as giving thanks or blessing God. It is hard to imagine thanksgiving as absent from the joyful action that bubbled over as the Jerusalem church broke bread "with glad and generous hearts" (Acts 2:46).

Paul makes the sense of **communion** or **fellowship** apparent in such passages as I Corinthians 10:16-17: "When we bless the 'cup of blessing,' is it not a means of sharing [*koinonía*] in the blood of Christ? When we break the bread, is it not a means of sharing (*koinonía*) in the body of Christ? Because there is one loaf, we, many as we are, are one body; for it is one loaf of which we all partake." The church built on the Jewish concept of the unity of those eating together. In its sharing, the community receives Christ, and the one loaf becomes a sign of the unity of the communicants.

The focal point of Jewish prayer is a think-thank process of **commemoration** with thanksgiving. The key phrase used both by Paul and Luke, "in my *anámnesis,*" is an underscoring of this process. To remember, recall, know again, or experience anew is certainly one of the main purposes for doing the eucharist (Luke 22:19 and I Cor. 11:24-25). Commemoration extends to all the works of Christ beginning with creation, including both testaments, and reaching until Christ's coming again (I Cor. 11:26).

The words of institution use the language of **sacrifice** in recalling a covenant established by the pouring out of blood. Hebrews is particularly rich in sacrificial imagery, comparing Christ to both high priest and victim: "he offered himself without blemish to God, a spiritual and eternal sacrifice" (9:14). The church's early appropriation of Malachi 1:11, "a pure sacrifice," shows how natural such imagery was to apply to the eucharist. Hebrews 13:15 also speaks of "the sacrifice of praise," though there is no unambiguous relating of sacrifice and the eucharist in Hebrews. More important is Paul's understanding of Christ's whole ministry as making "himself

223

nothing, assuming the nature of a slave" (Phil. 2:7). This obedient sacrifice is memorialized by the eucharist.

In the words of the Last Supper, Christ states his **presence** by identifying bread and wine with his body and blood. Paul, in words quoted above, identifies eating and drinking with sharing in the body and blood of Christ. Some would cite the John 6:51 passage as eucharistic ("the bread which I will give is my own flesh").

The eucharist as a **locus of the Holy Spirit's work** is not clear in scripture. The **eschatological** dimension is explicit in the Last Supper accounts, all of which speak of what Jesus is doing as finding "fulfillment in the kingdom of God" (Luke 22:16) or "until he comes" (I Cor. 11:26). Of course, the context of the Passover anticipates the messianic banquet when all things will be accomplished through the coming of the Messiah. In the New Testament accounts of the eucharist, anticipation seems to be as strong a theme as commemoration.

A fairly good balance of these basic themes appears in the early church, never worked out into full theologies, never precisely balanced, but mentioned frequently enough to show that these concepts were current in the understanding of why Christians gathered to "do this." Even Justin's short accounts in the *First Apology* speak of the eucharist in which the president "offers thanksgiving" and gives evidence of fellowship as all salute "each other with a kiss," share in the "amen," and partake together. The scriptures are read, and the eucharistic action is introduced as being done "for my memorial." A realistic (i.e., identifying bread and wine literally with body and blood) concept of presence is suggested in calling the bread and wine "the flesh and blood of that incarnate Jesus."[18] The *Didache* prays eschatologically: "Let your Church be brought together from the ends of the earth into your kingdom."[19] Sacrificial references appear very early; the *Didache* compares the eucharist to the "pure sacrifice" of Malachi 1:11, while First Clement speaks of those who make offerings (*prosphorá*) or gifts (*dôra*), presumably as ministers of the eucharist.[20]

Ignatius gives us one of the strongest images of presence in speaking of the eucharist as "the medicine of immortality" and insists against the Docetists that "the Eucharist is the flesh of our Saviour."[21] He is equally firm that the fellowship of the church is centered in the bishop. **Irenaeus** declares the presence of Christ is the cup, which "is his own blood," and the bread, which "is his own body."[22] **Cyprian** speaks of fellowship in poetic terms: "as many grains, collected, and ground, and mixed together into one mass, make one bread; so in Christ, who is the heavenly bread, we may know that there is one body, with which our number is joined and united."[23]

The work of the Holy Spirit is expressed by Hippolytus, who, in his eucharistic prayer, invokes the Father to send the Holy Spirit on the offering of the holy Church and to fill those gathered to strengthen their faith in truth. Such activity is defined more explicitly over a century later in Cyril of Jerusalem's mystagogical catecheses. He tells the newly initiated that in the eucharist "we call upon the merciful God to send forth His Holy Spirit upon the gifts lying before Him; that He may make the bread the Body of Christ, and the Wine the Blood of Christ; for whatsoever the Holy Ghost has touched, is sanctified and changed [*metabébletai*]."[24] This suggests the direction the Orthodox churches subsequently took in understanding the function of the Holy Spirit in making holy and transforming the eucharistic elements. Cyril is a portent of an approach that became highly important in the East though neglected in the West until recently.

We, aware of latter developments, find puzzling the ways early Christians spoke of the presence in terms both realistic and symbolic. Cyril speaks in the same lecture of the bread and wine as the "sign [*antitýpon*] of the Body and Blood of Christ." Augustine uses language that sounds realistic at times and, at other times, obviously symbolic. Unfortunately such ambiguity is no longer a possibility for us, but it is refreshing to see the latitude of expression still possible in the fourth century.

Augustine gives us insights into the theme of sacrifice. Building on the concepts of Christ's eternal sacrifice (Heb. 9:14) and the Christians' union to Christ, Augustine says, "This is the sacrifice of Christians; we being many, are one body in Christ. . . . [The Church] herself is offered in the offering she makes to God."[25] Thus the eucharist is a joining of the church's worship with Christ's own eternal offering on its behalf. This concept of sacrifice was overshadowed in subsequent centuries.

The first thousand years of Christianity are characterized by the absence of tight theological distinctions about understanding the eucharist. Even the vocabulary for technical theological discussion of the eucharist is lacking. A variety of terms is used, each author choosing what suits his purpose best. A portent for the West appears in Ambrose's suggestion that it is the recitation of the words of institution that accomplishes consecration: "And by what words and whose sayings does consecration take place? The Lord Jesus's. . . . So the word of Christ accomplishes this sacrament."[26] But the early period has a marvelous freedom in expressing what it experienced in the heart, not what had to be defined in the head. The church experienced the eucharist rather than debated it.

Two monks started the debate in the West, **Paschasius Radbertus** and **Ratramnus,** both monks of Corbie, France, in the ninth century. Paschasius, trying to compress into words Christ's presence experienced in the eucharist, used language that we would call literal or realistic; somewhat later Ratramnus tried to express the same experience in more spiritual or symbolic language. Two centuries later controversy again erupted, this time much less friendly. Flatly rejected were the efforts of **Berengarius** to express in symbolic terms the experience of the presence of Christ in the eucharist. A crude confession was forced on him, affirming that the body of Christ is handled and broken by the priest's hands and crushed by the communicant's teeth. From the eleventh century onward, the eucharist became the subject not just of devout experience but also of intellectual speculation.

There is nothing wrong in this, but unfortunately the more controversial themes came to the forefront and others quietly withered away both in piety and in doctrinal development. A penitential and introspective piety prevailed rather than a joyful spirit of thanksgiving. The mass had come to focus almost entirely on the passion, death, and resurrection with the sorrowful mysteries predominating in the West. As the rite became increasingly clericalized and communion became a once-a-year affair, any strong sense of communal celebration was dissipated. The Old Testament lessons were gone, and no references to creation and the rest of the old covenant salvation history appeared in the Roman canon. Thus commemoration of Christ's work was drastically reduced. The eschatological dimension had long since disappeared, and the Roman rite simply overlooked any statement of the Holy Spirit's eucharistic activity.

Left were two areas: how Christ was present and how the eucharist was a sacrifice. Late medieval theologians devoted their attention to these two areas. The most significant development was agreeing on the word that described the experience of bread and wine as conveying the reality of Christ. As we have seen in Berengarius' case, the church was groping its way toward realistic language of a spatial variety. But the word **transubstantiation** arrived late, long after the idea had been striving for expression. It was not used definitively until 1215, when the Fourth Lateran Council spoke of "the transubstantiation of bread into body and wine into blood."[27] The term itself has undergone changing meaning in subsequent history. Using the best of philosophical tools available, especially Aristotle, the thirteenth century described this miracle so that it could be expressed: "the substance of the bread is turned into the body of Christ and the substance of the wine into his blood."[28] The accidents (what is perceptible to the senses) remain unchanged, but the substance (inner reality) is miraculously transformed, contrary to all else in the natural world, where all accidents and substance conform. This triumph of rationalism tried to explain the mystery rather than accept and adore it.

Hand in hand with such theological definitions went practices that increasingly removed the sacred elements from contact with the people except for a dramatic showing at the **elevation,** when the bread and cup were raised for all to see. The doctrine of **concomitance** made it clear that the whole Christ is present in every drop and crumb of the consecrated elements, so it was no longer considered necessary for the laity to receive the cup with all the danger of spilling Christ's blood that that entailed. With infrequent communion, the laity's role was minimal. The priest offered mass on their behalf in a language few people understood.

Thought about the eucharist as sacrifice also developed so that the mass was seen as propitiatory, being performed to bring about desired purposes. Sophisticated explanations that the mass was a memorial and not a repetition of the unique sacrifice of Calvary too often were lost on lay people. Current theories of the atonement focused almost exclusively on the death of Jesus as satisfying God's justice, and the eucharist dovetailed too neatly into this scheme of things. Too easily, this narrow concept of sacrifice made the eucharist a means of securing God's favor instead of a proclamation of such favor already accomplished for all eternity.

Presence and sacrifice were aspects highly developed by the late medieval period, but this spurt of doctrinal construction was at the expense of a balanced interpretation. If ample concern had been given to the eucharist as the proclamation of thanksgiving, the sacrament of unity, the commemoration of all salvation history, the present work of the Holy Spirit, or the foretaste of the messianic banquet, doctrinal developments would have been far different.

A reshuffling of priorities occurred in the Reformation with limited success achieved in some instances in restoring a balanced eucharistic understanding. There were few things the Reformers were unanimous about, but rejecting late medieval approaches to understanding presence and sacrifice was one of them. The Reformation (facilitated by the use of the vernacular) saw tremendous gains in recovery of a sense of fellowship, some improvement in the breadth of commemoration, and reforms in the concepts of presence and sacrifice. Brilioth says: "The rediscovery of the idea of communion [fellowship] is the greatest positive contribution of the Reformation in regard to the eucharist."[29] Accomplishments in recovering a joyful sense of thanksgiving were mixed, acknowledgment of the work of the Holy Spirit recovered by some, and eschatological perception rare except under persecution.

Luther, who discarded the canon of the mass because it reeked of sacrifice and who saw sacrifice as the "third captivity" of the mass, was not able to accomplish anything positive in this dimension.[30] He did, however, wrestle with the concept of presence and, though rejecting the idea of transubstantiation ("the second captivity"), did insist that the bread and wine became the substance of Christ's body and blood though still remaining natural substances of bread and wine, just as a red-hot iron can be both iron and fire. Since Christ is everywhere present by his divine nature (*ubiquity*), and all the powers of his divine nature are communicated to his human nature, Christ can be present on a thousand altar-tables simultaneously. This solves some problems, though it still retains the concept of presence in spatial terms; Christ is present "in, with, and under" bread and wine. Even in rebellion, Luther is captive to medieval concepts of the presence. Luther recovered much congregational participation in the restoration of the chalice, for centuries denied to the laity ("the first captivity"), the use of vernacular, and rich congregational hymnody.

Surely the greatest single tragedy of the Reformation was the conflict between Luther and Zwingli over the concept of presence, a fight that erupted at the **Marburg Colloquy** (1529). Zwingli, impatient with any concept that the physical could convey the spiritual, repudiated Luther's teaching on presence with the view that Christ is only present spiritually by his divine nature. Zwingli's strength was emphasis on fellowship and the spiritual union of the participants together confessing their faith. Luther was caught between the rationalism of the right (Scholasticism) and the left (Zwinglian humanism), and so the two reformers split over the sacrament of unity. Clearly they were, indeed, of a different spirit. For Luther the eucharist is clearly a God-given means of grace; for Zwingli it is, instead, a corporate confession of human faith.

Calvin's role was as something of a mediator between the two, but he added much that is his own, or rather recovered something of the early church. God, who knows us best, uses outward signs to give Godself to us. Because of our sin and lack of faith, such signs are necessary; because of God's love for us, they are effective. We feed on Christ in the eucharist, but it is made possible only through the operation of the Holy Spirit, who raises our souls to heaven. The means of feeding on Christ is a "mystery, which plainly neither the mind is able to conceive nor the tongue to express."[31] In stressing the role of the Holy Spirit and the sense of mystery, Calvin picks up some authentic early Christian strands that medieval developments had overlooked. Calvin also stresses that the Lord's Supper implies mutual love or fellowship: "For what sharper goad could there be to arouse mutual love among us than when Christ, giving himself to us, not only invites us by his own example to pledge and give ourselves to one another, but inasmuch as he makes himself common to all, also makes all of us one in himself."[32] His spatial location of Christ in heaven is crude, nor does he contribute much that is positive on concepts of sacrifice, thanksgiving, commemoration, or eschatology. But Calvin affirms the centrality of the Holy Spirit's work.

Among the Anabaptists an intense sense of fellowship thrived, reinforced by the ban on those who lapsed. The pure church was also a church under persecution, a reality reflected in their hymnody. Under the threat of persecution and conscious of their martyrs, the Anabaptists conducted worship that reflected a vivid eschatological fervor.

There has been much controversy over Cranmer's eucharistic doctrine as expressed in the first two BCPs. In general, his position is seen as somewhat similar to Zwingli's but with a stronger view of the value of frequent communion. "Yet he is distinguished from the Zurich reformer in esteeming the Lord's Supper more highly and in emphasizing that its faithful observance is accompanied by the operation of God's grace."[33] Zwingli's feelings for fellowship are present too, as well as a rather strong dimension of commemoration, though like most of the Reformation materials this focuses narrowly on the passion. In 1637, the Anglicans of Scotland regained the 1549 *epiclesis*. Reinforced by the nonjurors in the eighteenth century, this canon influenced the 1764 Scottish canon, adopted for the first American BCP.

John Wesley had the advantages of living in a time after the Reformation controversies and possessing a deep knowledge of patristics. Though close to Calvin in many aspects, Wesley achieved a balance that even the Genevan reformer lacked. This is reflected in the divisions of John and Charles Wesley's *Hymns on the Lord's Supper:* "As it is a Memorial of the

Sufferings and Death of Christ," "As it is a Sign and a Means of Grace," "The Sacrament a Pledge of Heaven," "The Holy Eucharist as it implies a Sacrifice," "Concerning the Sacrifice of our Persons," and "After the Sacrament."[34] At last a strong positive Protestant statement of eucharistic sacrifice occurs in Wesley, coupled with a patristic-Calvinistic sense of presence as mystery. The eschatological and pneumatological aspects are vividly present, too, as is fellowship, though commemoration and thanksgiving are still narrowly focused on Christ's passion and death.

Recent years have seen extraordinary development in understanding of the eucharist, especially in the direction of a more carefully balanced approach. Brilioth's *Eucharistic Faith and Practice,* utilized by such Roman Catholics as Louis Bouyer, has been itself a contributor to this process; but much has come about through broader ecumenical contacts and greater study of the biblical, historical, and theological aspects of eucharistic theology. The problem areas of presence and sacrifice have received the most attention, but in all areas our understanding has been greatly increased.

Vatican II made a notable contribution in restating the whole question of presence by declaring that Christ is present in the mass, not in one way but in a variety of ways: in the person of the minister, in the bread and wine, in the sacramental action, in the word, and in the congregation (CSL, 7). How different history would have been had this insight come a thousand years sooner!

Catholic theologians have picked up another trail in developing the concept of **transsignification,** in which emphasis is on the meaning or purpose of the sacramental signs in the eucharist.[35] Earlier Odo Casel had opened new possibilities in portraying the mass as a time mystery rather than a spatial one. According to the idea of transsignification, if the meaning of something is a major component of its very being, then it can be said that the bread and wine undergo an ontological change in the eucharist by coming to signify the body and blood of Christ. Similarly, a box of chocolates becomes a gift through the sign-act of giving and thus is no longer just confections but a means of self-giving. These newer concepts, which virtually equate being with meaning, admit the insights of recent phenomenological philosophy and sometimes seem to reflect Calvin's understanding of God's use of signs to accommodate to human capacity. Such new approaches are far from being unanimously accepted by Roman Catholics but have great appeal to many Protestants.

Our understanding of sacrifice has been immeasurably broadened by equating it not with just the passion-atonement aspect, but with the whole incarnation of Christ, who emptied himself of deity to take the form of a slave (Phil. 2:7). The presence of sacrificial terminology in the New Testament and early church has been more widely recognized. Recovery of such images as Augustine's picture of the church in union with Christ in Christ's eternal offering for us have made a more positive approach widely possible without undercutting the unique character of Christ's work already accomplished. Currently, sacrifice is also seen as the memorial of Christ's work, all that Christians have or could hope to have to offer God. Commemoration and sacrifice are closely related.

Commemoration is now seen in its broadest aspects as encompassing all the work of Christ from creation to final judgment. Important new developments are the inclusion of Old Testament lessons and psalmody in the Lord's Supper once again and the recovery in Western eucharistic prayers of recital of the saving works of God of the Old Covenant. Commemoration is far broader than recalling just Good Friday and Easter.

Thanksgiving has been expressed abundantly in many modern liturgies concurrent with the broadening understanding of commemoration. Eucharists once again have become joyful occasions of praise. Part of this is due to contacts with the Eastern churches, which have always maintained that one comes to church primarily to praise God for what God has done, not to tell God what sinners we are. Perhaps some experimental services have gone overboard in stressing joy, but even the sorrowful mysteries of Christ's suffering and death ultimately are joyful.

The Eastern churches, too, have made Westerners aware of how vital is the understanding of the eucharist as the work of the Holy Spirit. Virtually all new eucharistic prayers have a distinct *epiclesis.* Pentecostalists, operating from experience rather than from theological reflection, have cherished these insights since the beginning of this century.

Evidence of new value for fellowship is abundant, as in the Vatican II reforms of a vernacular liturgy, communion in the hand and in both species, and general congregational participation. As have Roman Catholics, the churches of the Reformation have regained the kiss of peace as a congregational act.

It is not quite as apparent, but there has also been increased concern with the eucharist as anticipation, looking in an eschatological direction to the heavenly banquet, which will mark the completion of all things in Jesus Christ. An acclamation, recovered by Catholics and Protestants alike, is one sign of this: "Christ will come again."

There is much to rejoice over in these new understandings of what the church experiences at the Lord's Supper. These interpretations bring Christians closer not only to the witness of the Bible and early church, but also to one another.

III

Pastoral practice should reflect how the church has grown in rites and understanding in recent years so that one can exercise the fullest ministry in this area. There is close relationship between theory and practice for those responsible for planning, preparing for, and celebrating the eucharist.

In the first place, the **architectural setting** will dictate many, if not all, of the possibilities open to us. All traditions have moved in recent years to demanding a free-standing altar-table so the priest or minister can face the people across it. This became mandatory in new Roman Catholic churches in 1964, and most Protestant churches have followed suit. Once one has celebrated facing the people across the Lord's table, it is hard ever again to turn one's back on them.

Not only must one be able to face the people, but it must be easy for them to come to the altar-table if this is the practice of one's tradition. Some traditions, such as the Reformed and portions of the Free Church, are recovering the action of gathering around the Lord's table whether to stand, to kneel, or to sit around extensions of it. The very act of coming forward in the company of one's neighbors is a powerful nonverbal sign of offering of self. The altar-table must be not only visible but accessible. Increasingly in many churches, even on non-eucharistic occasions, the altar-table is the focus of all acts of prayer and offering, while proclamation centers in the pulpit. This implies a ministerial altar-table, cleared for action, that is designed to be used and is used. It does not indicate a monumental altar-table, conspicuous but unused and covered by an unused Bible, flowers, or candles.

The Lord's Supper is basically **action** supplemented by words. How careful are we to let the actions speak? An excellent learning experience is to celebrate the eucharist in silence, forcing the actions, vessels, elements, setting, vestments, and every other available medium of communication except the audible to speak for itself.

All the new eucharistic rites are based on the fourfold pattern of actions described above. Does the taking or preparing draw attention to the fact that a meal is to follow and altar-table and elements must be prepared? Do we use our hands as well as our voices to express that we are giving thanks to God over the elements? Is the breaking of bread a clear sign of the unity of the one loaf broken for many? Is there an actual touch of hands as the bread is given into the hand of the recipient? All these acts call for careful attention so that their sign value is expressed, not concealed. Good communication demands sensitive preparation.

The eucharist is a happening. God works through celebrant and people, but it is up to the clergy to make the communication as clear as possible. We would not mumble while preaching the sermon; we should not underplay while acting the eucharist. These sign-acts are not decoration; they are a vital part of ministry in bringing people to communion with God. At the Lord's table we understand how completely God knows and loves people as full human beings. The glory and majesty of God's being is accommodated to our humble human capacity. Thus what we do with our hands, bodies, and voices in leading the eucharist is a vital ministry that demands sensitivity to how humans relate and communicate. There is a body language as well as a vocal one, and we must learn to speak both with eloquence.

The **bread and wine** themselves are also an important part of the action. It has been sometimes said that it takes more faith to make Roman Catholic schoolchildren believe that communion wafers are bread than it does to believe that the bread becomes Christ's body. Real bread they have seen. The use of common food is at the heart of the eucharist. Christ did not choose nectar and ambrosia, the food of gods, but bread and wine, the food of humans. Much of the sign value is lost when the bread becomes cardboard wafers, plastic fish food, or anything else than bread as it normally appears, tastes, and smells. The same is true of the wine. The bread must be bread that can be broken easily, neither too fresh nor too stale. The act of breaking it can be one of the most meaningful parts of the service if carefully done. The act of giving is important, to. Giving a gift can be a real art; giving bread and wine are no exceptions.

Particular problems apply to giving the cup. Certainly the highest sign value of unity is in giving the wine from a common chalice. But people in most segments of American culture believe most devoutly in germs, though few have seen one. The American Medical Association now maintains that when a chalice of wine is turned and wiped after each communicant, such practice "seems to remove any danger."[36] But for those with overwhelming anxieties, one way to evade these fears is by dipping the bread in a common chalice (**intinction**), or pouring from the chalice into individual cups, or by giving the wine in individual cups. (People who believe this is the most sanitary method have never seen how such cups usually get washed!) Until modern times, the amount of bread and wine consumed was not tiny crumbs and drops but somewhat more generous portions. If we are given something, let it be more than minimal.

Special problems arise in ministering to the sick. The Roman Catholics have developed a system of special ministers (lay people) who are trained to bring eucharistic bread to the sick, sometimes daily. Surprisingly, some Protestants are much too clerical to allow this. Perhaps the best arrangement is to have several people from the congregation join the minister or priest in a sickroom celebration, abbreviated to be sure, but nevertheless a real common discerning of the body. This is especially meaningful on those Sundays when the rest of the congregation has also joined in the sacrament. The bringing of consecrated bread and wine to the sick has been an important ministry ever since Justin Martyr.

Much planning, preparation, and care in conducting the eucharist in all its outward and visible aspects is necessary that it may best communicate the inward reality of God's self-giving.

VIII
Passages

The mountain peaks and valleys of life are occasions for Christian worship just as surely as the flat plains of day-by-day living. We have already seen how initiation marks entrance into the life of the Christian community. Initiation can come at any age. For most Christians, it comes at birth; for many others, it occurs at the onset of puberty. These and other crisis points of life are marked by times when the community of faith gathers around individuals to express its love as they pass through various stages: marriage (for most), ordination (for some), serious sickness (for many), and death (for all). Each passage reflects three stages in varying degrees: separation from a past way of life; transition, or the moment when one crosses the threshold into a new order of being; and incorporation into a new way of life. Several are accompanied by transition periods of time (engagement, seminary studies, declining health) as well as transitions in space (new home, hospitalization, cemetery).

For Christians, none of these passages is a purely private moment but rather a concern shared by the whole Christian community. A wedding signalizes the formation of a new family and potentially adds to the body of Christ. Even the loneliness of dying is mitigated by the belief that death does not remove one from the church but only transfers one into the larger portion, the Church Triumphant. As communal concerns, these intensely personal moments are usually celebrated in the midst of the Christian community. The community of love surrounds and supports us both in the joys of marriage and ordination and in the sorrows of sickness and death.

God reaches out through the human community to establish new relationships of love at these special times. These new relationships are expressed in varying ways in different relationships and kinds of love: conjugal, pastoral, caring, and in memories. The eucharist can be an important part of the church's ministry of love in all four of these moments of passage. But other appropriate rites are used by Christians for each event, and these special rites are our present concern.

Except for ordination, these passages are by no means uniquely Christian but affect all people. In the ways life crises are observed, we see more clearly than anywhere else in Christian worship the influence of local culture. A great variety of customs and local practices functions at these moments, occasionally in conflict with Christian faith, sometimes concurring with it, and frequently indifferent to it. Christians have no monopoly in commemorating these passages, but they certainly are influenced by the ways others observe such events. It is important to know what is the distinctive Christian witness on such occasions and what is culturally determined, so one can make informed decisions in dealing with specific situations.

We shall consider in sequence the Christian wedding, ordination, ministry to the sick, and burial. Each deals with effective ministry in a moment of deep human need. Our survey will be quick but will indicate contemporary directions of converging faith and practice in each area.

I

There are few, if any, occasions more joyful than a **wedding.** Yet the church's approach to weddings has been a slow and cautious one, always willing to leave most of the festivities outside the church door. Even now the wedding service is a curious amalgam of Christian and pagan elements. The words are an unlikely match of liturgical language and legal jargon. The minister functions both as pastor and civil servant, subject to the canons or laws of both ecclesiastical and civil societies.

Weddings are a strange combination of Christ and culture.

The New Testament, though it frequently uses wedding imagery, tells us nothing about Christian weddings. We do have an account of the Jewish wedding feast Jesus attended at Cana (John 2:1-11), where occurred "the first of the signs by which Jesus revealed his glory"; but all we learn is that it was not a somber and sober occasion. The early fathers tell us little more. Apparently the early church was content to allow local customs to persist. These included the Roman betrothal ceremony in which promises for the future wedding were made and a ring given. The Roman wedding rite contained the joining of hands, sacrifice at the family altar, the wedding banquet with a wedding cake, and marriage bed rites. These ceremonies started at the home of the bride and concluded at the new home of the couple. The betrothal vows, joining of hands, and giving of rings still persist in Christian weddings today. The church's role for many centuries seems to have been limited to influencing Christians to marry Christians. Ignatius says, "It is right for men and women who marry to be united with the bishop's approval." Christian blessings were substituted for those in the name of pagan deities, and the eucharist might be celebrated in place of pagan sacrifice.[1]

Other pagan rites accumulated as the church converted northern Europe: rice as a fertility symbol, giving away the bride, bridesmaids dressed to confuse evil spirits who might hex the bride (apparently evil spirits were none too perceptive), the wedding veil as similar protection, and the offering of money. For centuries, weddings continued to take place in homes or taverns, and the church's involvement was minimal. Many weddings today make one envy the church's wisdom then!

The church's encroachment was unintentional. With the growth of legal systems out of chaos, it became increasingly necessary to have written records of weddings to prevent clandestine marriages and to provide for the legitimacy of offspring and uncontested inheritances. Wealthy people could afford painted portraits as a record (cf. Jan van Eyck's portrait of Giovanni Arnolfini and bride); ordinary people needed a written certificate. In most villages, the only literate person was the priest ("clergy" meant learned), and his presence became increasingly necessary at weddings simply to witness and record them legally. A **nuptial mass** (distinct from the wedding itself) would frequently be celebrated at the parish church after the wedding and the newly married couple blessed just before the fraction.

The legal character of the wedding ceremony is its most distinctive feature. Weddings consist essentially of a **public contract** freely and mutually assented to before witnesses. The traditional language—"to have and to hold"—is language still used in conveyance of property. "From this day forward" dates the contract. Then follows the unconditional nature of said contract: "for better for worse." "Till death us do part" terminates the above, and "I give thee my troth" is the pledge of faithfulness to it. All this is lawyers' talk, not liturgists'. Almost identical words appear in English in fourteenth-century manuscripts, long before other liturgical documents were translated into the vernacular. The center of this most joyful occasion is a legal transaction.

By the twelfth century, weddings were moving to the church door or porch, where most of a village's legal transactions took place in the sight of God. The priest had by now become requisite for the wedding itself. A nuptial mass and blessing inside the church often followed the wedding. The nuptial mass was prohibited in Advent and Lent. Chaucer tells us his Wife of Bath "husbands at the church door she had five" and was ready for more. Luther's wedding rite (1529) still took place at the church door and then moved inside for scripture reading and blessing. In the English Reformation, the full wedding service finally (after fifteen hundred years) took place inside the church building.

Eastern Orthodox churches have conserved distinctive ceremonies such as exchanging the vows and rings in the vestibule (the world), processing inside the church (the kingdom), crowning both bride and groom as a symbol of the kingdom of God (their future family), both drinking from a single cup, and a triple procession around the altar-table. Theologically, the priest is considered the actual minister of the sacrament. He represents Christ, who acts in this sacrament within his body, the church.

By and large, the Reformation found few changes necessary beyond substituting the vernacular for the entire service and simplifying it somewhat. Wedding rites have always tended to be conservative, since society has such an enormous stake in their proper observance. The Church of England continued to require three prior readings of **banns** (public announcements of the forthcoming wedding), thus underscoring society's involvement. The woman's promise in the *Sarum Manuale*—"to be bonere and buxum in bedde and at te borde"—was dropped, but much of the medieval service was retained. Psalm 128, asking that they may "see thy childers children," and a prayer for the fruitfulness of the union were retained, but the Church did not press for a miracle; these items could be omitted "where the woman is past childe byrth." Rubrics called upon the couple to receive the eucharist "the same daye of their mariage."

Puritan objections brought removal of some ceremonies (rings), but most of them have quietly been replaced in subsequent years. The tendency in Protestantism in the past hundred years seems to have been to retain or to recover much of the pre-Reformation contours of the service. Protestants have been reluctant to accept the frankly sexual nature of the rite as it appeared in the Reformation. At least the medieval-Reformation rites acknowledged that marriage involved sex and usually produced children. The Church of England still uses that wonderful line in the vows—"with this ring I thee wed, with my body I thee worship"—but that proved too much for eighteenth-century American Episcopalians. From Luther's "Order of Marriage" comes the use of Matthew 19:6: "What God hath joined together, let not man put asunder" and the declaration: "I pronounce them joined in marriage."[2] Cranmer and most Protestants have followed suit. English-speaking Protestantism generally follows the medieval-Anglican versions of the vows, including the **betrothal vows** (future: "*N.*, Wilt thou have . . ."); the **nuptial vows** (present: "I, *N.*, take thee . . ."); and the giving of the rings ("With this Ring . . ."). Wesley omitted giving away the bride and the giving of rings; his descendants restored both.

Recent revisions of the marriage rite have so much in

common it is hard to distinguish between them. In most of them, the obligations of the community are underlined, such as the congregation's taking a vow "to uphold these two persons in their marriage" (BCP, 425). Many new versions try to make the wedding rite a full service with hymns, lessons, and other acts of worship provided to place it in the context of normal Christian worship. Too often, a fifteen-minute ceremony has sufficed to seal a fifty-year covenant.

There has been a marked shift among Protestants toward suggesting the eucharist as part of the service for all when Christian couples marry. Roman Catholics encourage the eucharist for Catholics. Propers for nuptial eucharists are provided in several instances (Sac, 759-67; BCP, 432; SWR #5). In most cases, there are numerous options and far greater possibilities for flexibility than ever existed before. Several (BCP, 433-34; Wb, 69-70; SWR #5) make provision for the blessing of a civil service held previously. A few contain materials for wedding anniversaries and the renewal of marriage vows (Sac, 768-70; *A Service of Christian Marriage,* SWR #5).

Another common characteristic is emphasis on equality. Women no longer promise to "obey him, and serve him," and the giving away of the bride has disappeared in some (LBW, 202-5; Rites, 539-70; SWR #5; Wb, 65-70), though made an option in others (BCP, 423-32; SoC #4). A positive statement of God's goodness in creating us male and female appears in the new Episcopal, Lutheran, and United Methodist rites, though most are still reticent about mentioning the possibility (or current existence) of a family, except the Roman Catholic.

Certainly the most obvious common feature is the nuptial vow itself, worded so as to state lifelong intent ("until death do us part"). This is specifically stated in all the chief new official rites and is a clear sign of a split between much of contemporary culture and Christian ideals.

The church's thinking about the wedding service has been greatly influenced by the fact that so much canon law focuses on questions of marriage. This has tended to make reflection on marriage revolve more around legalistic controversies than liturgical ones. Indeed, except for the Reformation debate over whether matrimony was a sacrament or not, controversies over the rite itself have been almost nil.

Two New Testament passages have been of prominence in the church's thinking about marriage: the sayings of Jesus with regard to the indissolubility of marriage (Matt. 19:9 and 5:32; and Eph. 5:22-23). The rites of the Western church have ignored the eschatological references to Christ comparing himself to the bridegroom and his disciples as sharing in the wedding feast (Matt. 9:15; 25:1-13), an allusion to the coming kingdom of God. The Ephesians passage calls marriage "a great mystery [*mystérion*] . . . with respect to Christ and the Church" (5:32, literally). The church has relied on this passage as indicating the completeness of the union between husband and wife, though it may tell us even more about the union between Christ and church. *Mystérion* became *sacramentum* in Latin, thus ensuring eventual inclusion among the seven sacraments.

The early church had few problems in interpreting marriage in a monogamous culture. Even Tertullian could find little to complain about in the pagan marriage rites as long as Christian blessings and sacrifice were substituted. The church, in time, even modeled its rites for the consecration of virgins on the marriage rite, a bit more cheerful than monastic profession with its parallel to the burial rites. From earliest times, virgins and widows were given honored roles in the church's life.

Peter Lombard puts matrimony last and has little to tell us. He follows Augustine in noting that marriage was the only sacrament instituted before the fall, being initiated originally as a duty and, after the fall, being regarded as a remedy.[3] Augustine understood quite well the evils of which he spoke but is hardly positive in recommending marriage as "a remedy for the sick." But Lombard mentions the creation narrative, Cana, and Ephesians 5 to show "that marriage is a good thing otherwise it would not be a sacrament; for a sacrament is a sacred sign."[4] Lombard shows that sexual union is necessary to reflect the fullness of the union between Christ and the church.

Indeed, some medieval theologians came to believe that the actual sexual union was the real matter of the sacrament, an act rather difficult for the church to administer. But the actual giving of the contract "by mutual consent uttered aloud at the spot" came to be considered the true form and matter of this sacrament. Since Christ left no form, the church is free to change the actual words used but not the necessity of a mutual free consent. The church may forbid marriage because of various **impediments** such as clandestinity, or marriage under duress, or simulated consent. The amount of canon law dealing with marriage is complex.

The resulting consensus (in the West) was that the husband and wife themselves are the only proper ministrants of this sacrament, it being the one sacrament a Roman Catholic priest or bishop cannot perform, though he may administer a nuptial mass and bless the union. In practice, Protestants tend to be more clerical in the conduct of weddings than Roman Catholics, though this is lessening.

According to the *Decree for the Armenians,* the purposes of marriage are threefold: "first, the begetting of children, and their bringing up in the worship of the Lord; secondly, the fidelity that husband and wife should each maintain toward the other; thirdly, the indissoluble character of marriage, for this typifies the indissoluble union of Christ and the Church."[5]

The chief change the Reformation made was to deny that marriage was a sacrament. Calvin speaks for all the Reformers:

No man ever saw it [matrimony] administered as a sacrament until the time of Gregory [VII]. And what sober man would ever have thought it such? Marriage is a good and holy ordinance of God; and farming, building, cobbling, and barbering are lawful ordinances of God, and yet not sacraments. For it is required that a sacrament be not only a work of God but an outward ceremony appointed by God to confirm a promise. Even children can discern that there is no such thing in matrimony.[6]

The Reformation, however, was almost as conservative in understanding the experience as it was with regard to the rite itself. The first BCP tells us the ends of marriage are firstly "the procreacion of children, to be brought up in the feare and nurture of the Lord, and prayse of God. Secondly it was ordeined for a remedie agaynst sinne, and to auoide fornication. . . . Thirdelye for the mutuall societie, helpe, and coumfort, that the one oughte to haue of thother, both in prosperitie and aduersitie." This is hardly a romantic view of marriage! It was actually the English Puritans who reversed this order and put first mutual help and comfort. Finally I Corinthians 13 took precedence over I Corinthians 7. Modern thought has accepted the Puritan reordering of priorities in the purpose of marriage, though popular culture is prone to stress romantic infatuation. If one had to choose between a purely romantic notion of love, based solely on mutual attractiveness, and love based on mutual responsibility, then the medieval-Reformation purposes do not sound so bad. Society's need for procreation in order to ensure survival, though, is less urgent today.

The most important change in recent years has been a new emphasis on marriage as **covenant** rather than as contract. This represents a return to a biblical and early Christian (and pagan Roman) perspective in which God is seen as acting to witness and guarantee that a covenant will be carried out with all fidelity. The medieval tendency, pursued by the Scholastic theologians, to think of marriage in terms of contract instead of covenant, made it easy for the Reformers to deny that matrimony was a sacrament. After all, most contracts deal with impersonal matters in which the action of God is not at all apparent. Rarely do contracts involve love. Each of my Puritan foremothers in seventeenth-century Massachusetts had her future husband sign a contract providing for disposition of her property and care of any children born to her in the event that she died before her husband. A covenant relationship, on the other hand, is based upon a lifelong ideal of mutual love, not the prudence of a legal contract. It is significant that Vatican II always speaks of marriage in terms of covenant rather than as contract.

Several other concerns are prominent in recent thought about the marriage rite. Vatican II mandated that various local "praiseworthy customs and ceremonies" not only be retained but encouraged (CSL, 77). Indigenization is clearly favored as long as there is clear articulation of consent to the vows on the part of both parties. The gross inequalities of the old nuptial blessing (which prayed that the woman only "be faithful and chaste" and "fortify herself against her weakness") are changed to "equal obligation to remain faithful to each other" (78). Roman Catholics have been less subject to pressures to secularize weddings by the addition of sentimentalities, especially in music. Whether such banalities that have often plagued Protestant weddings will be a problem for Roman Catholics remains to be seen. In theory, indigenization is an excellent idea, but if it means singing "O Promise Me" or "Sweetheart of Sigma Chi" at church weddings, one might have second thoughts.

The question of whether the church should perform weddings must be raised. After all, for most of its history the church let society do this. The best argument in its favor seems to be that the church as a community of faith has an intimate concern in surrounding a Christian couple with love and in ministering to them. A new relationship of love is established when one enters the marriage covenant, just as when one enters the church covenant through initiation. The wedding is a visible sign of this new relationship of love and calls others to nurture this love just as when we baptize babies or adults the church undertakes in love to nurture their faith. In both cases, the relationship of love is a permanent one. Not only does the wedding couple contract with each other, but the community itself covenants to uphold them too. The reading of the banns and asking if there is any impediment at the start of the wedding help underscore the social nature of marriage. The family, inaugurated at marriage, is in essence a small church modeled on mutual love within the body of Christ. The eschatological image of the Eastern churches of the family as a foretaste and small model of the kingdom of God is instructive.

The non-Christian who wants a church wedding presents a different situation. Perhaps churches ought to devise a frankly non-Christian wedding service to perform as a social service (just as we bury non-Christian dead) and avoid the pretense of speaking Christian words to those for whom they are meaningless.

Other problems abound in modern society. How can the church minister to nearly half of society who have undergone the agony of divorce without compromising its stand against divorce? This is especially perplexing in the case of remarriage. The Eastern churches make provision for such with integrity. More radical is the question of homosexual unions, which the major churches have refused to sanction. Pressures for celebrating such contracts will undoubtedly grow. The churches, long so squeamish about even mentioning sexuality in wedding rites, have undercut a sure position here. The Reformation rites, with their frank acknowledgment of the goodness of the created order and God's purposes in instituting matrimony, may once again give fresh insights. As social structures change, the church will face new problems about the marriage relationship.

One consensus seems clear, if one can judge from the new rites. The Christian wedding is conceived of as a public contract before witnesses by a man and woman who, by their free and mutual consent, make unconditional promises of lifelong fidelity to each other with the help of God. There is nothing new or novel about this; it represents an understanding present ever since the New Testament. Luther (and some of the Gallican rites before him) simply reinforced this view by adding Matthew 19:6 to the rite itself: "What God hath joined together, let not man put asunder," words that most of the new rites contain (except SoC #4). These words certainly imply a sacramental view of marriage, even though Luther repudiated such. They indicate that God works through the church's actions to bring about a new and permanent relationship of love.

Numerous pastoral concerns arise out of the need to show forth this distinctive nature of Christian marriage and the rite itself. Presiding at weddings is certainly one of the most joyful pastoral roles ministers or priests have, but it is also one of the most demanding in complexity.

First of all, this ministry demands considerable time and skill in **counseling** those desiring to be married. The state has its own laws regarding who may be married, and most churches have additional standards. The priest's or minister's role is to be faithful to the standards of his or her church, and this involves the ability to say no. Certainly this must be the case where there is no willingness or time for counseling. Refusing to perform a

247

walk-in wedding is actually performing a service for people, though unlikely to be so understood.

The positive side of counseling, both premarital and after marriage has begun, is the ability to present the church's witness to the meaning of responsible love, so widely trivialized in our society. The pastoral role, of course, is contingent upon having a flock and the congregation's support in upholding a couple's intention of a Christian marriage. We have not just the church's doctrines to present but the church as living community.

When clergy perform a wedding they also act as unpaid civil servants of the state. That means they are subject to the **laws of the state** in which the wedding is performed. Violation of these laws, either through ignorance or knowingly, is a criminal activity for which there are fines and penalties. There is no substitute for familiarizing oneself with the laws of the state in which the wedding is to be performed. No uniformity exists as to when and where a wedding license is valid, the number of witnesses needed, or the method for filing the wedding certificate. The only way to be sure is to check with a county clerk in the state in which the wedding is to be performed. For example, in some states, the wedding may be performed only in the county issuing the license.

Due respect to ministerial etiquette ought to be observed when performing a wedding in another parish than one's own. This ought to be done only at the pastor's invitation and deserves a letter of thanks.

All the skills of a diplomat are needed in helping to **plan a wedding.** Various matters, such as the music, can easily get out of hand unless there are standards of excellence and appropriateness to suggest. A general rule is that the pastor should be consulted from the beginning of wedding plans. Friendly persuasion can often prevent distortion of the religious meaning of the service and lapses in good taste. Printed materials have some authority in convincing the skeptical. One's denomination can usually supply a list of recommended wedding music. Each congregation ought to publish rules for the use of its property for weddings, including such items as who can use the organ, a schedule of fees for use of the church building and janitorial services, where and how flowers and candles may be placed so as not to damage the furnishings or conceal liturgical centers, and rules about photographers. The minister or priest is in a much better position to enforce printed rules passed by the local parish council, vestry, elders, or official board than rules based only on his or her own authority.

Most Christian couples are open to suggestions as to how to make their wedding the finest possible act of Christian worship. The priest or minister must be familiar with the options available. Most new rites give a number of possibilities and leave much to the clergy's discretion. This is more demanding of pastoral leadership but also provides a better opportunity for ministering. One needs to be familiar with the possibilities (and problems) of celebrating the eucharist with a wedding congregation, some of whom may not be Christians. Since Western Christianity teaches that the couple marry each other and the clergy only preside, this should shape the entire service. Certainly the couple should face each other in saying their vows and in giving the rings.

One would have to be very bold, not to say foolhardy, to try a wedding without a **rehearsal.** If nothing else, the rehearsal ought to build confidence in the couple, who often are terrified at the time of the actual wedding. The minister or priest should rehearse all the problem areas that nervous people can flub: the entrance procession, the taking of hands, the exchange of vows, the giving of rings, and the recession.

Once the wedding is over and the legal details cared for, there are equally important pastoral responsibilities in marriage counseling and integrating the couple in new ways into the life of the congregation. Most of these are happy responsibilities as one watches the maturing of love. Marriage is indeed a "great mystery" through which God works and the clergy are privileged to have a part.

II

The majority of Christians have probably never seen an **ordination;** yet most Christians are served by ordained men and women. In some churches only bishops perform ordinations and ministers and priests may rarely be present at an ordination other than their own. Yet nowhere else does the church make so explicit its understanding of the purpose of the church and its ministry. Even though ordination is a rite of passage reserved for the tiny minority of Christians who enter ordained ministry, it ought to be better understood by all Christians as the occasion on which the church expresses most clearly its understanding of its mission in the world.

The witness of the New Testament to the rites of ordination is minimal. It consists in the laying on of hands with prayer after election or appointment by the apostles (Acts 6:1-6; 13:3; 14:23; I Tim. 4:14; 5:22; and II Tim. 1:6). It was accompanied by fasting and likely included a charge to those ordained (Acts 20:28). The act of laying on of hands, as we have seen in initiation, is a sign of the tradition of power, blessing, or the setting apart of another person by one authorized to do so.

The New Testament tells us of a variety of ministries (I Cor. 12:28). There is development within its pages of a smaller but by no means decisive list that hardly distinguishes lay from ordained ministries. The *Didache* speaks of prophets, obviously people of special gifts, and we learn from Hippolytus of confessors who had suffered for the faith, which was considered sufficient consecration without laying on of hands unless one were to become bishop. Widows and virgins constituted recognized states of life but not orders; and readers, subdeacons, and healers were recognized rather than ordained. For Hippolytus, only three receive ordination: bishops, presbyters, and deacons.

Once again we rely on Hippolytus for the first substantial evidence as to how ordination took place in the early church. Hippolytus gives a full account of ordination of bishop, presbyter, and deacon.[7] Ordination occurs in the context of the eucharist in the place of the ministry of the word. Apparently the new **bishop** is chosen by the people some time prior to the actual ordination, which takes place on a Sunday with other bishops present. The people give their assent, probably by acclamation. Then the bishops lay hands on him while one bishop prays the prayer of ordination. The prayer begins with a recital of God's saving acts, then invokes that the Holy Spirit be

250

poured out on the new bishop so that he may serve properly in his responsibilities (which are listed). The new bishop is greeted with the kiss of peace, and then he presides over the eucharist.

For the ordination of a **presbyter,** Hippolytus notes that the bishop lays hands on him while other presbyters also touch him. The bishop prays, perhaps using some of the same language as in the ordination of a bishop but specifically invoking the Spirit for the ministry of a presbyter. The prayer cites Moses' choice of the seventy (Num. 11:17-25; cf. also Luke 10:1-17). The ordinand's new colleagues in the order of presbyters also share the laying on of hands (though not in reciting the prayer). But, in the case of the **deacon,** only the bishop lays on hands since, Hippolytus tells us, the deacon serves the bishop and is not a member of the council of presbyters. Prayer invoking the Holy Spirit for the work of a deacon is used. For all three orders, the central act is the **ordination prayer,** said during the **laying on of hands.** Other ceremonial is minimal.

The sacramentaries[8] contain appropriate prayers for ordination of all three orders: usually a bidding prayer, a collect, and the ordination prayer itself. Usually the last are a catena of scriptural preferences, beginning with Moses and culminating in invocation of the Holy Spirit for the work of the appropriate order.

In the third century, only three orders were ordained. But the early Middle Ages saw the elaboration of four **minor orders: porter, lector, exorcist,** and **acolyte.** At first, these were simply instituted by being given the tools of their trade, i.e., the **tradition of instruments** (key, book of lessons, book of exorcism, and candle, candlestick, and cruet). The ceremony of **tonsure** (cutting of hair) marked the pledge of celibacy and entrance into **major orders,** which came to be reckoned as: subdeacon, deacon, and priest. Rites for each minor order developed with an address, a formula as they were given the symbols of their office, and two prayers of blessing. The **subdeacon** shares in the ministry of the altar-table, so celibacy was imposed at this stage. Originally these orders were permanent and not stepping stones to a "higher" order. For centuries, bishops of Rome were chosen from among the Roman deacons.

251

The latest revision of the *Roman Pontifical* (English translation, 1978) has abolished the tonsure, the minor orders of porter and exorcist, and the major order of subdeacon, and produced rites of "Institution" of readers and of acolytes and a rite of "Admission to Candidacy for Ordination as Deacons and Priests" (Rites, 723-75; *Pontifical,* 133-48).[9] Ordination rites for three major orders follow: bishop, priest, and deacon (*Pontifical,* 149-254) plus the "Blessing of an Abbot" or "Blessing of an Abbess" (257-80) and "Consecration to a Life of Virginity" (283-325).

Abolition of several orders is not the only drastic simplification that has occurred in the new Roman Pontifical. The Middle Ages saw the accretion of a number of subsidiary ceremonies, largely the result of fusing ninth- and tenth-century Gallican practices to the more restrained Roman rites. Such ceremonies included anointing the hands of the priest, vesting ordinands in the appropriate vestment, and tradition of instruments. These found their way via the tenth-century Romano-Germanic Pontifical back to Rome itself in the eleventh century. They were further elaborated by the great Bishop William **Durandus** of Mende, France, during the late thirteenth century, by the Roman curia late in the fifteenth, and became part of the post-Tridentine *Roman Pontifical,* published in 1596. Until recently, such subsidiary ceremonies have tended to overshadow the ordination prayer and laying on of hands. A series of short prayers and an imperative formula had taken the place of the primitive great ordination prayer. This has now been restored. The ancient role of the people in election of the candidates and in acclaiming them "worthy" had disappeared but is now recovered somewhat.

The rites the Reformers inherited were of confused priorities. It is not surprising that they had only moderate success in unraveling the historical complexities of ordination. Much of the ceremonial was eliminated. Laying on of hands seems to have been generally maintained, though even this was avoided for a time in Geneva and Scotland because of fear of superstition. Minor orders and the subdiaconate were everywhere abolished. Luther performed one of the earliest Protestant ordinations in 1525; and the rite that he eventually devised, though he never published it, became the source of most Lutheran ordination. His text of 1539 for "Ordination of Ministers of the Word" consists largely of scripture, admonitions, prayer, and the laying on of hands while reciting the Lord's Prayer.[10] The first Anglican collection of ordination rites (the **ordinal**) dates from 1550 and was revised in 1552. It contained more ceremonial. The ordination formula is imperative ("Take thou" or "Receive"), rather than a prayer, and is addressed to each candidate during the laying on of hands.

For many in the Free Church tradition the great change was that ordination became an act of the local congregation, with election once again a real practice. Frequently ordination was practiced by members of the congregation or by ministers of neighboring churches. Most Quakers, of course, dispensed altogether with ordained ministry.

Recent revisions, both Protestant and Roman Catholic, have shown a return to the priorities of the early church as witnessed to in Hippolytus. The new *Roman Pontifical,* the Episcopal services (BCP, 511-47), the United Methodist *Proposed Ordinal for Alternative Use,* the United Church of Christ rite (SoC #6) all agree in making the great prayer of ordination the center of the rite with simultaneous laying on of hands. These central prayers are modeled on Hippolytus' examples and replace imperative formulas with invocation. Most of these rites indicate that ordination should occur in the context of the eucharist, with those being ordained exercising their proper roles in the eucharist. The role of the congregation is magnified with opportunity for acclaiming the candidates or promising support to the ordained (Wb, 89-95). Subsidiary ceremonies are retained in most cases but made clearly secondary to the ordination prayer and laying on of hands. These new rites are more remarkable for their similarity than their diversity.

How have Christians understood the rite of ordination as functioning within the life of the church? One could easily develop an ecclesiology from the rites themselves, but our concern is with how the rites function.

It is clear from the New Testament onward that ordination is accomplished through prayer and laying on of hands. Our earliest examples of the prayer (Hippolytus) fall into a familiar pattern: thanksgiving to God for what God has already done in times past, and invocation of further work in giving requisite gifts to those being ordained. Thanksgiving and supplication form this prayer much as they do the eucharistic prayer. The church has been much more consistent in ordinations in testifying to the work of the Holy Spirit.

The other biblical act, the laying on of hands, signifies the power and authority received by the ordinand to be exercised within the church. Varying views explain how this power and authority relate to continuity and succession whether through persons or through teachings. The variety of gifts that Paul mentions in I Corinthians 12 are all given by the Spirit for one purpose: to be used for the edification of the church. Hippolytus speaks repeatedly of the "Holy Spirit in the holy Church," and his prayers are for gifts of the Holy Spirit to be used in ministry within the holy church.

The early understanding of ordination got confused in the course of history. The Scholastic urge to fit ordination into the same pattern as the other sacraments eventuated in the Council of Florence's decree that the matter "for the priesthood is the cup with the wine and the paten with the bread; for the diaconate, the books of the Gospel, for the subdiaconate, an empty cup placed upon an empty paten."[11] The form for priests, it declared, was "receive the power to offer sacrifice in the Church for the living and the dead, in the name of the Father, and of the Son, and of the Holy Ghost." Since Christ did not specify the form or matter of ordination, the church could revise its practices. In 1947 Pius XII in *The Apostolic Constitution on Holy Orders* reaffirmed that the matter was laying on of hands. The form he prescribed now appears within the ordination prayer in the new *Pontifical*.

The Reformers had difficulty accepting the concept that ordination conveys an indelible character. Luther saw ordination as functional in designating one Christian to do what all have the authority to do and indeed any could if stranded on a desert island without benefit of clergy: "We are all priests, and there is no difference between us; that is to say we have the same power in respect to the Word and all the sacraments."[12]

Ordination remained for Luther a public calling to "the ministry of the Word." Some of the Free Churches took this even further in making ordination really equal to installation into the pastoral office in a local church. Reordination, however, is rarely practiced when one moves to serve another congregation or when one changes denominations. It was, however, a major problem in the Anglican-Methodist unity talks of the 1960s. These talks produced one of the finest new ordinals, although unused.[13]

In general, Protestants have avoided the belief that ordination brings specific graces and have looked at it largely as designating people to certain functions. One could argue that the apostolic practice of laying on of hands suggests a higher concept of authority than the words of theologians may concede. On the other hand, election and acclamation by the people certainly show that whatever power and authority are conferred have meaning only as used in ministry to the church. It is vital to recognize that *ordination is something done for the church and not just to individuals.* Only in recent years have we realized that preoccupation with what the individual receives misses the point and that what the community itself receives is the real focus of this sacrament.

Ordination functions within the community of faith as a way of making visible a new relationship of love. The congregation rejoices in someone's being called by God to serve it through ordained ministry and for the gifts of leadership he or she brings. It is a service of thanksgiving in that ordination acknowledges and thanks God for God's **providential call** of a person to ministry and invokes God's further blessing on that individual. Ordination also functions as a formal **ecclesiastical call** by which the church recognizes that a person has been called of God and is now set aside as one who is suitable to represent the Christian community.

It is indeed strange that Christianity has never developed rites to commemorate entrance into nonecclesiastical vocations. Luther and most Protestants have maintained that every vocation that serves others is a valid priestly vocation. Luther reminds us that the milkmaid has as holy a vocation as the nun. Each and every person in an honest occupation serves his or her neighbor and thus is involved in ministry. But the churches have never developed rites comparable to ordination for those who choose other ways to serve humanity.

Most pastors will not have opportunity to plan ordinations, but there are a few practical matters in most of the new rites that deserve mention. In the first place, since ordination is for the people, the people themselves need to have opportunity for active participation. Spontaneous acclamations when the candidates are presented, even applause, ought to be encouraged. Hymns and unison prayers should be shared in fully by those gathered. Representatives of the laity may be involved in some acts, especially in greeting those newly ordained. This ought not to be left only to parents and family but, as much as possible, done also by those whom the ones ordained will actually serve.

The ancient use of the eucharist as the context in which ordination is done has much to commend it. Ordination is almost as joyful an occasion as a wedding; the congregation is almost certainly all Christian and thus for them the eucharist is the most suitable sign of joy and thanksgiving. The eucharist also gives those ordained the first public opportunity to exercise important parts of their ministry of word and sacrament.

Much has happened in recent years to make the new ordination rites converge. If the various churches were as close in their understanding of orders and ministry as they are in practice of ordination, Christians would indeed have reached a happy stage for the reunion of Christianity. But doing sometimes precedes thinking, and use of the new rites is certainly a major step toward unity.

III

The church's **ministry to the sick** has involved a variety of cultic acts over the centuries. These have ranged from simple bedside prayer to public healing services. Recent years have seen a major shift in practice on the part of Roman Catholics and increased interest among Protestants in exploring new ways of ministering to the sick. Both have had to avoid the bizarre and spectacular.

The Gospels are full of accounts of Jesus' healing ministry, and Acts makes it clear that the Apostles continued in this work. Mark 6:13 tells us: "many sick people they anointed with oil and cured" while Jesus was still with them. Apostolic practice is abundantly chronicled, but the key passage for subsequent developments is James 5:14-16. Several matters stand out in this passage. The elders or presbyters (the council presiding over a church) are those with the ministry of healing. Their function is "to pray over" the sick person and to "anoint him with oil in the name of the Lord." The purpose is definitely healing of the body, but it is also accompanied by forgiveness of sins. Therefore all Christians are advised to confess their sins to one another and to pray for one another, for thus they will be healed physically.

The use of oil for healing purposes was widespread in the ancient world and was both used for anointing and taken internally. For Christians, such use was natural since "Messiah" or "Christ" meant anointed one.

Both human prayer and divine activity are joined: prayer to save and the Lord to raise up. The statement of the power to heal is strong, though no more so than Mark 16:18.

The most striking part of the passage, of course, is the linkage of physical healing to forgiveness of sin. We are inclined to distinguish sharply between these two, but the writer is concerned with full restoration, both bodily and spiritual. Quite clearly the purpose of anointing and prayer is both physical and spiritual healing.

Our next major insight into anointing of the sick comes in Hippolytus. After the eucharistic prayer, someone may offer oil. The bishop gives thanks over the oil, and God is asked to grant that "it may give strength to all that taste of it and health to all that use it."[14] The oil is obviously meant both to be drunk and to be applied externally for the purpose of healing. More than a century later, Sarapion gives us more detail; he includes a prayer over the oil after the eucharistic prayer: "that every fever and every evil spirit and every sickness may depart through the drinking and anointing."[15] A subsequent prayer in Sarapion's collection is even more explicit in listing the medicinal and exorcistic virtues ascribed to the oil. In these early centuries, persons in need of healing (or their friends) would bring oil to church, have it blessed, and then drink it or anoint themselves. The Eastern churches were more insistent on having priests do the anointing.

Eventually, Maundy Thursday came to be the normal time for blessing the **three sacramental oils:** olive oil for use at baptism, olive oil for anointing the sick, and chrism (olive oil and balm) used at confirmation. Among Roman Catholics, these are blessed by the bishop at the cathedral on Maundy Thursday morning with all the priests in the diocese present.

Well into the Middle Ages, the purpose of anointing of the sick was seen as restoration to health, both physical and spiritual. Peter Lombard says it has "a double purpose, namely for the remission of sins, and for the relief of bodily infirmity." The one who receives it properly is "relieved both in body and in soul, provided it is expedient that he be relieved in both."[16] Lombard then launches into a long defense of repetition of the sacrament in case of recurring illness. But the later twelfth century increasingly saw anointing solely as preparation of the dying soul for entrance into heaven as implied by the name **extreme unction.** This was a drastic change from the earlier conception and practice, which saw anointing as involving healing for both soul and body. Until recently, the Scholastics were appealed to in supporting the approach that unction was the "sacrament of consecration for death."

Whereas the earliest method of anointing seems to have been wherever there was pain, by the late Middle Ages it came to be on the eyes, ears, nostrils, mouth, hands, feet, and loins, all capable of sin. By the fifteenth century, it was determined that it should be given only to those in danger of death. The form was: "Through this holy unction and his most tender compassion, the Lord grants thee forgiveness of whatever sins thou hast committed by the sight," etc., the matter being olive oil blessed by the bishop.[17] The benefit is "the healing of the mind and, so far as is expedient, of the body also," a rather dubious second thought.

Subsidiary sacraments and sacramentals also grew up as part of the church's ministry to the sick and dying. These include a series of psalms, prayers, lessons, and sprinkling with holy water for use when visiting the sick. Confession may be heard, if possible. Confirmation is to be given if not done previously. Communion is to be given (the **viaticum**). An apostolic blessing is provided, and, at death, the soul of the dying is commended to God with the prayer: "Depart, O Christian soul." In all, just as the catechumenate ritualized the whole process of conversion, so the rites of the sick ritualized the whole process of dying as a Christian.

Little of this survived the Reformation. Calvin denounced anointing as "playacting, by which, without reason and without benefit, they wish to resemble the apostles."[18] The apostles' gift of healing was a "temporary gift," and Calvin will have none of the current way "these fellows [Catholics] smear with their grease not the sick but half-dead corpses." Cranmer preserved portions of the Sarum "order for visiting a sick man," though abbreviating it greatly. The BCP retained a psalm, prayers, an exhortation, the Creed in interrogatory form (as at baptism), confession and absolution, psalmody, and anointing "upon the forehead or breast only." Bucer had problems with the anointing, and it disappeared in 1552. But Bucer had no such problem with Cranmer's rite for "The Communion of the Sicke," which provided that on communion days some of the elements should be reserved and brought from the church celebration to the sickroom. On other days, there was to be an abbreviated celebration "in the sicke mans house." Calvin, however, disagreed: reservation was "useless" since the sick cannot hear the institution and promises. If these are recited in the sickroom this "is a true consecration," but prior consecration is of no effect.[19] Peter Martyr sided with Calvin, and any mention of reservation vanished in the 1552 BCP.

All traditions continued informal forms of **visitation of the sick,** and most of these involved prayers and probably confession for those anxious to die well. Early Methodism saw frequent sickroom communion celebrations. Anointing reappeared among the Church of the Brethren early in the eighteenth century. The current rite includes reading of scripture, an invitation to confession, and the anointing with oil on the head thrice: "for the forgiveness of your sins, for the strengthening of your faith, and for healing and wholeness according to God's grace and wisdom."[20]

Within the past century, there have developed in both Protestant and Roman Catholic circles public healing services. Outside the United States these are sometimes associated with shrines. Radio and television ministries have enormously spread the popularity of such services. Christian Science provides a healing ministry. All these efforts, though occasionally not above criticism, reflect the persistence of deep human need in this area and the frequent failure of mainline parishes to provide for it. Some of the most interesting experiments have been done among charismatics in this country and in new Christian sects in Africa, many of which have mass anointings. Sporadic concerns arise, but public healing services seem to appear at local initiative rather than as official rites promoted by any church.

The situation with sickroom rites is more positive. Vatican II gave instructions to broaden the sacrament and rename it the "anointing of the sick" for anyone "in danger of death from sickness or old age" (CSL, 73). Today there has been apparent success in reversing the twelfth-century narrowing, so that the sacrament is given for anyone seriously ill and may be repeated. The new rites include "Visitation and Communion of the Sick"; "Rite of Anointing a Sick Person"; "Viaticum"; "Rite of the Sacraments for Those Near Death—Continuous Rite of Penance, Anointing, and Viaticum"; "Confirmation of a Person in Danger of Death"; "Rite for the Commendation of the Dying"; and assorted texts (Rites, 573-642). Many options are provided to adapt the rites to varying circumstances. For those dying baptized, three or even four sacraments are provided as forms of ministry.

The Episcopal Church has renamed and extensively revised its "Ministration to the Sick" (BCP, 453-61). Anointing is now provided as an integral (though optional) part of the rite. There is provision for either sickroom celebration of the eucharist or use of the reserved sacrament. There is also "Ministration at the Time of Death" (462-67) with the traditional commendation "Depart, O Christian soul" and prayers for a vigil. United Methodists are working on supplemental worship resources for use with the sick and dying.

There are many touchy theological issues involved in the ministry of healing, and the church has not always been willing to deal with them. The late medieval narrowing of anointing to a final catchall sacrament of penance simplified things considerably but solved nothing. It meant the church tended to lose sight of the unity of spiritual and physical affliction about which the Bible was so realistic. It means a convenient but unrealistic dualism between body and soul. Though the New Testament is generally careful not to make illness the result of sin, it does show a close relation of the two, as when Jesus heals by forgiving sin (Matt. 9:2-6) or the James 5:14-16 passage. Penance, too, was described in the early church as a healing medicine (Tertullian, "On Penance"). The church's ministry is to the healing of both the body and the soul. Christians are called to save people and not just souls. A large part of the ministry of Jesus and the apostles was spent healing people's bodies as well as souls.

There are certainly difficulties in the modern world to recover for anointing the sign value it once had in a culture when everyone associated anointing with healing and personal hygiene. But there would seem to be real pastoral values in having such an objective act as part of ministry to the sick in order to do something visible and concrete beside verbalizing prayers.

The problems with regard to the reserved sacrament have changed drastically since the Reformation. As early as Justin Martyr, communion elements were sent to those absent (sick and imprisoned).[21] The fears the Reformation had of adoration of the consecrated elements seem hardly a present danger today. It would seem that fresh possibilities of ministry have opened up here. Of course, a sickroom celebration with a small group present is a fuller sign when feasible.

A central problem in ministry to the sick is how to express adequately the church's loving concern for both body and soul, the whole person. James 5:16 suggests that all Christians are to participate in confessing and praying for one another "and then you will be healed." Our Christian neighbor, to whom we are united in baptism, has a claim on us and we on him or her, to share in sustaining health. In this sense, ministry to the sick is an important relationship of love within the community of faith. Healing is a concern in which the whole community of faith makes its love for an ailing member visible. Relationships of love demand honesty and peace of conscience for which mutual confession becomes a part of healing of both mind and body.

Though only a few may have the ministry of anointing or bringing communion, all are called to engage in intercessory prayer for the sick member of the body. Ministry to the sick is by the whole Christian community, though most of it will take place outside the sickroom. Every Sunday service ought to include the sick and injured in the corporate prayers of intercession, and all members ought to engage in this ministry in their personal devotions. Ministry to the sick is an important part of making love visible as God acts through the community of faith.

A few pastoral dimensions are clear. Ministry to the sick involves the participation of all the congregation, but much of the actual visitation will be the responsibility of the clergy. Much could be said about the need for more **objective acts** of ministry, such as anointing and communion. The Church of the Brethren *Pastor's Manual,* as well as the new Roman Catholic and Episcopalian rites, is well worth study. There are many places where actions speak louder than words, and the sickroom is often one of these. One often despairs of saying the right thing but sometimes an expressive gesture can be more nearly adequate. Frequently just one's presence, just being there, is the foremost sign we have of concern. But a general sensitivity to what we do as well as to what we say ought to be cultivated. Taking the patient's hand, placing one's hand on his or her forehead, anointing with prayer, and giving communion are important forms of this ministry. Often these objective acts communicate even when hearing is impossible.

Clergy never engage in ministry alone but share it with the rest of the Christian community. Concern for the sick ought to flow over into both public and private worship. More structures need to be devised to encourage lay people to visit the sick, many of whom a pastor cannot reach regularly. This is an important part of the ministry of the laity, too important to leave to chance.

Churches need to develop public **services of healing** of body and soul which do take seriously that God does act to give Godself to people in public worship. Not the least of God's gifts is the gift of healing of body and soul.

IV

Christian burial is practiced to console the bereaved and to commend the deceased to God. This may not seem a cheerful subject with which to end our study of Christian worship, but it does show that the Christian's whole life involves the praise of God from baptism to burial. And the observance of Christian death has much to tell about Christian life itself.

Attitudes about Christian burial, historically, seem to have evolved through three quite different stages: hope, fear, and refusal to think about it. These are reflected in the rites themselves in various ways, some subtle and others less so. The services themselves are often crystallized attitudes about death itself.

We have no New Testament information about Christian burial and very little from the first three centuries A.D. Even Hippolytus tells us nothing except to indicate that there was a Christian cemetery and that the price of burial was to be kept reasonable. Tertullian indicates a funeral eucharist and a yearly eucharist on the anniversary of death ("Of the Crowns," 3). Sarapion gives us a prayer for a dead person before burial. It is mostly a recital of God's acts but turns to supplication for the rest of the deceased, for his or her final resurrection, for forgiveness of sins, for consolation of the bereaved, and ends with a petition to "grant unto us all a good end."[22] Augustine tells of the burial of his mother, Monica, mentioning few details except his restraint in tears and the prayers of the funeral eucharist.[23]

Several general observations can be made about early Christian burial practices. The general atmosphere of Christian burial was that of *hope* in the resurrection. Augustine's dry-eyed statement may be a bit extreme but not too much so. The dead Christian who had kept the faith was treated as a victor, and the funeral procession had the character of the triumph accorded a victorious general on return home. Since cemeteries, by Christian times, were outside the city walls, the carrying forth was a major part of the rite. It was done to the accompaniment of psalms of hope and praise and shouts of alleluia. White garments were worn, palm leaves and lights were carried, and incense burned as the community marched to the cemetery in broad daylight (unlike the nighttime funerals of pagans). Previously the body had been washed, anointed, and wrapped in linen at the home of the deceased while prayers were said.

At the grave there was prayer and celebration of the eucharist. Augustine notes: "The sacrifice of our ransom was offered for her [Monica], when now the corpse was by the grave's side." After the corpse was given the final kiss of peace, it was buried with the feet toward the rising sun. An *agape* might follow immediately, and there were services on various days after death and on the anniversary of the death. For heroes of the faith such as martyrs, these anniversaries could be important occasions. The account of the second-century death of Polycarp, "Martyrdom of Polycarp," speaks of the community's intention "to gather together in joy and gladness to celebrate the day of his martyrdom as a birthday, in memory of those athletes who have gone before, and to train and make ready those who are to come hereafter."[24]

Death, for the Christian, was a "heavenly birthday," and the saints were commemorated on their birthdays (*natalis*) into eternity rather than their mundane birthdays into finite time. Chronicles of their lives and deaths were collected in martyrologies, from which selections were read on each heavenly birthday (death day).

Like weddings, the funeral services of the church were much influenced by Roman customs, though many were rejected (such as cremation). The practice of commemoration of the dead by funeral meals at the gravesite (*refrigerium*) the church turned into a eucharist and gave the food to the poor. The sense of continuity of the family through generations, centering on the family burial plot, still is strong in Rome. Even today, All Saints' Day and All Souls' Day are kept as reunions of generations across time.

The medieval ethos of Christian burial took a different turn; that of *fear*. Burial came to be draped with the medieval imagination of hell and purgatory and the terrors of dying unprepared. The eucharist has suffered whenever it has been used for disciplinary purposes; funerals were also abused. The medieval mind tended to feel that if one could scare the hell out of people, it might be possible to scare them out of hell. Death became a threat used to discipline the living. Who could ignore a prayer such as that used in the York province: "Deliver him from the cruel fire of the boiling pit"? Most medieval parish churches had graphic mural paintings of the last judgment (the doom) over the chancel arch with the torments of the damned displayed with gusto. Late medieval drama often included a hell's mouth into which unrepentant sinners were dragged. Dante shows us the whole scheme at its most sophisticated level; for others it was equally vivid and real.

The burial rites came to be permeated wih awe and fear over the destination of the soul. The **office of the dead** developed out of psalms originally sung at funerals and eventually had forms for vespers, matins, and lauds. Medieval burials were usually in churchyards. The body was met at the churchyard lych-gate (corpse gate) and carried into the church with psalms; the eucharist was celebrated, and the dead was granted absolution, incensed, and sprinkled with holy water. Interment followed in the churchyard or beneath the church. The absolution shows the change from the early church's sense of triumphant victory. The *dies irae* (day of wrath) chant from the twelfth or thirteenth century reflects the late medieval focus on judgment and the possibility of damnation, so different from the clear confidence of early Christians.

The Reformation did not find it easy to shake loose these attitudes, even though fear of purgatory was no longer a sanction. Luther deplored the mournful character of funerals and wanted to make them stronger expressions of hope. He condemned "popish abominations, such as vigils, masses for the dead, processions, purgatory, and all other hocus-pocus on behalf of the dead" in favor of services stressing the resurrection of the dead with "comforting hymns of the forgiveness of sins, of rest, sleep, life, and of the resurrection of departed Christians."[25] Luther left no burial rite but seems to have utilized hymns, psalms, a sermon, and simple ceremonial.

A low ebb was reached in the *Westminster Directory* of 1644, which decreed that the body be "decently attended" to the cemetery but immediately buried "without any ceremony." Even funeral sermons became controversial among both the Scots and English Puritans, for they often degenerated into eulogies of virtues real and imaginary. Some in the Free Church tradition regarded burial as purely a secular matter and conducted no services. Calvin had approved of funeral sermons but never provided a liturgy for Christian burial. Usually the Reformed tradition tolerated a service of scripture and sermon after the burial. Out of this possibility and borrowing from the Anglican rite eventually developed the Free Church practice of a service of psalmody, lessons, a sermon, and prayer, concluding with a graveside committal service.

Anglican revisions of the burial rite were more conservative, though there was a further lurch to the left in 1552. Cranmer, in 1549, condensed the office of the dead and assimilated the churchyard procession, the committal, and an optional eucharist (for which propers were given). The service might take place entirely in the graveyard or partly in the church. A conscious effort was made to stress hope through Christ and the resurrection. In 1552, reference to the eucharist disappeared, and the service took place almost wholly at the graveside. The cautious prayers for the dead in the 1549 version had also vanished. The brief rite that remained consisted of sentences, prayers, Revelation 14:13, I Corinthians 15:20-58, and words of committal while earth was cast upon the body. Subsequent history brought expanded psalmody and more prayers. Wesley kept the 1662 rite basically, though omitting Psalm 39, a prayer, and the committal. The great change Methodism brought was the addition of fervent hymns of hope.

Modern Christianity, all too often, has forgotten both hope and fear and has *refused to think about death* as part of the Christian message. Cemeteries are now located out in the suburbs of our consciousness, and burial customs have been largely commercialized. The seventeenth century saw the introduction of tombstones and private burial plots for ordinary people. Previously, like Hamlet's Yorick, one could occupy a bit of earth for thirty years and then it was another's turn. Caskets became common for ordinary people in the nineteenth century and embalming at the time of the Civil War. The result is that moderns have become more superstitious about death than our medieval ancestors, though much less colorful and imaginative. To pretend that we can preserve even our names, let alone our bodies, would doubtless have amused medieval people. Yet modern practice tries to camouflage the reality of death and ends up creating more fictions than any previous age.

Too often, this has been the fault of the church, which has substituted sentimental funeral services of flowers and poetry for the witness of the gospel. And the church, too often, politely sidesteps mention of death in its weekly life, even during the season of Easter, the period focusing on resurrection. The teaching ministry also has neglected treating something as offensive as death.

Recent services have recaptured many of the more affirmative elements of the early Christian attitude to death. Vatican II mandated that "the rite for the burial of the dead should express more clearly the paschal character of Christian death" (CSL, 81). This resurrection emphasis has been largely accomplished in the new rites. The visual change from black vestments to white (Christ and resurrection) or green (growth) marks a major shift in emphasis. The new rites, which encourage the following of local custom, provide for all or parts of the service to occur at stations in the home of the deceased, in the parish church, at the cemetery chapel, at the grave, or combinations of these (Rites, 645-720). There is also a vigil service, and provision for funerals of children. Many options are provided, including celebration of a funeral mass, anniversary masses, various commemorations, and prayers for the dead (Sac, 857-89).

Other churches have followed the same emphasis on the Paschal nature of the Christian understanding of death. The new Presbyterian rite is entitled "Witness to the Resurrection" (Wb, 71-88), and the United Methodist is *A Service of Death and Resurrection* (SWR #7). The new BCP has two rites for the "Burial of the Dead" and the outline of a third (pp. 469-507).

All three rites contain the possibility of a eucharist, as do the new United Methodist and Lutheran services. Prayers for the dead are an option in the BCP. The greater part of these services consists of psalmody and the reading of the scriptural promises.

Both the new Lutheran "Burial of the Dead" (LBW, 206-14) and the new United Methodist service begin with reference to a Christian's baptism into Christ's death and resurrection and relate baptism and burial. The Methodist service tries to personalize the occasion by a naming and witnessing ceremony in which those who knew the deceased best can commemorate his or her life. The United Church of Christ service asks that the "coffin be closed" (SoC #5), a rubric repeated by United Methodists, Lutherans, and Episcopalians.

How does Christian faith understand the funeral? Its past has been a changing one. As late as the Third Lateran Council of 1179, it was possible to speak of burial of the dead as a sacrament, that is, for most of the church's history. But Christian burial never received the Scholastic attention the seven did and the failure of both Luther and Calvin to develop funeral rites shows that they had more pressing things to do. Thus the funeral has never received as much theological consideration as it deserves, though psychologists, sociologists, and popular writers have leaped in to fill the void. The Christian understanding of death has received somewhat more careful theological examination.[26]

What are the possibilities for understanding the function of Christian burial apart from the utilitarian matter of disposal of the body? Two concerns stand out: to show forth God's love and the community's support in consoling the bereaved, and to commend the deceased to God's gracious care.

The church works best by honesty as it **consoles the bereaved.** We must beware of knowing too much about death. It remains a mystery. Efforts to probe beyond its dark veil, either in modern scientific terms or in speculative pictorial imagery, loosely based on scripture, are all unproductive undertakings. But there are two affirmations that Christian faith can make in all honesty for the benefit of the bereaved. The first of these may seem to be of little comfort, but it is a vital part of the grief process and can only cause prolonged trouble if ignored. This is the reality of death itself. The Bible is clear: "We shall all die; we shall be like water that is spilt on the ground and lost" (II Sam. 14:14), a far more Christian affirmation than any stone monument. For this reason, it is generally better, when possible, to have the body present at a funeral than to have a memorial service. The reality of death is not denied by a religion with the crucifixion at its heart.

But the second affirmation is the trustworthiness of God. This is not a doctrine about death (about which we know very little) but a doctrine of God's trustworthiness (about which we know a great deal). Death makes humans realize how completely dependent they are upon God when all else fails. Whatever lies beyond death is also created by God and experienced before us by Jesus Christ. Christians are not bereft of hope even in the face of death; they are comforted by the only real source of hope in the world, God's gracious love.

The Christian funeral, then, testifies to the realities of death and resurrection. The strong affirmations of scripture are far more potent than any poetry about sleep, passage, or crossing the bar. God's words in scripture and actions in sacraments are the strong medicine needed at this time, not poetry, flowers, or sentimental statements. It is important that the funeral occur in the context of the beloved community, especially in the familiarity of the church building where words and actions of hope have been experienced on the first day of each week throughout one's lifetime.

The presence of the community itself is a strong witness to God's action in love here. Other Christians being there are a visible sign of love. The community together marks the transition of the deceased to a new relationship in the church as that one moves to the Church Triumphant from the Church Militant on earth. The role of other Christians at the funeral is to make visible by their presence the environment of love that encompasses the bereaved.

The second function of the funeral is to **commend the deceased to God.** Potentially, each of the baptized has already died and been raised with Christ in baptism (Rom. 6:3-4). Now is time to remember that God has already shown God's acceptance of us, an acceptance first made visible in our baptism. It is only natural to wish to commend those we love to God's keeping. Concepts of purgatory are very unlikely for modern Protestants (and probably for many Roman Catholics, too, today). But the hope of resurrection in Christ is so central in Christian faith that we can hardly refrain from praying that God will accomplish God's purpose for the deceased. It is most unnatural to pray for a person up to the moment of death and then be dumb. God's love continues after death as well as before, and carefully worded prayers can commend the dead to God's keeping without implying a belief in purgatory.

The Christian funeral, then, has two functions: ministry to the living and ministry to the dead, though it is impossible to separate these. Both are made possible through the understanding that God acts in Christian burial, as in the sacraments, to give Godself afresh to us even at the end of life. The community of faith, entered through the waters of baptism, now for the last time again unites around one to manifest divine love made visible through the community's caring actions.

A few pastoral consequences may be briefly noted. The occasion of death is a time of a sustaining and continuing relationship for which the pastor is likely to have chief responsibility. Counseling with the family before burial and long afterward is an essential ministry. The **grief process** cannot be rushed; the worst danger of all is when people refuse to grieve and it catches up with them unawares. "Putting up a good front" is an invitation to catastrophe. There are few areas of greater need for pastoral sensitivity than counseling the bereaved.

Much of this ministry begins long before death in the **teaching ministry,** which helps church members understand death from a Christian perspective. Through various media, the congregation can be helped to think through the most desirable forms of funerals. None of us is fully mature until he or she knows with certainty that he or she is going to die eventually. Making plans for one's funeral is not necessarily a morbid preoccupation; it can be a witness to one's faith and a splendid way to advance in understanding of life. Members of one retirement home weave their own funeral palls, a magnificent final affirmation.

Pastoral care does not come alone; it presupposes a flock. Others need to share with the pastor in this ministry so as to represent to the bereaved the concern and support of the community. Much can be done to enlist and train members of the congregation in ministry to those of their number who have been bereaved.

The Christian funeral is worship above all else and not primarily a grief therapy session. It should stress the strong promises of scripture as to God's trustworthiness and not rely on anything less. Some form of ministry of the Word seems essential to proclaim and give thanks for God's goodness. Psalmody and scripture are basic, supported by sermon, hymns, prayers, and creed. The eucharist can proclaim the continuing relationship between those in life and those in death within the body of Christ.

The presence of the body at the funeral service and the attendance of people at the committal service are to be encouraged as ways of testifying to the reality of death. Rarely should the body be displayed. It is far better to cover the casket with a **pall,** a cloth about ten feet long and six feet wide with a large cross on it. It testifies far better than cut flowers to the source of our hope in Christ. The pall also cuts down on ostentatious display of coffins. Even when the body is to be given to medical research or to be cremated it can usually be present at the funeral.

Funerals are a very personal occasion, and some means must be found in stressing that it was this particular person who died. This can be done without extravagant praise. But some form of personal identification from someone who knew the deceased well, can be valuable. Sometimes mementos or photographs of things or people central in the life of the deceased may be displayed. Christians are identified by name in baptism and ought to be named as well in their funerals.

Notes

1. What Do We Mean by "Christian Worship"?

1. Paul W. Hoon, *The Integrity of Worship* (Nashville: Abingdon, 1971), p. 77.
2. Peter Brunner, *Worship in the Name of Jesus.* Originally published in German in 1954. Trans. M. H. Bertram (St. Louis: Concordia, 1968), p. 125.
3. Jean-Jacques von Allmen, *Worship: Its Theology and Practice* (New York: Oxford University Press, 1965), p. 33.
4. Evelyn Underhill, *Worship* (London: Nisbet & Co., 1936), p. 339.
5. Godfrey Diekmann, O.S.B., *Personal Prayer and the Liturgy* (London: Geoffrey Chapman, 1969), p. 57.
6. Odo Casel, *The Mystery of Christian Worship* (Westminster, Md.: Newman Press, 1962).
7. For more detailed discussion of this definition, see my *New Forms of Worship* (Nashville: Abingdon, 1971), pp. 40-50.
8. The revisions decreed by the Council of Trent and entrusted to the papacy appeared as the Roman breviary, 1568; missal, 1570; martyrology, 1584; pontifical, 1596; *Caeremoniale Episcoporum*, 1600; and ritual, 1614.
9. Other books that might be combined with these included: the passional (the sufferings of the martyrs), the homily-book (excerpts from the Fathers' expositions of scripture), the *legenda* (accounts of the saints' lives), the responsory (with responds for use after the lessons), the collectar (containing the collects for the day), and the *ordo* (to show how to put it all together for the proper day and hour).
10. These were sometimes separated as an *epistolarium*, containing the Old Testament and Epistle lections, and the *evangelarium*, for the Gospels.
11. Separate collections of graduals, tropes, kyries, and sequences were sometimes used.
12. For a more detailed delineation of these, see my *Christian Worship in Transition* (Nashville: Abingdon, 1976), pp. 61-75.

2. The Language of Time

1. *Early Christian Fathers*, Cyril Richardson, ed. (Philadelphia: Westminster Press, 1953), p. 96.

2. *The Apostolic Fathers,* Kirsopp Lake, trans. (Cambridge: Harvard University Press, 1965), I, 331.
3. *Documents of the Christian Church,* Henry Bettenson, ed. (New York: Oxford University Press, 1952), p. 6.
4. *Early Christian Fathers,* p. 287.
5. *The Apostolic Fathers,* I, 397.
6. *Documents of the Christian Church,* p. 27.
7. *Early Christian Fathers,* p. 174.
8. James Donaldson, ed., ANF, VII, 469.
9. *Baptismal Instructions,* 17. Paul W. Harkins, trans. (Westminster, Md.: Newman Press, 1963), 127.
10. "On Baptism," 19, S. Thelwall, trans., ANF, III, 678.
11. Eusebius, *The History of the Church,* V, 23. G. A. Williamson, trans. (Baltimore: Penguin Books, 1965), p. 230.
12. *Egeria's Travels,* xxx, i; xxxi, 2. John Wilkinson, trans. (London: S.P.C.K., 1971), pp. 132-33.
13. *Letters,* Wilfrid Parsons, trans. (New York: Fathers of the Church, 1951), p. 283.
14. *Cyril of Jerusalem and Nemesius of Emesa,* William Telfer, trans. (Philadelphia: Westminster Press, 1955), p. 68.
15. *Letters,* pp. 284-85.
16. "On Baptism," ANF, III, 678.
17. "Life of Constantine the Great," E. C. Richardson, trans., NPNF, 2nd series, I, 557.
18. John Chrysostom, *Opera Omnia,* Bernard de Montfaucon, ed. (Paris: Gaume, 1834), II, 418.
19. *Ibid.,* II, 436.
20. Cited by L. Duchesne, *Christian Worship,* 5th ed. (London: S.P.C.K., 1923), p. 260, n. 3.
21. "De Corona," 3, ANF, III, 94.
22. *Opera Omnia,* I, 608.
23. Gregory Dix, *Shape of the Liturgy* (Westminster: Dacre, 1945), p. 305.
24. "Formula Missae," in Bard Thompson, ed., *Liturgies of the Western Church* (Cleveland: Meridian Books, 1961), p. 109.
25. "Book of Discipline," *John Knox's History of the Reformation in Scotland* (London: Thomas Nelson and Sons, 1949), II, 281.
26. "The Sunday Service," Thompson, *Liturgies of the Western Church,* p. 417.
27. *The Christian Year: A Suggestive Guide for the Worship of the Church,* drafted and revised by Fred Winslow Adams (New York: Committee on Worship, Federal Council of the Churches of Christ in America; 2nd ed., rev., 1940), p. 9.
28. *The Christian Year and Lectionary Reform* (London: SCM Press, 1958).
29. Pius Parsch, *The Church's Year of Grace* (Collegeville, Minn.: Liturgical Press, 1964–65), 5 vols.
30. Cf. *Proclamation* series (Philadelphia: Fortress Press, 1973–1978), 26 vols.
   Reginald Fuller, *Preaching the New Lectionary* (Collegeville, Minn.: Liturgical Press, 1974).
   Gerard Sloyan, *Commentary on the New Lectionary* (New York: Paulist Press, 1975).

3. The Language of Space

1. Historically, there has always been a close relationship between book artists and religious expression, and in no tradition has such been stronger than in Christianity. And within the context of the book arts, one of the most visible expressions of devotion through art has been in the field of bookbinding. The historic evidence is overwhelming, and it is a tradition that is very much alive today. But the tradition exists now through the support of private patrons or university libraries rather than commissions from the church.
2. For a more detailed account, see my *Protestant Worship and Church Architecture* (New York: Oxford University Press, 1964), chaps. 3-6.
3. In these simplified floor plans, A = altar-table; F = font; P = pulpit; C = choir; L = lectern; D = reading desk.
4. *The Letters of Stephen Gardiner,* ed. James A. Muller (New York: Macmillan, 1933), p. 355.
5. John Ruskin, *The Seven Lamps of Architecture* (London: George Allen, 1903), p. 233.
6. Tillich, "Protestantism and Artistic Style," *Theology of Culture* (New York: Oxford University Press, 1964), pp. 68-75.
7. Cyril Richardson, "Some Reflections on Liturgical Art," *Union Seminary Quarterly Review,* VIII (Spring, 1953), 24-28.
8. Within the past ten years, many bookbinders have completed important, at times brilliant, bindings for Bibles or liturgical books. Some of the most significant have been Bibles or Gospels by Philip Smith, Jeff Clements, William Matthews, Bernard Middleton, Ivor Robinson, and Sydney Cockerell.
9. See my *New Forms of Worship* on vestments, pp. 119-21; on banners, pp. 139-44.
10. For a fuller discussion, cf. the article "Vestments," in *A Dictionary of Liturgy and Worship,* J. G. Davies, ed. (Philadelphia: Westminster Press, 1979), pp. 365-83.
11. Modern classics of typography, both in design and execution, include Daniel Berkely Updike's printing of the *Book of Common Prayer* (1930), Bruce Rogers' *Oxford Lectern Bible* (1935), and Andrew Hoyem's *Psalms of David* (1977).

4. The Spoken Word

1. Chap. 8; *Early Christian Fathers,* Cyril Richardson, ed., p. 174.
2. *The Stromata or Miscellanies* VII, 7; ANF, II, 534.
3. Tertullian, *On Fasting* 10, *On Prayer* 25; Origen, *On Prayer* XII, 2; Cyprian, *On the Lord's Prayer,* 34.
4. Bernard Botte, *La Tradition Apostolique de Saint Hippolyte* (Münster: Aschendorffsche, 1963) for introduction, text, notes, and French translation. English translation: Gregory Dix, ed., *The Apostolic Tradition,* reissued by Henry Chadwick (London: S.P.C.K., 1968); or Burton Scott Easter, *The Apostolic Tradition of Saint Hippolytus* (Hamden: Archon, 1962).
5. Chap. XXXVI; Dix, ed., *The Apostolic Tradition,* p. 63.
6. Chap. XXXIII; *Ibid.,* p. 60. Cf. also chap. XXXV, p. 61.
7. *Commentary on Psalm 64,* verse 10. *Patrologiae Graecae* (Paris: J.-P. Migne, 1857), XXIII, 640.

8. *Apostolic Constitutions,* II, 59; ANF, VII, 423; ANF VIII, 35; VII, 496.
9. *Baptismal Instructions,* 17. Paul W. Harkins, trans., pp. 126-27.
10. *Egeria's Travels,* XXIV; John Wilkinson, trans., pp. 123-24.
11. *Institutes of the Coenobia,* II, 3; NPNF; 2nd series, XI, 206.
12. *Ascetical Works,* Sister M. Monica Wagner, C.S.C., trans. (New York: Fathers of the Church, 1950), pp. 309-10.
13. *Homilies on First Timothy,* #14. NPNF, 1st series, XIII, 456.
14. *Institutes,* III, iv, NPNF, 2nd series, XI, 215.
15. "The Rule," *Western Asceticism* (Philadelphia: Westminster Press, 1958), p. 327.
16. E. C. Ratcliff, "The Choir Offices," in *Liturgy and Worship,* W. K. Lowther Clarke and Charles Harris, eds. (London: S.P.C.K., 1932), p. 266.
17. *The Second Recension of the Quignon Breviary,* J. Wickham Legg, ed. (London: Henry Bradshaw Society, 1908), v. 35; and J. Wickham Legg, *Liturgical Introduction with Life of Quignon* (Henry Bradshaw Society, 1912), v. 42.
18. *Liturgy of the Hours: The General Instruction* (London: Geoffrey Chapman, 1971), p. 35, par. 77.
19. Cf. "Formula Missae" and "Deutsche Messe," *Liturgies of the Western Church,* Bard Thompson, ed., pp. 120-21 and 129-30.
20. *The First and Second Prayer Books of Edward VI* (London: J. M. Dent, 1952), p. 3.
21. *Ibid.,* p. 4.
22. "First Apology," 67, *Early Christian Fathers,* Richardson, ed., p. 287.
23. This is Baumstark's famous second law, explicated in his *Comparative Liturgiology* (London: A. R. Mowbray, 1958), p. 27. The first law is that ancient elements in time tend to be duplicated by more modern items; then, when the redundancy is eventually noted, the earlier ones are eliminated (p. 23).
24. Sermon #325, *Patrologiae Latina* (Paris: J.-P. Migne, 1863), XXXVIII, 1449.
25. Thompson, *Liturgies of the Western Church,* pp. 106-22.
26. *Ibid.,* pp. 123-37.
27. *Ibid.,* pp. 197-208.
28. Hughes O. Old, *The Patristic Roots of Reformed Worship* (Zurich: Theologischer Verlag, 1975), pp. 208-18.
29. Thompson, *Liturgies of the Western Church,* pp. 354-71.
30. *Ibid.,* pp. 245-68.
31. *Ibid.,* pp. 269-84.
32. *Ibid.,* pp. 422-33.
33. Cf. John Knox, *Integrity of Preaching* (Nashville: Abingdon, 1957).
Ronald Sleeth, *Proclaiming the Word* (Abingdon, 1964).
Gustaf Wingren, *The Living Word* (Philadelphia: Muhlenberg, 1960).
Karl Barth, *The Preaching of the Gospel* (Philadelphia: Westminster Press, 1963).
P. T. Forsyth, *Positive Preaching and the Modern Mind* (London: Independent Press, 1960).
Reginald Fuller, *What Is Liturgical Preaching?* (London: SCM Press, 1957).
Heinrich Ott, *Theology and Preaching* (Westminster Press, 1965).
H. H. Farmer, *Servant of the Word* (Philadelphia: Fortress Press, 1964).

Domenico Grasso, *Proclaiming God's Message* (Notre Dame, Ind.: University of Notre Dame Press, 1965).

Dietrich Ritschl, *A Theology of Proclamation* (Richmond: John Knox Press, 1963).

5. The Acted Sign

1. "Tractus on John," LXXX, 3, NPNF, 1st series, VII, 344, and *Institutes*, IV, xiv, 4; *Library of Christian Classics*, XXI, 1279.
2. The central thesis of E. Schillebeeckx, *Christ the Sacrament of the Encounter with God* (New York: Sheed & Ward, 1963).
3. Cf. Joachim Jeremias, *Eucharistic Words of Jesus* (New York: Scribner's, 1966), pp. 106-37.
4. *Institutes*, IV, xvii, 32, p. 1403.
5. Text in Elizabeth Frances Rogers, ed. *Peter Lombard and the Sacramental System* (Merrick, N.Y.: Richwood, 1976), IV, ii, 1; p. 85.
6. *Ibid.*, IV, i, 6. Rogers, p. 82.
7. *Ibid.*, IV, i, 4; Rogers, p. 80.
8. *Ibid.*, IV, xxiii, 3; Rogers, p. 221.
9. Text in *A History of Christianity*, Ray C. Petry, ed. (Englewood Cliffs, N.J.: Prentice-Hall, 1962), p. 324.
10. *Ibid.*, p. 325.
11. For an important discussion of this term and its shifting meanings, cf. Piet Schoonenberg, "Transubstantiation: How Far Is This Doctrine Historically Determined?" *The Sacraments, an Ecumenical Dilemma* (New York: Paulist Press, 1966), *Concilium*, XXIV, 78-91.
12. "Canons and Dogmatic Decrees of the Council of Trent," *The Creeds of Christendom*, Philip Schaff, ed. (Grand Rapids: Baker, n.d.), II, 119.
13. *Institutes*, IV, xvii, 1, p. 1361.
14. *The Mystery of Christian Worship and Other Writings*, Burkhard Neunheuser, ed. (Westminster, Md.: Newman Press, 1962), p. 124.
15. Cf. also Schillebeeckx's *Eucharist* (New York: Sheed & Ward, 1968).
16. *Institutes*, IV, xiv, 3, p. 1278.

6. Initiation and Reconciliation

1. Mandate IV, iii, 6. *The Apostolic Fathers*, Kirsopp Lake, trans., II, 85.
2. Kurt Aland, *Did the Early Church Baptize Infants?* (London: SCM Press, 1963), p. 10.
3. Cf. Oscar Cullmann, *Baptism in the New Testament* (London: SCM Press, 1950).
4. *Didache*, 9 and 7; in *Early Christian Fathers*, Cyril Richardson, ed., pp. 174-75.
5. *First Apology*, 61 and 65; Richardson, *Early Christian Fathers*, pp. 282, 285.
6. *On Baptism*, 20; ANF, III, 678-79.
7. *Ibid.*, 17; ANF, III, p. 677.
8. *Of the Crowns*, 3, in *Documents of the Baptismal Liturgy*, E. C. Whitaker, ed. (London: S.P.C.K., 1970), p. 10.
9. *On Baptism*, 8; ANF, III, 672.
10. Gregory Dix, ed., *The Apostolic Tradition*, p. 38.

11. *Didascalia Apostolorum,* 16, R. Hugh Connolly, ed. (Oxford: Clarendon Press, 1969), p. 147.
12. *Egeria's Travels,* xlv-xlvii; John Wilkinson, trans., pp. 143-46.
13. *Concerning the Sacraments,* I, 4; in *Documents of the Baptismal Liturgy,* Whitaker, ed., p. 128.
14. *Mystagogical Catechesis* 2; in Whitaker, *Documents,* p. 29.
15. Whitaker, pp. 40-41. Cf. also Edward Yarnold, *The Awe-Inspiring Rites of Initiation* (London: St. Paul, 1972).
16. *Concerning the Sacraments,* III, 8; Whitaker, *Documents,* p. 131.
17. J. D. C. Fisher, *Christian Initiation: Baptism in the Medieval West* (London: S.P.C.K., 1970), p. 148.
18. *Ibid.,* p. 106.
19. Cf. John T. McNeill and Helena M. Gamer, *Medieval Handbooks of Penance* (New York: Columbia University Press, 1938).
20. *Luther's Works,* Ulrich S. Leopold, ed. (Philadelphia: Fortress Press, 1965), LIII, 107-9.
21. Rubrics in "The Form of Prayers and . . . Manner of Administering the Sacraments," text in *Christian Initiation: The Reformation Period,* J. D. C. Fisher, ed. (London: S.P.C.K., 1970), p. 117.
22. Text cited by Rollin S. Armour, *Anabaptist Baptism* (Scottdale, Pa.: Herald Press, 1966), pp. 143-44.
23. G. R. Beasley-Murray, *Baptism in the New Testament* (Exeter: Paternoster Press, 1962), p. 125.
24. Fisher, *Reformation Period,* p. 173.
25. *Ibid.,* pp. 174-78.
26. *Institutes,* IV, xix, 13, p. 1461.
27. *Luther's Works,* LIII, 116-21.
28. For a more detailed account, cf. my *Worldliness of Worship* (New York: Oxford University Press, 1967), pp. 132-45.
29. *First Apology,* 61 and 65, in Richardson, *Early Christian Fathers,* pp. 282-83, 285.
30. *Vs. Heresies,* III, xvii, 2 in Henry Bettenson, *The Early Christian Fathers* (London: Oxford University Press, 1963), p. 129.
31. *Enchiridion,* XLIII-LII; NPNF, 1st series, III, 252-54.
32. *Sentences,* IV, ii-vi, in Elizabeth Rogers, ed., *Peter Lombard and the Sacramental System,* pp. 85-116.
33. *Ibid.,* IV, vii, 3; Rogers, ed., p. 117.
34. In *A History of Christianity,* Ray C. Petry, ed., p. 326.
35. IV, xiv, 4; Rogers, ed., *Peter Lombard,* p. 158.
36. *Decree for the Armenians,* Petry, *A History,* p. 328.
37. "The Holy and Blessed Sacrament of Baptism," *Luther's Works,* XXXV, 36.
38. *Ibid.,* p. 34.
39. "Of Baptism," *Zwingli and Bullinger,* G. W. Bromiley, ed. (Philadelphia: Westminster Press, 1953), p. 156.
40. *Institutes,* IV, xv, 1, p. 1303.
41. Menno Simons, "Foundation of Christian Doctrine," *Complete Writings,* J. C. Wenger, ed. (Scottdale, Pa.: Herald Press, 1956), p. 120.
42. Karl Barth, *The Teaching of the Church Regarding Baptism* (London: SCM Press, 1948).
43. Oscar Cullmann, *Baptism in the New Testament.*
44. Jeremias, *Infant Baptism in the First Four Centuries* (Philadelphia:

Westminster Press, 1962) and *The Origins of Infant Baptism* (Philadelphia: Westminster Press, 1963); Aland, *Did the Early Church Baptize Infants?* (London: SCM Press, 1963).

45. Gregory Dix, *The Theology of Confirmation in Relation to Baptism* (London: Dacre, 1946), p. 32.
46. G. W. H. Lampe, *The Seal of the Spirit*, 2nd. ed. (London: S.P.C.K., 1967).

7. The Eucharist

1. Joachim Jeremias, *Eucharistic Words of Jesus*, p. 173.
2. Gregory Dix, *The Shape of the Liturgy*. This book, Joseph Jungmann's *Mass of the Roman Rite* (New York: Benziger, 1951–55), 2 vols., and Brilioth's *Eucharistic Faith and Practice* (London: S.P.C.K., 1953) are modern classics of eucharistic studies. Dix's influence has been profound on almost all liturgical revision ever since the Church of South India rite first appeared in 1950.
3. Church of the Brethren, *Pastor's Manual* (Elgin: Brethren Press, 1978), pp. 27-58; *Sac.*, 208; BCP, 274; LBW-Ministers Desk Edition, 138; SWR #4 (*Ritual for a New Day*) and #8.
4. For a good resumé of this discussion, cf. A. J. B. Higgins, *The Lord's Supper in the New Testament* (London: S. C. M. Press, 1952), pp. 13-23; also Jeremias, *Eucharistic Words*, pp. 41-84.
5. Hans Lietzmann, *Mass and Lord's Supper* (Leiden: L. J. Brill, 1953–), 11 fascicles; also Oscar Cullmann and F. J. Leenhardt, *Essays on the Lord's Supper* (Richmond: John Knox, 1958).
6. Church of the Brethren, *Pastor's Manual*, pp. 27-58.
7. *Didache*, 9-10, 14; Cyril Richardson, ed., *Early Christian Fathers*, pp. 175-76, 178.
8. *First Apology* 65; Richardson, *Early Christian Fathers*, pp. 285-86.
9. Most conveniently available in R. D. C. Jasper and G. J. Cuming, *Prayers of the Eucharist: Early and Reformed* (London: Collins, 1975), pp. 21-25. For original languages, cf. A. Hänggi and I. Pahl, *Prex Eucharistica* (Fribourg: Editions Universitaires, 1968), pp. 80-81. Both books will be most useful throughout the following pages.
10. Jasper and Cuming, *Prayers of the Eucharist*, p. 22.
11. Bernard Botte, *La Tradition Apostolique de Saint Hippolyte*, p. 28.
12. "To the Smyrnaeans," 8; Richardson, *Early Christian Fathers*, p. 115.
13. *Bishop Sarapion's Prayer-Book*, John Wordsworth, ed. (Hamden, Conn.: Archon, 1964), p. 63.
14. Dix, *Shape of the Liturgy*, p. 48.
15. The chronology of the most important Protestant liturgies during the five first crucial years of effort to produce a reformed eucharist is:

1521	Andreas Karlstadt, Wittenberg Christmas Mass (German)
1522	Kaspar Kantz, "Evangelical Mass" (German)
1523	Martin Luther, *Formula Missae*
	Thomas Müntzer, "German Evangelical Mass"
	Ulrich Zwingli, *De Canone Missae Epicheiresis*
	John Oecolampadius, *Das Testament Jesu Christi*
1524	Diobald Schwarz, *Teutsche Messe*
	Guillaume Farel, *La Maniere et fasson*
	"Worms Mass" (German)

1524   Martin Bucer, *Grund und Ursach*
1525   John Oecolampadius, *Form und Gstalt*
      Ulrich Zwingli, *Action oder Bruch des Nachtmals*
      Döber, Mass for Nuremberg Hospital Chapel (German)
      Martin Luther, *Deutsche Messe.*
For a complete list see D. Julius Smend, *Die evangelischen deutschen Messen bis zu Luthers Deutscher Messe* (Göttingen: Vanderhoeck & Ruprecht, 1896), pp. 2-11.

16. "Formula Missae," in Bard Thompson, *Liturgies of the Western Church*, p. 108. This book, and Jasper and Cuming, *Prayers of the Eucharist*, should be consulted for the texts of Protestant rites.
17. Cf. two important works: John McKenna, *Eucharist and Holy Spirit* (London: Alcuin Club, 1975) and Geoffrey Wainwright, *Eucharist and Eschatology* (London: Epworth Press, 1971).
18. *First Apology*, 65-67; Richardson, *Early Christian Fathers*, pp. 286-87.
19. *Didache* 9; Richardson, p. 175.
20. *First Clement* 40 and 44; Richardson, pp. 62, 64.
21. "To the Smyrnaeans" 7; Richardson, p. 114.
22. "Against Heresies" V, 2; Richardson, p. 388.
23. Epistle LXII, 13; ANF, VIII, 217.
24. "Mystagogical Catechesis V," *St. Cyril of Jerusalem's Lectures on the Christian Sacraments* (London: S.P.C.K., 1960), p. 74.
25. "City of God," X, 6; NPNF, lst series, II, 184.
26. *On the Sacraments*, IV, 14; Jasper and Cuming, *Prayers of the Eucharist*, p. 98.
27. Henry Denzinger and Adolf Schönmetzer, *Enchiridion Symbolorum*, 33rd ed. (Rome: Herder, 1965), p. 260.
28. *Decree for the Armenians*, in *A History of Christianity*, Ray C. Petry, ed., p. 328.
29. Brilioth, *Eucharistic Faith and Practice*, p. 97.
30. It is all the more ironic that Luther discarded the canon of the mass except the words of institution which, to us, seem to be such explicit sacrificial language.
31. *Institutes*, IV, xvii, 7, p. 1367.
32. *Ibid.*, IV, xvii, 38, pp. 1415-16.
33. Cyril Richardson, *Zwingli and Cranmer on the Eucharist* (Evanston: Seabury-Western Theological Seminary, 1949), p. 48.
34. J. E. Rattenbury, *The Eucharistic Hymns of John and Charles Wesley* (London: Epworth, 1948), pp. 195-249.
35. E. Schillebeeckx, *The Eucharist;* Joseph Powers, *Eucharistic Theology* (New York: Herder and Herder, 1967), and *Spirit and Sacrament* (New York: Seabury, 1973).
36. *Bishops' Committee on the Liturgy Newsletter*, XV, January 1979, 147.

8. Passages

1. "To Polycarp," 5; Richardson, *Early Christian Fathers*, p. 119.
2. *Luther's Works*, Ulrich S. Leopold, ed., LIII, 110-15.
3. *Sentences*, IV, xxvi, 2; in Elizabeth Rogers, *Peter Lombard and the Sacramental System*, p. 243.
4. *Ibid.*, IV, xxvi, 5; Rogers, p. 245.
5. *Decree for the Armenians*, in *A History of Christianity*, Ray C. Petry, ed., p. 329.

6. *Institutes,* IV, xix, 34, p. 1481.
7. Gregory Dix, ed., *The Apostolic Tradition,* pp. 4-19. Cf. also H. B. Porter, *Ordination Prayers of the Ancient Western Churches* (London: S.P.C.K., 1967), pp. 1-11.
8. Porter, *Ordination Prayers,* pp. 12-35.
9. *Roman Pontifical* (Washington, D.C.: International Commission on English in the Liturgy, 1978).
10. *Luther's Works,* LIII, 124-26.
11. *Decree for the Armenians;* Petry, *History of Christianity,* p. 329.
12. "Babylonian Captivity," *Three Treatises* (Philadelphia: Muhlenberg Press, 1947), p. 234.
13. *Anglican-Methodist Unity: Part I, the Ordinal* (London: S.P.C.K. and Epworth Press, 1968).
14. V, Dix, ed. *The Apostolic Tradition,* p. 10.
15. I, 5, *Bishop Sarapion's Prayer Book,* John Wordsworth, ed., p. 67. Cf. also III, 17; pp. 77-78.
16. *Sentences,* IV, xxiii, 3; in Rogers, *Peter Lombard,* p. 222.
17. *Decree for the Armenians;* Petry, *History of Christianity,* p. 329.
18. *Institutes* IV, xix, 18, p. 1466.
19. *Ibid.,* IV, xvii, 39, pp. 1416-17.
20. Church of the Brethren, *Pastor's Manual,* pp. 63-71 including a sound introduction. This rite ought to be more widely known.
21. *First Apology,* 65-67; Richardson, *Early Christian Fathers,* pp. 286-87.
22. V, 18, *Bishop Sarapion's Prayer Book,* Wordsworth, ed., pp. 79-80.
23. *Confessions* IX, xii. F. J. Sheed, trans. (New York: Sheed & Ward, 1942), p. 167.
24. "Martyrdom of Polycarp," V, 18, Richardson, *Early Christian Fathers,* p. 156.
25. "Preface to the Burial Hymns," *Luther's Works,* LIII, 326.
26. John Hick, *Death and Eternal Life* (New York: Harper, 1976).

For Further Reading

I. What Do We Mean by "Christian Worship"?

Bishop, Edmund. *Liturgica Historica.* Oxford: Clarendon Press, 1918.

Bouyer, Louis. *Liturgical Piety.* University of Notre Dame Press, 1955.

Cabrol, Abbot. *The Books of the Latin Liturgy.* St. Louis: B. Herder, 1932.

Davies, J. G., ed. *A Dictionary of Liturgy and Worship.* Philadelphia: Westminster Press, 1979.

Guardini, Romano. *The Church and the Catholic and the Spirit of the Liturgy.* New York: Sheed & Ward, 1935.

Jones, Cheslyn; Wainwright, Geoffrey; and Yarnold, Edward, eds. *The Study of Liturgy.* New York: Oxford University Press, 1978.

Shepherd, M. H. *Worship of the Church.* Greenwich, Conn.: Seabury Press, 1952.

Swete, Henry B. *Church Services and Service-Books Before the Reformation.* London: S.P.C.K., 1930.

II. The Language of Time

Inter-Lutheran Commission on Worship. *Contemporary Worship #6, The Church Year.* Minneapolis: Augsburg, 1973.

McArthur, A. A. *The Evolution of the Christian Year.* London: SCM, 1953.

Nocent, Adrian. *The Liturgical Year.* Collegeville, Minn.: Liturgical Press, 1977. 4 vols.

Porter, Boone. *Keeping the Church Year.* New York: Seabury Press, 1978.

Seasons of the Gospel. Nashville: Abingdon, 1979.

III. The Language of Space

Bishops' Committee on the Liturgy. *Environment and Art in Catholic Worship.* Washington: National Conference of Catholic Bishops, 1978.

———. *Music in Catholic Worship.* Washington: National Conference of Catholic Bishops, 1972.

Bruggink, Donald J. and Carl H. Droppers. *Christ and Architecture.* Grand Rapids: Eerdmans, 1965.

———. *When Faith Takes Form.* Grand Rapids: Eerdmans, 1971.

Introduction to Christian Worship

Debuyst, Fréderic. *Modern Architecture and Christian Celebration.* New York: Pueblo, 1979.
Hammond, Peter. *Liturgy and Architecture.* London: Barrie & Rockliff, 1960.
———, ed. *Towards a Church Architecture.* London: Architectural Press, 1962.
Maguire, Robert and Keith Murray. *Modern Churches of the World.* New York: Dutton, 1965.
Sövik, Edward. *Architecture and Worship.* Minneapolis: Augsburg, 1973.
White, James F. *The Cambridge Movement.* Cambridge: Cambridge University Press, 1962 and 1979.

IV. The Spoken Word

Batiffol, P. *History of the Roman Breviary.* London: Longmans, Green, 1898.
Bradshaw, Paul F. "The Origins of the Daily Office," *Annual Reports 1978.* London: Alcuin Club, 1978.
Brightman, F. E. *The English Rite.* London: Rivingtons, 1921. 2 vols.
Cuming, G. J. *A History of Anglican Liturgy.* London: Macmillan, 1969.
Dugmore, C. W. *The Influence of the Synagogue upon the Divine Office.* Westminster: Faith Press, 1964.
Jungmann, Joseph A. *Pastoral Liturgy.* London: Challoner, 1962.
Jasper, R. C. C., ed. *The Daily Office.* London: S.P.C.K. and Epworth, 1968.
Lamb, J. A. *The Psalms in Christian Worship.* London: Faith Press, 1962.
Mateos, Juan. "The Origins of the Divine Office," *Worship,* October 1967, pp. 477-85.
———. "The Morning and Evening Office," *Worship,* January 1968, pp. 31-47.
Reed, Luther. *The Lutheran Liturgy.* Philadelphia: Muhlenberg, 1947.
Salmon, Pierre. *The Breviary through the Centuries.* Collegeville, Minn.: Liturgical Press, 1962.
Van Dijk, S. J. P., and Walker, J. H. *The Origins of the Modern Roman Liturgy.* London: Darton, Longman, and Todd, 1960.

V. The Acted Sign

Baillie, Donald. *Theology of the Sacraments.* New York: Scribner's, 1957.
Gelpi, Donald L. *Charism and Sacrament.* New York: Paulist, 1976.
Hellwig, Monika. *The Meaning of the Sacraments.* Dayton: Pflaum/Standard, 1972.
Leeming, Bernard. *Principles of Sacramental Theology.* London: Longmans, 1960.
Rahner, Karl. *The Church and the Sacraments.* London: Burns & Oates, 1963.
Worden, T., ed. *Sacraments in Scripture.* London: Geoffrey Chapman, 1966.

VI. Initiation and Reconciliation

Baptism in the New Testament. Baltimore: Helicon Press, 1964.
Beasley-Murray, G. R. *Baptism in the New Testament.* London: Macmillan, 1962.
Cully, Kendig Brubaker, ed. *Confirmation: History, Doctrine, and Practice.* Greenwich, Conn.: Seabury, 1962.
Fisher, J. D. C. *Confirmation Then and Now.* London: S.P.C.K., 1978.
Gilmore, Alec, ed. *Christian Baptism.* London: Lutterworth, 1959.
Kavanagh, Aidan. *The Shape of Baptism: The Rite of Christian Initiation.* New York: Pueblo, 1978.

282

Made, Not Born. Notre Dame: University of Notre Dame Press, 1976.

Mitchell, L. L. *Baptismal Anointing.* University of Notre Dame Press, 1978.

Neunheuser, Burkhard. *Baptism and Confirmation.* New York: Herder & Herder, 1964.

Riley, Hugh. *Christian Initiation.* Washington: Catholic University Press, 1974.

Rite of Penance: Commentaries. Washington: Liturgical Conference, 1975-77. 3 vols.

Schnackenburg, Rudolf. *Baptism in the Thought of St. Paul.* Oxford: Blackwell, 1964.

Wainwright, Geoffrey. *Christian Initiation.* London: Lutterworth, 1969.

VII. The Eucharist

Bouyer, Louis. *Eucharist.* Notre Dame: University of Notre Dame Press, 1968.

Buxton, R. F. *Eucharist and Institution Narrative.* London: Alcuin Club, 1976.

Church of England Doctrine Commission. *Thinking about the Eucharist.* London: SCM, 1972.

Clements, R. E., *et al. Eucharistic Theology, Then and Now.* London: S.P.C.K., 1968.

COCU. *Word, Bread, Cup.* Cincinnati: Forward Movement, 1978.

Delorme, H., *et al. The Eucharist in the N. T.* Baltimore: Helicon, 1964.

Jungmann, Joseph. *The Early Liturgy.* University of Notre Dame Press, 1959.

Klauser, Theodor. *A Short History of the Western Liturgy.* London: Oxford University Press, 1969.

Martimort, A. G. *The Church at Prayer: The Eucharist.* Shannon: Irish University Press, 1973.

Ratcliff, E. C. *Liturgical Studies.* London: S.P.C.K., 1976.

Ryan, John Barry. *The Eucharistic Prayer.* New York: Paulist Press, 1974.

Srawley, J. H. *Early History of the Liturgy.* Cambridge Univ. Press, 1957.

Vagaggini, C. *The Canon of the Mass and Liturgical Reform.* London: Geoffrey Chapman, 1967.

Watkins, Keith. *The Feast of Joy.* St. Louis: Bethany Press, 1977.

VIII. Passages

Bradshaw, Paul F. *The Anglican Ordinal.* London: S.P.C.K., 1971.

Cope, Gilbert, ed. *Dying, Death, and Disposal.* London: S.P.C.K., 1970.

Dwyer, Walter W., ed. *The Churches' Handbook for Spiritual Healing.* New York: Ascension Press, 1965.

Irion, Paul E. *The Funeral: Vestige or Value?* Nashville: Abingdon, 1966.

Jackson, Edgar. *The Christian Funeral.* New York: Channel Press, 1966.

Knauber, Adolf. *Pastoral Theology of the Anointing of the Sick.* Collegeville, Minn.: Liturgical Press, 1975.

McNeill, John T. *A History of the Cure of Souls.* New York: Harper, 1977.

Palmer, Paul F. "Christian Marriage: Contract or Covenant?" *Theological Studies,* December 1972, pp. 617-65.

Power, David, and Maldonado, Luis, eds. *Liturgy and Human Passage.* New York: Seabury Press, 1979.

Prayer Book Studies #20. *The Ordination of Bishops, Priests, and Deacons.* New York: Church Hymnal Corporation, 1970.

Rowell, Geoffrey. *The Liturgy of Christian Burial.* London: S.P.C.K., 1977.

Van Gennep, Arnold. *Rites of Passage.* London: Routledge & Kegan Paul, 1960.

Willimon, William H. *Worship as Pastoral Care.* Nashville: Abingdon, 1979.

Index

Acoustics, 97-104
Actions as worship, 200, 207, 234
Adams, Fred Winslow, 59
Advent, 57, 64, 188
Agape, 209-10, 264
Agnus Dei, 217, 219
Aland, Kurt, 176, 197
Alexandrine rites, 38, 214-15
All Saints' Day, 58, 65, 68, 264
Altar-table, 82-83, 233-34
Ambrose, 54, 152, 179-81,216, 226
Anabaptists, 134, 183-85, 195-96, 218-19, 230
Anamnesis, 207, 212-13, 223, 232
Anaphora. *See* Eucharistic prayer
Anglican worship, 42-43
Annunciation, 56, 57, 69
Anointing, 173-75, 179-80, 201, 257, 259-62
Apostolic Constitutions, 48, 55, 116-17, 214
Architecture, church: criteria for, 93-97; history of, 84-97; and worship, 77-78, 96-97; theology of, 78-84. *See also* Acoustics
Art, liturgical, 104-6
Arts, visual, 73-75, 104-9
Ascension, 54-55, 58, 68
Ash Wednesday, 52, 68, 164, 188-89
Augustine, 52-53, 98, 102, 145, 152-53, 155, 161, 166, 192-93, 225, 232, 243, 263-64

Baptism, 50, 170-202, 270; formula, 174-75, 177; believer's, 134, 183-85, 195-98; method of, 183-84, 200-201; NT witness to, 174-77; of infants, 176-77, 195-96; renewal of, 186-87, 201; rites, Roman Catholic, 186, 199
Baptism of the Lord, 60, 64, 68, 187, 199
Baptistery, 85, 87, 190. *See also* Font, baptismal
Baptists, 184, 197
Barth, Karl, 197
Basilica, 86-87
Baumstark, Anton, 126, 275
Berengarius, 154, 226
Bible in worship, 141-42. *See also* Lectionary
Bishops' liturgy, 35, 185, 194, 211, 249-56
Bookbinding, 83, 108, 274
Book of Common Prayer
   1549: 32, 34-35, 37, 122-23, 134, 183, 185, 188, 196, 200, 220, 241, 244, 253, 259, 266
   1552: 183, 185, 196, 253, 259, 266
   1662: 123, 188-89, 220, 266
   1979: 10, 70, 72, 124, 133-34, 186, 188-89, 221, 242, 260
Book of Worship, 10, 124, 134, 222
Books, service, 31-37, 272
Breviary, 34, 120-21

Index

Brilioth, Yngve, 222-24, 231
Brunner, Peter, 17
Bucer, Martin, 131-32, 184-85, 219, 259
Burial, Christian, 263-71
Byzantine liturgy, 40

Calendar, 33, 44, 50-60, 62-69
Calvin, John, 131, 145, 154, 161, 165-66, 183, 185, 195-96, 219, 229-30, 244, 259, 266
Canon. *See* Eucharistic prayer
Casel, Odo, 21, 164-65, 231
Cassian, 118-19
Catechesis, mystagogical, 54, 179-80, 199, 225
Catechumenate, 171, 178, 181, 186, 199
Cathedral office, 116-17
Centers, liturgical, 82-97
Chair, presidential, 83-84
Chancels, 89-92
Choir, 82, 89, 101
Christmas, 56-58, 64
Christ the King, 60, 68
Christological feasts, 51, 59, 65, 69
Christology, 17, 71, 73
Chrysostom, St. John, 38, 41, 50, 54, 56, 58, 71, 117-18, 179, 216
Churches of Christ, 42
Circumcision, 57, 59, 172-73
Clement of Alexandria, 115, 192
COCU, 70, 125
Collects, 128
Colors, liturgical, 74
Communion, first, 50, 181-82, 201
Community, sacramental, 166-70
Confirmation, 50, 160, 171, 181-82, 184-85, 187, 193-94, 196, 198, 259
Constantine, 48, 53, 59, 86
Constitution on Sacred Liturgy, 20, 81-83, 90, 121, 136, 231, 245, 260, 267
Cranmer, Thomas, 122-24, 133, 230, 259. See also *Book of Common Prayer*
Creeds: Apostles' 144, 178; Athanasian, 144; Nicene, 129-30, 144, 191
Cyprian, 115, 211, 225
Cyril of Jerusalem, 52-53, 152, 179-80, 225

Dance, liturgical, 98, 103
Day, Christian, 49-50
Decree for the Armenians. See Florence, Council of
Devotions, 26-27, 115-16
Didache, 48-49, 83, 115, 175, 177, 210-11, 214, 224, 250
Didascalia Apostolorum, 178
Disciples of Christ, 42
Dix, Gregory, 58-59, 198, 207-8, 214, 221, 278
Donatism, 153, 166
Dura-Europos, 85
Durandus, William, 35, 252

Easter: Day, 49, 50-51, 58, 180, 199; Season, 52, 64, 267; Triduum, 54; Vigil, 54, 68, 71, 177-78, 180, 187; Week, 51-55
Egeria, 50-51, 53, 117-18, 178-79
Enlightenment, 161-63, 166
Epiclesis, 212-16, 225, 233
Epiphany: Day, 56-58, 59, 68; Season after the, 57-58, 61, 64
Eschatology and eucharist, 224, 227-28, 230, 233
Eucharist, 36, 203-36, 256; biblical themes, 222-24; bread and wine of, 235; funeral, 264, 271; history of, 206-22; institution of, 206-8; nuptial, 240-42; practice of, 233-36; theology of, 222-33
Eucharistic prayer, 211-13, 218
Eusebius, 55, 116
Evangelism, 183, 199
Ex opere operato, 153, 157, 161-63, 166

Fasting, 48, 177
Fellowship, eucharistic, 223, 228, 233
Florence, Council of, 156, 194, 244, 254
Font, baptismal, 82-83, 190, 200
Foot washing, 54, 208
Forgiveness of sins, 191-94, 257
Free Church worship, 42-43, 131, 134-35, 185, 188, 196, 200, 220, 233, 253, 265
Funerals. *See* Burial, Christian

Index

Order of worship, 28, 141-42
Ordinal, 35, 253
Ordinary parts, 65
Ordinary Time, 50, 64
Ordination, 160, 249-56
Ordines, 36
Ordo, 28
Orthodoxy, Eastern, 12, 38, 56, 103, 225, 232, 240, 246, 258

Palm/Passion Sunday, 50, 54, 68, 71
Paschal candle, 54, 75
Passage, rites of, 29-30, 237-71
Passover, 50, 206, 208
Pastoral offices. See *Rituale*
Penance. *See* Reconciliation
Penitentials, 34, 182
Pentecostal worship, 30, 31, 42-43, 135, 184, 220
Pentecost: Day of, 52, 54, 58, 60, 199; season after, 64
Phenomenology, 29-43
Pius X, Saint Pope, 20
Pius XII, Pope, 22, 53, 254
Pliny, 48, 209
Pluralism, 33, 135, 221. *See also* Indigenization
Pontifical, 35, 252-53
Prayer, 18; of confession, 129, 142; forms of, 139; Jewish, 114; intercessions, 126, 127, 144, 212, 262; opening, 72; pastoral, 142; private, 116; synagogue, 205; types of, 142. *See also* Collects, Eucharistic prayer
Preaching, 138-39, 161. *See also* Lectionary, Sermon
Presbyterian Worship. *See* Reformed worship, *Worshipbook*
Presence, eucharistic, 81-83, 224, 227-29, 231
Presentation, 57, 59, 69
Proclamation, theology of, 136-40
Propers, 65-66, 217
Psalmody, 72, 118, 120, 123, 129, 139-40, 142-43, 205, 232, 265

Quaker worship, 30-31, 42-43, 91-92, 97, 134, 158, 184, 253
Quartodeciman, 51
Quinones, Francisco de, 121-23

Radbertus, Paschasius, 154, 226
Ratramnus, 154, 226
Reconciliation, 159-60, 171-72, 175-76, 180, 182, 184-85, 187-89, 191, 196, 198, 201-2, 259
Reformation, 34-35, 37, 90, 111, 130-34, 156, 159-62, 183-85, 194-96, 228, 241, 244, 265, 278-79
Reformation Sunday, 69
Reformed worship, 42-43, 131-32, 135, 143, 219, 233
Reformers, Protestant, 37, 130-31, 136-37, 161, 183-85, 252
Renunciation, baptismal, 177-78
Resurrection, 47-49, 53, 71
Revivalism, 92-93, 135
Rituale (book), 34
Rituale Romanum, 35
Roman rite, 38, 41, 216
Rouault, Georges, 105, 107
Rubrics, 28, 36, 140
Sacramental system, 158-60
Sacramentary, 34, 36, 53, 72, 211, 216, 221, 242, 267
Sacraments: apostolic practice, 150; character, 156-57; Christ as primordial, 149, 165; contemporary statement of, 166-70; institution of, 149-50, 156, 159; number of, 147, 152-53, 158, 166; old covenant, 155; practice, 154-55; *res,* 155, 166, 169
Sacrifice, eucharistic, 148, 204-5, 223-25, 227-28, 231-32, 279
Saints' days, 59, 264
Sanctus, 211-12, 219
Santos, 105
Sarapion, 214, 257, 263
Sarum Manuale, 35
Schillebeeckx, Edward, 165
Scholastic theology, 156-57, 162, 193, 227, 229, 254, 258
Schoonenberg, Piet, 165, 276
Scotland, Church of, 59-60
Sermon, 72, 126-27
Services of the Church, 10, 242, 247, 253, 268
Shakers, 103, 105
Shepherd of Hermes, 176
Sick, ministry to the, 160, 235-36, 257-63

287